On Blackness, Liveliness,
and What It Means to Be Human

SUNY series, Critical Race Studies in Education
———
Derrick R. Brooms, editor

On Blackness, Liveliness, and What It Means to Be Human

Toward Black Specificity in Higher Education

WILSON KWAMOGI OKELLO

SUNY PRESS

Cover Credit: *The Flying African* by Mikael Owunna. Used with permission.

Published by State University of New York Press, Albany

© 2024 State University of New York

All rights reserved

Printed in the United States of America

No part of this book may be used or reproduced in any manner whatsoever without written permission. No part of this book may be stored in a retrieval system or transmitted in any form or by any means including electronic, electrostatic, magnetic tape, mechanical, photocopying, recording, or otherwise without the prior permission in writing of the publisher.

Links to third-party websites are provided as a convenience and for informational purposes only. They do not constitute an endorsement or an approval of any of the products, services, or opinions of the organization, companies, or individuals. SUNY Press bears no responsibility for the accuracy, legality, or content of a URL, the external website, or for that of subsequent websites.

For information, contact State University of New York Press, Albany, NY
www.sunypress.edu

Library of Congress Cataloging-in-Publication Data

Name: Okello, Wilson K., author.
Title: On Blackness, liveliness, and what it means to be human : toward Black specificity in higher education / Wilson Kwamogi Okello.
Description: Albany : State University of New York Press, [2024]. | Series: SUNY series, critical race studies in education | Includes bibliographical references and index.
Identifiers: LCCN 2024005818 | ISBN 9781438499659 (hardcover : alk. paper) | ISBN 9781438499666 (ebook)
Subjects: LCSH: African Americans—Education, Higher—Philosophy. | Black people—Education, Higher—Philosophy. | African Americans—Race identity. | Black people—Race identity. | Humanism.
Classification: LCC LC2781 .O54 2024 | DDC 305.896/0071173—dc23/eng/20240718
LC record available at https://lccn.loc.gov/2024005818

To August

Contents

Introduction: Preliminary Vocabulary toward Black Specificity   1

Part I.
On What It Means to Be Human

1. Loving Black Flesh in Higher Education   15

2. Breathing, Being, and Human Development   45

3. "Look a Negro!" Explicating Self-Definition   73

Part II.
Black Ontological Possibility:
The Praxes of Self-Definition

4. Invention: Narrating the Impossibility of Black Ontology   101

5. Toward an Ontology of Black Intimacy   123

6. Presence: Black Ontology as Image-Making and Imagination amid the "Uninhabitable"   145

7. "Make it intact": Toward Ethical Regard in Higher Education   169

Part III.
Carcerality and the
Radical Imagination of Self-Definition

8. On the Possibility of Black Thought to Guide Educational
    Policy and Practice   199

9. "I can't be a pessimist": Carcerality, Black Study, and
    Staging Black Futures   229

Gratitude   255

Notes   259

References   267

Index   285

Introduction

Preliminary Vocabulary toward Black Specificity

Words are to be taken seriously. I try to take seriously acts of language. Words set things in motion. I've seen them doing it. Words set up atmospheres, electrical fields, charges. I've felt them doing it. Words conjure. I try not to be careless about what I utter, write, sing. I'm careful about what I give voice to.

—Toni Cade Bambara, *What It Is I Think I Am Doing Anyhow*

I've seen some preliminary thoughts . . . I need to say that if you haven't read, not a single thing written by Saidiya Hartman or Hortense Spillers. And if you have no knowledge, never heard of Negritude or how it's related to surrealism. If you don't know who Senghor is or why he would have anything to do with art. If you never spent anytime figuring out who was and wasn't at FESTAC 77. If you have no idea what critical fabulation is. If you didn't know what I meant when I said In the Wake. If you never studied Independence architecture. If you don't know why Pauline Lumumba walked through the streets of Kinshasha bare breasted. If you have no idea who Katherine Dunham is or her scholarship . . . If the words Black Feminist Thought bring absolutely zero concepts to mind . . . If you don't know what story I'm referring to when I talk about A Question of Power. If you thought I was being weird when I told you I was too busy sharpening my oyster knife. If you've never heard of the Herero Genocide. Then you lack the knowledge to recognize the radical gestures in my work. And that is why, instead of mentioning these things, I have politely said black women are my primary audience.

—Simone Leigh

Specificity.

noun: the quality or condition of being specific; distinctive; something peculiarly adapted to a purpose or use.

Black Specificity.

Noun; adjective; verb: abolitionist; aesthetic; atemporal and (Black) Atlantic; of breaks and breaths; capacious; carnival; the clearing; compositional and critique of dominant systems; "every line of the text is sutured to Black life"; freedom dreams; dance and grooves; diasporic; imagines and indexes and invents; long and wide and deep; and small and cramped; 9 x 7 x 3; liveliness and living; is mad and madness; Mathematics; marronages; memory; music—Aretha, Betty, Bob, Cole, and Erykah, Gil, Kendrick, Missy, and Nas, and Nina, and Paul, and, Roots, and Sly, and Tina, and Whitney, and so on; ongoing and quotidian; it is pause; and Palestine; poetic and poesies; radically relational and rebellious; rhythmic; it is sharing; slow; unthought and ungeographic; where we know from; *Zong!*[1]

The question circulated, hovered, and looped; it lingered and repeated as if to say, I deserve a clear and reasoned response. It is a question that required care and full regard—care as meticulous and unflinchingly observant, as in I care about this matter, this question, I care about you; care as an alternative to state imposition, and, instead, a living tenderness. "Wilson, how do you feel about being Black in this country?" It has been years since Winston, a seventeen-year-old first-year student, asked me this question at an opening convocation, and for years, I have followed the question to logical conclusions. What remains consistent in this line of thinking is precarity. What are the words and phrases, what is the language of precarity—of creating amid negation? What is the grammar—the language, inflection, relation, and function—of the possible amid constraint? Seeking a response to Winston's questions, and my own, I have read, and thought, and lived, and written about what it has meant to exist in this world in a Black body. Never at once, always in pieces, in my rereading, thinking again, living into, and writing through, I am noticing otherwise. Whereas the academic journal demands forms of legibility that can never fulfill the depth and breadth of Black intellectual thought and praxis because Western social science protocols often reduce Black ways of knowing and being to that which is in excess of standardization, my response to Winston (see Okello 2018) hints at something I was feeling, and yet, still clarifying. I am convinced as much now as I was then, that the answer won't be found by turning to Western social science protocols that are rooted in racial and colonial logics. Instead, the ongoing, and evolving response to Winston ought to take up praxis, a form of intellectual practice concerned with "the imaging and material realizing of otherwise worlds, otherwise possibilities" (Crawley, 2016, p. 236). This book is a meditation on otherwise attunement, of looking for and locating methods of Black liveliness in Black being in the break and beat drop, the rhythm and refrain, in the hum. I think, the riot and chorus, the merge of text and textiles, drums and shouts, noise, and dancing wavelengths of the praise song signal the unfolding, blossoming attributes that are Black liveliness; indeed, Black being is in the garret and attic space, as both confinement and vessel of care, of fugitivity, of escape; it is in the whispers of the brush, the rhythmic sound of the tambourine, the whooping moment of "yonder they do not love it," the unspeakable; it is in the mourning, weep, and laugh; the answer, if we listen for it, perhaps, if we attune to it, is in being, is in the richness of Black dimensional interiority. Understanding and appreciating that richness doesn't align with predictive algorithms or methodologies incapable of attending to Black vitality. Attunement requires specificity.

In the epigraph above, Black artist and curator, Simone Leigh, responds to white art critics who, after viewing an exhibition featuring mostly nonwhite artists, including her own work, labeled it "not radical enough." The white critics' formulation suggested that the works did not meet the threshold of meaningful artistry. While an in-depth examination of Leigh's statement for its political implications in the realm of art criticism is beyond the scope of these analyses, the more important work, as I understand it, is to take seriously Leigh's call to consider how we know and where we know from. In doing so, I am contemplating how intellectual work in education might forge a "radical" interdisciplinarity that undoes analytic mechanisms in favor of Black specificity as praxis.

Interdisciplinary work, to riff on Bambara (1980), is an exercise in liveliness and living; they are ways of knowing and constructing worlds; Working across, sharing, deep reading, and study is how I stay in touch with the genealogy of Black possibility—the chorus of writers, thinkers, cultural workers, and voices that have contributed and continue to add shape and texture, weight, and substance to the archive of Black memories, current conditions, and futures. I am indebted to the archive of Black being that overflows with clues and lessons, anecdotes, and coordinates about how to refuse anti-Black constraint, materially, aesthetically, and grammatically. For Sylvia Wynter (2015), "being human is always a doing, a praxis" (p. 196), and it is in the liveliness of Black being that I bear witness to utterances, enunciations, and pronouncements of how to be, that are *untranslatable* (see Sharpe, 2023) in the inherited grammar of Western knowledge systems. By grammar, I am suggesting that the rules of science, the rituals, and techniques of academic writing in particular, are rehearsed in many ways to bring order to that which is not perceived as legible, and, as such, is at odds with the ways transformation unfolds. Whereas writing across genres and deep reading are some of the ways I stay accountable to diverse knowledges and literacies for the "usable wisdoms they yield," in this text, I, like Bambara (1980), am trying to work out a "fusion of disciplines that might break with fragmentations and distortions" (p. 154). This book, then, is a gathering, a ceremony (Wynter, 2015), or critique of the ways normative systems of knowledge form and shape the knowledge and social order. I believe that ceremonies hold within them the potential to transform how we know in the world. In ceremony, I am after methods that allow for one to attend to the embodied, and quotidian, everyday formations of liveliness and to that end, I engage personal memory and stories, media, literature, history, science, and art and aesthetics to draw out the ways readers might reimagine humanity and trace a praxis for living.

Storytelling methods assist in triangulating the data, bridging an analysis of Black Aesthetics/Black Arts movement letters/literature and contemporary scenes of anti-Blackness to consider what it means for Black people to exist across time and space. Storytelling as a method both situates me in the text and offers readers another entry point. One of the ways I stage this opportunity for reimagination is by deploying Black art as that which revalues and resuscitates Black living.

For Black creative intellectuals, aesthetics are a medium, instrument, and form for becoming the "living site of intervention" (Spillers, 2003, p. 456), a method for reading and locating liveliness in excess of what is swept up in the normative capture, consumption, and circulation of Blackness. Aesthetics are frames for understanding that images/texts/compositions not only speak, but do so in a particular tone, timbre, and pitch. Aesthetics locate the voice of an image/text/composition in the language that it intends to be known. Aesthetics assume the objects of study possess a liveliness that moves between, over, against that which it encounters, in other terms, the object is agentic, a *doing* project, dynamic in the way that it escapes stillness, takes shape, and animates. If then, an object is doing, producing, of multiple voices, and shifting, then locating meaning must mean the deployment of a range of aesthetic strategies if one is to ethically attend to the capacious, heterogeneity of an object's rendering. I take to be true, what Black creative intellectuals have long understood and taught, which is representing Blackness and Black being demands specificity. Black specificity, is to push against contracting, rigid imaginaries that reiterate normative scripts about what Blackness is, is not, and what Black people can do and be. Thus, this book is not a study or review of Black people, histories, or experiences. It is a project that intends to consider how Blackness has (not) been taken up in theory and practice, the consequences of such, and how educators and researchers might orient themselves to the matter, grammar, and vocabularies of Black living in higher education.

Animated by a series of aesthetic strategies, ways of reading Black livingness, in this book I consider how the production of Blackness dictates the ways Black people are rendered, made to move and be in education, namely, in student/early-adult development discourses, though not exclusively. While the theoretical approaches may seem disparate and dissonant, I believe, as other transdisciplinary scholars do, that the collective placement of various practices across this text produce a "generative friction" (King, 2019) that emphasizes how the concept of the human is constructed in relation to Black people. As the relationship to the question of human shifts, an alternative terrain emerges for ontologically theorizing more expansively with Blackness, such that one might notice, render visible and unsettle modes of violence acting on Black living and otherwise possibilities alongside such violence. Mikael Owunna performs one such work.

Whereas, Black people are often examined as objects of study, "the point of consumption," Owunna constructs a transgressive series that argues for thinking about Blackness at the point of production, or what I elaborate on throughout this text as the epistemological level. His approach anticipates the ways the United States social imaginary relates to Black people, and, by way of aesthetic errantry, works against those controlling forces that would render Black subjectivity secondary at best, and invisible at worst. His work in the *Infinite Essence* series subverts logics that methodically labor to control the movement and representation of Blackness and Black being, and, as such, is indicative of the care ethic that directs my thinking across this text. Each chapter begins with a piece of

Black art from Mikael Owunna's *Infinite Essence* series. Annotating each image is Owunna's corresponding title and descriptive caption. Beneath each description, I meditate on the images' force with prose as I make meaning of the photographs and the contribution each makes to its corresponding chapter. This juxtaposition invites readers/viewers to grapple with how art and aesthetics can orient and instruct.

Moreover, I cannot forget Winston's question, nor can I shake the angst and curiosities that it provokes, and so I write from and with the assumptions of Blackness as capacious, and full of possibility—creative, expressive, infinite, liberatory, and otherwise. I write to orient readers to the ways Blackness structures what it means to be human, and to demonstrate how this rendering shifts how we think about human development and knowledge production. In this text, I conclude each chapter with a meditation to and for my Black son, August, who at this writing is two years old. I am writing to offer some insight on how the matters of theorizing, human development, and knowledge production come to bear on one everyday life that is fleshed with ongoing questions, tensions, and commitments. The writings to my son also function as a summation of larger themes in the chapter.

The vocabulary that follows includes oft-used language, phrases, and recitations for reading and understanding this book's principle ideas.

Anti-Blackness.

verb: an antagonistic relationship in relation to Black people
noun: a structural condition that organizes the lives of Black people
in this text: The term anti-Blackness is shorthand for epistemic, ideological, material, and/or spiritual violence against Black people. This harm is contoured by a hyperclimactic obsession with and disregard for Blackness as bonded to Black bodies, experiences, and knowledge.

Blackness.

verb: a frame for categorization and organization
noun: the quality or state of being Black
in this text: Scholars conceptualize Blackness in ways that are different from what I am arguing. Centrally, I take up Blackness as an economic, epistemic, social, and political matrix that orders society, and, also, a capacious rendering that emphasizes joy, waywardness, and possibility, toward the principal question: what does it mean to be human? This reading of Blackness is informed by the Humanities.

Black People.

noun: belonging to a population of people categorically understood as being Black (see Blackness)

in this text: When discussing Black people, I am referring to those whom the historical construction of Blackness has rendered Black people in a United States context.

Black Study.

verb: study is a process of contemplative being. Black Study is a rigorous communing with Black ideas in the service of Black people.

noun: a frame; a lens; an approach

noun: a reading, thinking, and practice orientation that makes room for aesthetic possibility and, therefore, humane framings that attend to the specificity of Black people.

in this text: I regard Black Study as the intellectual, social, relational, and political practice of advancing Black ideas about living in the world.

Ethics.

adjective: relating to standards of conduct and being

noun: a set of moral principles: a theory or system of moral values

in this text: the language ethic/ethical/ethics argues for principled, honest, and humane approaches to a matter.

Flesh.

noun: a structural position determined by Western colonialism

in this text: Flesh constitutes an historical-made-present understanding of Blackness as bound to being. Conceptually, it is a Black humanities recognition of the ways Black people were never considered those who might possess the social and political rights of full humans under the strain of Western colonial ideals.

Genre.

noun: a category of artistic, musical, or literary composition characterized by a particular style, form, or content

in this text: Genre represents the different and varied expressions of living (being human) in the world that are possible if and when those expressions are narrated outside of Western ways of knowing.

Human (also Man, Man-as-human, Western human, Western humanism).

adjective: of, relating to characteristics of humans; having human attributes
noun: Homo sapiens—capacity for articulate speech and abstract reasoning
in this text: A compounding category that defines the rational, reason-driven subject, epistemically configured through European conquest, the Judeo-Christian deity, and the age of Western Enlightenment; reflected as white, male, property-owning, a representation by which all other beings are measured in relation. The period of European imperial expansion marks the emergence of what Sylvia Wynter has called the emergence of Man,[2] whereas the European man embodies the quintessential, ideal version of self—or Man—and the all others, namely Black folks, represent mere approximations, or nonhuman, not-quite-human others. Part of Wynter's larger project chronicles the making of kinds of humans, which she has called genres, determined by Western humanism.

Love.

adjective: a posture of critical tenderness, respect, devotion, responsibility, and care.
verb: to act in the interest of cultivating someone else's spirit. Thank you, bell hooks.
noun: regarding, fully.
in this text: an orientation of bearing with, of being in relation to, with, and for Black people.

Map.

verb: a mode of settlement and spatialization (spatial coherence); cartographic ordering; mode of writing the self
noun: the act or process of drawing distinctions, making a map
in this text: mapping is a symbolic method of writing the self into relevance as possessing a legitimate placement in the sociopolitical hierarchies.

Otherwise.

adjective: dissimilar; partly or completely unlike in form
adverb: in a different manner
in this text: to think and imagine beyond set parameters.

Praxis.

noun: to do, or practice; practical application of theory
in this text: of iteration; complex habit formations of how to be in the world.

Refusal.

transitive verb: to express oneself as unwilling to accept or comply with
adjective: to put aside, decline
in this text: The essence of refusal does not lie in opposition or rejection, instead, refusal is in and of the creation of otherwise possibilities amid negation. Refusal is the renunciation of terms that have structured Black being and the articulation of new terms that might direct current and future actions, and nonactions. Thank you, Tina Campt.

Territory.

noun: an indeterminate geographic area; a field of knowledge
in this text: extant, normative systems of knowledge that are foundational to social order in the United States.

Where to and How: Chapter Overviews

In chapter 1, I extend Sylvia Wynter's critique of Man-as-human to student/early-adult development theory, positing that study with and about Black existence must intentionally take up Blackness as a set and seat of political relations, and with it, histories of violence and exclusion, love, possibility, and traditions toward the principal question: what does it mean to be human? Otherwise stated, student development theorizing ought to consider the "facticity of Blackness, that is, how certain groups of humans became Black through a multitude of material and discursive powers" (Weheliye, 2014, p. 6). Centrally, I ask, how might Black specificity reconstitute student development theorizing? In chapter 2, I consider how student development theory, and self-authorship, in particular, reinforces anti-Black degradation insofar as it is grounded in constructivist methods that do not attend to the specificity of Blackness. This chapter responds directly to this issue by, first, reviewing literature on self-authorship to identify anti-Black logics. Examination on the workings of anti-Blackness in a United States context shed light on the scopic regimes (Fleetwood, 2011), that is, the overarching experience of the gaze enacted on culture, which shapes the experiences of Black people in educational contexts. This analysis is necessary because, as Wynter (2006) noted, the order of knowledge, or the ways student/early-adult development research is constructed in education, reifies Western humanistic logic. Wynter points to the Black Studies/Arts/Power/Aesthetics movements, occurring during my period of investigation, as a site of Black specificity. Findings from these analyses support the call of third-wave student/early-adult development to infuse critical perspectives into theorizing (Abes et al., 2019).

To unpack the question of how Black people are to exist in their bodies, in a United States context, given the material histories attached to them, chapter 3 explicates invention—inventiveness as a way of knowing by asking, how does the invention of the Western Man render Black emotionality and being absent, as well as, how does Blackness bring Black being into view? Conceptually, *inventiveness* as otherwise narration, depends on reflexivity and historicizing one's *invention* as part and parcel to knowing and being. As a consequence of one's sociopolitical location, invention surmises that histories are tied and bound up in one's identity formation. One's way of knowing and being in the present, thus, demands a deliberate reckoning with how one's history is framing their contemporary choices and options. Herein, I interrogate Black masculinity's foundations as a way to add texture and complexity to the cause of knowing and being for Black people in particular, in a United States context. To accomplish this, I lift the veil on gendered and sexual violence committed against Black men. Theorizing in chapter 4 assumes that Black knowledge production exceeds the research practices and data regimes advanced by traditional social science protocols, locating possibility in the inwardness of Black existence. As such, this chapter builds on a tradition of Black socialization practices, such as *the talk* to propose the *Black intimate*, a conceptual frame for annotating Black interior patterns over and against reductive anti-Black logic enforced by traditional social science research. Pushing beyond the canonicity that has defined ways of knowing and being for Black living, chapter 5 explores and documents the radical creativity of Black presence in white institutions, particularly, Black image-making "as refusals to accede to the optics, the disciplines, and the deathly demands" (Sharpe, 2016, p. 115) of anti-Blackness that struggle to make them invisible. Next, I home in on the notion of ethics as part of the United

States social imaginary, and white educational institutions, in particular, to flesh revision as a praxis of ethics regarding the self. More pointedly, chapter 6 will clarify revision as the inclination, articulation, and activity of becoming something that did not exist before.

Locating Black ontological possibility requires frames that appreciate the capaciousness of Black liveliness and living. If educational leadership, and more specifically, how leaders craft policies and practices, are to meaningfully account for Black liveliness and living, it will require more than a rendering of race and racism. Instead, it will demand an explicit focus on Blackness and its negotiations; thus, chapter 7 considers the potentiality of a Black policy praxis. Finally, the last chapter grapples with how the carceral imagination structures the educational futures of Black people, toward the principle question, what are the tools for bringing *Black futures* into view, and, subsequently, harnessing Black futures as an epistemological orientation?

∼

This project pivots on a single premise: *Blackness unsettles*.[3] Generally, when I invite discussion on the question what does it mean to be human? the responses range from empathy and feeling, to laughter, to connectedness and community. In an anatomical and social sense, these responses are unsurprising. The activity of Blackness, however, disturbs the simplicity of this question, and, in doing so, calls forth habits of thinking, being, and doing that might engender otherwise genres—variations—of seeing and being human. The reader will sense my hesitancy[4] to name the details of those genres. While I understand the impulse to empirical evidence as that which is legitimate, and can translate to effective policy, the priority for this project, which in turn will lead to sharper, more precise considerations of educational transformation, is in shifting *how* we think and write and approach our work, as opposed to what we do.

Part I
On What It Means to Be Human

1

Loving Black Flesh in Higher Education

Figure 1.1. At the start of creation, the Dogon deity Amma emanates from Themself eight spiritual figures called Nommo, who are the androgynous, immortal, self-fertilizing, bisexual progenitors of humanity. Nommo Semi (The Sacrificed Nommo) is the third of this group, and They are sacrificed by Amma to purify the universe as atonement for the wicked deeds of Their twin Ogo. Planets and stars spool forth from Their blood. They are then resurrected and installed as the Guardian of Space. *Source*: *Nommo Semi, Guardian of Space* by Mikael Owunna. Used with permission of the artist.

The image demands an otherwise viewing practice. It requires us, the viewers, to look, and then, as if understanding that we might be tempted to theorize or project some manner of explanation, cause, rendering, or justification, the image invites us to stop, pause, and then look again. That one feels compelled to look, however, does not imply an invitation to question the veracity, legibility, or value of the image, nor is the image responding to negation. More precisely, it alleviates the burden of questioning and instead gathers us, the viewers, through the insistence and assertion of Black possibility without the need to prove its feasibility.[1] It presses on our pupils, attaching itself to our retinas. The scene is one of vastness and possibility, encompassed in what appears to be space, and yet it is more than space in the cosmic, universal, or spatial sense; the space seems to move back and forth across history, time, and place, both ephemeral and permanent. One might call this scene a world, a Black world, and still, the idea of a world feels too small, too final for the artistry. Theorizing Blackness, as Brand (2001) does, in her sacred re-memory of the "the door of no return," she writes that "the door of no return is on her retina" (Brand, 2001, p. 89); as such, it becomes a heuristic, an optic for seeing and understanding Black minds and bodies in the diaspora. I understand Brand to be discussing a kind of refusal and seizure. Regarding refusal, there is a sense that Brand refuses to unsee the meaning of "the door," where it led, what it destroyed, who could never return, and what it meant for her to bear witness. The door, in this way, is a holding place, keeping one's attention and requiring a reckoning with all that it means to be present, taken to, and responsible for, still; it suspends one in the in-between—a stepping away and into, from which one can never return. One does not just see or unsee this fixture, they encounter it—they experience it as lived through the body, and, as such, the body does not forget. I remember encountering the image at an urban research symposium—it felt like flight, unhinged and unashamed, like a people could fly, "climbin up on the gate. And they flew like blackbirds over the fields. Black, shiny wings flappin against the blue up there" (Hamilton, 1985, p. 1). As the tale goes, "the people who could fly kept their power, although they shed their wings. They kept their secret magic in the land of slavery" (p. 3), and this rendering, this encounter was evidence. The artist must have known the tale, had it told to them or read, shared, passed down. Even if not, they embodied the story and were sharing it anew so that folks, full of the sea's misery and longing to breathe freely might encounter their secret, might feel their magic and mystery. The image sounded like "whispers

Loving Black Flesh in Higher Education | 17

and sighs" (Hamilton, 1985) under the cover of night and a freedom song in the day. It was a refusal to stay and the blessing to go, to follow the tide "beyond the face of fear" to "open [one's] eyes to water/water waving forever" (Clifton, 2000). The image was fugitive and still, but not stuck in place. Seizure is the thrust of history and memory that comes to bear on the present and is always at work in shaping futures. One encounters history, and they live in it, this, the afterlife of the door, of slavery, in the wake. For Brand, the door on her retina is a "sitting in the room with history" (Brand, 2001, p. 24), whereas "one enters a room and history follows; one enters a room and history precedes. History is already seated in the chair in the empty room when one arrives. Where one stands in society seems always related to this historical experience" (p. 24). We, the people who could fly, perhaps, are (still) always and already arrested by history even as we transcend, however temporarily, its weight and grasp. The image was motivated seizure, whereas seizure is what it means to be pinned, and pressed down, and not destroyed. Seizure is enclosure, it is locked away, in the hold, it is occupation and confiscation, stripping away and never having had. What is it about seizure, the experience, memory, or threat of capture, and requisition that is capable of producing something so everlasting? I see in the image memory of revolution, of people that refused to be captured, so they fought, and jumped, walked, and flew away. Tracing the history of revolts by enslaved people in a Western context, the Haitian revolution enters history as that which, according to French colonizers, was unthinkable. Amid seizure, domination in its varied forms, freedom survived on the minds and spirits of enslaved people. To the rational mind, there existed no model or conceptual frame by which enslaved people in Haiti could imagine futures beyond the compliance of plantation logic. Freedom, or an alternative to enslavement, thus, was reasoned as more than a material impossibility; it was that which had no onto-epistemological framing. The image takes up this mystery of Black being, shedding notions of the docile and tranquil subject. The image rejects that which is unthinkable, opening itself up to everywhere and nowhere. Following McKittrick (2017), as it relates to Blackness, "There is no from. There is no there, or somewhere, or place that a black from is anchored to. This means that our historically present black geographies—the Africa's and the prisons and north stars—are from nowhere" (p. 97), they are fictions (Hartman, 2019), constructions dictated by the predicament of Black disavowal, or coding the human as the disavowal of Blackness. And yet, amid this disavowal, this nowhere, Blackness emerges.

18 | On Blackness, Liveliness, and What It Means to Be Human

> black is in the break, it is fantastic, it is an absented presence, it is a ghost, a mirror, it is water, air; black is flying and underground; it is time-traveling, supernatural, inter-planetary, otherworldly; it is in between the lines and it is postcolonial; black is bulletproof and magical and in every dark corner . . . soulful, neosoul, blues; it is negritude, postslave, always enslaved; black is like who/black is like me; black is everywhere and everything; it is make-believe and magic. (pp. 97–98)

The image, as a portal to nowhere, offers a template to reimagine the "production of space not through patriarchal and colonial project trappings (for example, we want our own space, to own space, give us a place) but instead as a project that engenders relations of uncertainty" (p. 99). The body in flight, floating, in an ocean of Blackness is luminous, a constellation in and to themselves, appears content. It seems as if galaxies and interstellar systems are coursing through veins or are the veins. Are they universe, who and what worlds are they holding? As a cluster of dark matter, I, as a viewer, am transfixed in their orbit, gravitationally bound to their presence and possibility. The artist intimates, insofar as the geographic space of canvas permits, that there is a world where Blackness exists unencumbered and, in this way, the nowhere of Blackness is not rendered nonexistent, rather, it fosters an outlook that is "structured by, but not necessarily beholden to, crass positivist cartographies" (McKittrick, 2017, p. 99). Invoking a Black world understands that Blackness exists in the "tussle of being, in reverie and terribleness, in exception and ordinariness" (Quashie, 2021, p. 1). A sovereignty set up for and of Black people, where question and resolution dwell with and of people who are Black. Conjuring this world, as the artist dreams it into being, pushes against societal instantiations of progress and liberalist renderings in the United States political imagination—a better world for Black people. I type these words against the reminders—insert myriad forms of anti-Black violence—of the exemption of Black humanity that proliferates indefensibly and as ordinary, a consistency that could otherwise give way to surrender. The image refuses to surrender; it is a breach that obliterates time and space, calls into question, and critiques methods that function to capture Blackness. As a rebellious offering and unsettling feat, it demands that we leap—move precipitously, to spring free from and toward possibility; it lifts aesthetics as life-making, and Blackness, form, and shape. Taking form, the project does not concede to reactive posture; instead, the artist deploys resonance and affect as the instantiation of Black world totality. Returning to Brand's (2001) meditation on the door of no return and sitting in the room with all that the door represents, the writer elevates the rightness of feeling as knowing as germane to living and encountering Black worlds, writing "where one can be observed is relative to that history. All human effort seems to emanate from this door. How do I know this? Only by self-observation, only by looking. Only by feeling. Only by being a part" (pp. 24–25). The implication, of course, should mean that aesthetics are not devoid of politics, or "racial formations are aesthetic phenomena and aesthetic practices are racialized structures" (Roelefs, 2005, p. 83). Plainly, my encounter with the image was, and yet is, both discursive and material, an invitation into "the everyday abstraction of Blackness" (Gillespie, 2016, p. 9). Society's lack of imagination for Black liveliness and living are part of the conditions that make for brutal reenactments on Black being. There is no assumption of Black humanity in the current order of knowledge (Wynter, 2003, 2006), and yet the image, the canvas, assumes otherwise. I am interested in clarifying the otherwise, or what the artist calls *infinite essence*.

Infinite, or that which might be defined as endless, immeasurable, or inconceivable. Divine, and present within. An inherent welling, and state of being. Encompassed and manifested in materiality. Everywhere and in everything. Immanence. Transcendence. Eternal and absolute. Everlasting, unending, and measureless. Incessant, as in persistent and given to vigor, not easily deterred. Incessant as opposed to blockage barred or segmented; ceaseless, unremitting, and perpetual; infinite as relentless and not easily broken. Black is unbroken, though Black skin was broken, and lineage, and family, and language, we rise, we rise, we rise, infinite and boundless, speculative, and future; a commitment to expanse and expansiveness; vast, and endless. Infinite, as in dispossession and no possession. Infinite: as opposed to static, intermittent, rigid. Cosmological and ascendant. Universal and always in development. Infinite as opposed to definitively captured, caged confined. To be free and unoccupied, an exercise in imagination and dreaming. Infinite: living, surviving; the wake and afterlife. Eternal as opposed to incarcerated, jailed, subjugated. To be consummated and liberatory. Against redlining, and redistricting, and written out of. Sovereign. Relational, connected. Ancestral and celestial, growth outward, and inward, and upward. Rooted. Breathing deeply and fully. Inexhaustible and indefatigable and diligent. Infinite: the abstract, embodied-affective range of emotionality, as opposed to the concrete and cemented, place-bound, and "stay in your place." Theory and formulation, shape-shifting, beauty, desire, and performative. Praised, worthy of celebration, and given to joy. Unconditional and under all conditions. Pertaining to the historical and future, omnipotent and a priori; lineage and inheritance; retrieval and remembrance. Essence. Mikael Owunna is a queer Nigerian-Swedish American artist and engineer whose work lives at the intersection of visual media with engineering, optics, Blackness, and African cosmologies. The meditations that led to the project "infinite essence" were borne of Black disregard and birthed in Black livingness. Describing his aesthetic offerings, Owunna suggested that he is responding to negative stereotypes and pervasive images of Black death depicted in the media. Owunna has been working to articulate an alternative vision of the Black body as immortal and transcendent. The vicious and sensational reel of Black death spilling out over public media channels struck up an aesthetic response from Owunna that assumed Black liveliness and living. The assumption is important—as will be explained, anti-Blackness, and more pointedly, the afterlife of slavery, by definition, does not make room for assumptive Black-humanness, which leaves Owunna, and all others who would dare to attend to something called Black "living" in excess of traditional representational modalities and frames to work with, and in need of alternative world-making tools. Owunna's otherwise imaginings, which signify a capacity "to create change, to be something else, to explore, to imagine, to live freely, fully, vibrantly" (Samatar, 2015, para. 2), militate against the normative world, by first stepping outside of it in the figurative sense, and beginning from Blackness in the literal. Owunna accomplishes infinite essence in the dark, said otherwise, he turns off the lights: "With this series, I've set about on a quest to recast the Black body as the cosmos and eternal. I hand paint the models' bodies with fluorescent paints and using my engineering background I have augmented a standard flash with an ultraviolet bandpass filter, to only pass ultraviolet light. Using this method, in total darkness, I click down on the shutter" (Owunna, 2020, para. 2). The approach is compelling for several reasons. First, Owunna does not take for granted that photography, as initiated by a practice of standard capture, can bring the interiority of Blackness into view. The instantiation, itself, is a kind of presumption that follows Western humanism[2] as the rational belief that one is already capable of being seen in full at will. Moreover, under standard settings that call for image stabilization, low noise/grain in images, and placing the white balance on auto, which is the process of removing unrealistic color casts from the photo, the vitality of Blackness that Owunna intends to illuminate cannot exist. By setting Blackness as the condition for viewing (that is, total darkness), for a fraction of a second or otherwise, dark bodies are iridescent, as Owunna introduces a method for thinking and being Black in excess of the violent domination of no-thingness (Moten, 2018). I am interested in that fraction of a second. From the space of Blackness, worlds are made/constructed and possible/narrated, over and against the colonial violence that intended to strip Blackness of meaning making potentialities.[3] I observe in Owunna's approach the essence of Black methodology (McKittrick, 2017), or methodology that begins in, and dreams in Black, how that "the dynamism between our biological selves (our flesh, our blood, our hearts, our muscles, and neurons) and the stories we tell about ourselves about our identities and our sense of place" (Prescod-Weinstein, 2021, para. 12) become praxis for living and doing freedom.

By assuming that an otherwise image existed—the Black body as transcendent, planetary, and of the cosmos and eternal—Owunna introduces a seeing, which runs counter to the idea of Blackness as a void, vacuous, and blank. It is the type of viewing practice that animates this text. Blackness, historically, however, is grounded in the discardable, anti-intellectual, and beholden to death, yet darkness (read: Blackness) as the animating frame, critiques these violent projections and elaborates an alternative on the presumption that other relations exist. Black knowledge traditions, here and throughout referred to interchangeably as Black onto-epistemologies, are sites of knowing and being and possibility. Blackness is of possibility, and makes possible. For Owunna, this occurred with and through ultraviolet light—a form of radiation, or radiated energy that emits but is often undetectable to the senses. However temporarily, Owunna makes visible the unseeable therein. Following this premise, I am interested in what Blackness makes visible, or "sights" (McKittrick, 2006). Sighting intimates that "imagination requires a return to and engagement with painful places, worlds where black people were and are denied humanity, belonging, and formal citizenship" (McKittrick, 2006, p. 6), thus I grapple with the where and how of Black inhabitation against the myriad forms of disavowal. I do this deliberately, yet cautiously, so as not to trivially participate in the convening of Black (social) death and dying.

I believe, as Perry (2021) does, that "hope won't get us out of the funk of history that we live with today.... The terror of now is as important a subject for the Black imagination as the speculatively beautiful tomorrow" (para. 19). In addition, that which is not visible, as in brought into view for understanding, is a part of larger settler colonial project that depends on displacing the centrality of Blackness. Thus, a broader import comes into focus for this project in my pursuit to call forth alternative notions of humanity, divorced from the Western Man-as-human, that begins with and accounts for Blackness, transforming the human "into a heuristic model and not an ontological fait accompli" (Weheliye, 2014, p. 8). Put differently, I ask, what does Blackness as a practice and disciplinary frame make possible for education, and more specifically, what is commonly understood as student/early-adult development theory? As one point of entry into Black specificity (there are others), I elaborate on anti-Blackness and social (political) death.

Groundings and Departures

Sylvia Wynter clarified how Blackness became the essential code for nonhuman (that is, no humans involved), articulating how the order of knowledge, rooted, and propagated by coloniality, transatlantic enslavement, and the convergences of Western conquest, generated a representation of the human as a bio-evolutionarily selected organism. In this order, conceptions of who fits within its bounds and those who do not (nonhuman/not-quite-human) (Wynter, 1994, 2003, 2006) are cemented. Thus, biological inscription took on sociopolitical implications, morphing race into a set of relations and organizing principles for society. Black *living* under the logic of "no humans involved," thus, is a dangerous overcalculation at best, and more befittingly, a refurbished misnomer circulated in educational spaces, and, specifically, student/early-adult development theory.

Critically then, this book extends Wynter's critique of Man-as-human to student/early-adult development theory, positing that study with and about Black life and existence must intentionally take up Blackness as a set, and seat, of political relations and with it, histories of violence and exclusion, joy, love, and possibility, toward the principal question: what does it mean to be human? On this premise, I am proposing that a Black Studies, specifically, Black feminist theories of the human (Spillers, 1987; Weheliye, 2014; Wynter, 1994, 2003) intervention can push theorizing to take up the fullness of Black living. In what follows, this book thinks with Wynter (1994, 2003, 2006) toward a Black Studies grounding in student/early-adult development theorizing, and educational research and practice broadly. Concerning the former, attention to and conversation with self-authorship at points throughout this book, is twofold. First, self-authorship has been the focal point of holistic development theorization in student/early-adult development theory. Because this text, too, is interested in student/early-adult development, it is necessary to engage the preeminent literature on the subject. Additionally, and more importantly, literature suggests self-authorship is fundamental to twenty-first-century learning outcomes (Baxter Magolda, 2001, 2008, 2009; Baxter Magolda & King, 2004; Berger, 2012) and thus the determined goal of higher education. While groundbreaking for the ways it pulled dimensions (that is, cognitive, intrapersonal, and interpersonal) together, fundamentally, self-authorship (and student development writ large) is reasoned on the presumption of Man-as-human, and as human, individuals possess the full faculties of the Western, white, bourgeois, propertied, male. The construction of Blackness as nonhuman in the Western imaginary interrupts how Black people exist, know, and can be known, inhibiting Black people's ability to lay claim to the human. Thus, any theorization that does not purposefully begin from and build on that/this place, may be too generic to respond to their condition.

The work of theorizing Blackness in the United States intellectual tradition is, partially, an investigation of the ongoing and sustained nature of Black exclusion from the sociopolitical dimensions of human regard; it reckons indefinitely with the insatiable thrust and established need for the denial of Black humanity in society. In doing so, I take seriously the ways chattel slavery, often contextually bound to a period since past in the United States, persists and overdetermines the life chances of Black people, and thus, reflect briefly on the roots of slavery and its relationship to social death as a mechanism for understanding its contemporary manifestations in understandings of human development and knowledge production.

The Autopoiesis of Biocentric Logics and Social Death

Confronting the prevalence of biocentric logics is daunting and always incomplete. Biocentric logics, and a biocentric conception of the human posit that the Black subject is already inferior, underdeveloped, and incapable of full regard. This conception of the human follows a biocentric knowledge system that presupposes that humans evolved differently along racial and ethnic lines. In this way, Blackness demarcates, and the biocentric order is enforced by ideologies, laws, methods, and science, implicating how we study and theorize about racialized violence. The biocentric belief system, thus, informs habits and traditions, and are tied up in and necessary to everyday understandings of how to be in society. In other words, the narrated and fictive truths of the biocentric belief system are ubiquitous and ordinary (McKittrick, 2021). Here, the notion of a closed and recursive system is a helpful frame for understanding how society organizes itself in relation to Black bodies (that is, the biocentric order). Because the practice—habits and traditions—of being human are enmeshed in a closed social system that is self-referential and recursive, one can only be human in accordance with the "parameters of the existing social system" (McKittrick, 2021, p. 133), giving way to autopoiesis. Following Maturana and Varela (1972), autopoiesis describes the ways living systems repeat their conditions—habits and traditions—to maintain the system. To put it differently, autopoiesis is the neuroscience of discipline and recursive behavior, and Black social death, as one such habit and tradition of society, is normal and ordinary.

Social death[4] functions to ground understandings of the Black as enslaved in a sociopolitical hierarchy that situates the Western Man as the authoritative ideal (that is, master-slave relationship), thereby foreclosing the possibility of citizenship to those beyond its proximity. As an entry point for grappling with the complexity of the biocentric belief system, autopoietics, and how a break toward Black liveliness might occur, Patterson's thinking provides important theoretical tools. It acknowledges and clarifies the violent dispossession and dehumanization of the Black subject as synonymous with slave and chattel, and, thus, subject to the economic, libidinal, and social desires of society. Moreover, society, or what might be understood as the public sphere, is rooted in and constructed on this "dispossession of Black bodies such that the world as we know it is constructed through the position of the Black as Not Human, or Anti-Human" (Dumas, 2018, p. 33), by which the idea of humanity finds coherence and possibility. Here, the ontological nature of the Black is intended to have no standing or placement in the world, and instantiations of Black existence do so against a social imaginary that vehemently denies the claim.

In this way, the Black body becomes "constitutive of suffering, and the suffering of the Black is a constant testimony" (Dumas, 2018, p. 34) to the reified unfolding narration of dispossession and enslavement that made and shapes the (non-)life chances of Black subjects in the United States. This grounding ensures that the Black in the United States imaginary conjures "the sheer weight of a history of terror . . . inseparable from the tortured body of the enslaved" (Hartman, 1997, p. 58). As Dumas concluded, this proportion facilitates a tolerance of Black suffering, whereas a Black body, in the biocentric system, as nonhuman can withstand greater degrees of pain, much more than what is humanly (compared to white bodies) possible. In this established historicity, Black people are open to the whims, rationalizations, and, for the purpose of this text, theorizations and discourses absent of complexity to their sociopolitical station.

Wynter (n.d.) noted that enslavement represented the "first large-scale intensive attempt at the mechanization of human existence" (p. 107), which functioned to solidify Black nonpersonhood as necessary and normal. Enslavement, thus, built a unique structure of organizing society that required and legitimated Black suffering and nonbeing, or as Gordon (2000) wrote, "Blacks here suffer the phobogenic reality posed by the spirit of racial seriousness. In effect, they more than symbolize or signify various social pathologies—they become them. In our antiblack world, blacks are pathology" (p. 87). This observation transcends social ideology and structure (for example, laws, policies, and practices); Black bodies are racially coded as anxiety producing, engendering physiological and neurobiological responses (that is, indicative of desires, feelings, and emotions) that are implicit to the anti-Black, biocentric belief system (Fanon, 1952; Wynter, n.d.). Again, in essence, within a racially coded biocentric belief system, anti-Blackness is ingrained as common sense.

Hortense Spillers (1987) grounds this idea in her always timely contribution, "Mama's Baby, Papa's Maybe," where she sketches and exposes the onto-epistemological project of chattel slavery across the twentieth century and clarifies the exclusion of Black folks from societal definitions of personhood, or the capacity, as the protracted captive, to take ownership or belong to a community. If we are theorizing about otherwise possibilities of Black being in the United States, contextualizing the condition of enslavement and "theft of the captive body" (Spillers, 1987, p. 67) is important insofar as one is able to trace the legacies terror of anti-Blackness and coloniality as they play out in perpetuity.[5] Spillers (1987) contextualized this point, writing, "I would make a distinction in this case between 'body' and 'flesh' and impose that distinction as the central one between captive and liberated subject-positions. In that sense, before the 'body' there is 'flesh,' that zero degree of social conceptualization that does not escape concealment under the brush of discourse, or the reflexes of iconography" (p. 67). The unmaking that delineates the body and flesh, as noted above, is materialized in and on the captive body, whereas the captive body brought into view a method and precedence for the attribution of personhood. In conversation with Spillers's (1987) notion of the body, Sylvia Wynter's (1994, 2003, 2006) intellectual work animates this larger project as it raises critical questions about the adoption of Western humanism, particularly how the entrapments of the body legitimated the making of the quintessential human.

Defining the Human

Following Weheliye (2014), the study of Black life that emerged at the end of the nineteenth century aligns with the emergence of the human sciences, understood here as positivist discourses that cut across several disciplines such as anthropology, sociology, and history, to name a few. The human sciences, thus, established the disciplinary grounds by which the Negro and its relationship to humanity would be cemented. It was in these empirical waters that "the human emerges as an object of knowledge . . . in the quest to ascertain Black people's humanity" (p. 20). The underlining thought here is that constructions of humanity shift, fluctuate, and recalibrate at the precise moment that Black people are part of, or come close to its (read: humanity's) conceptual bounds. Critiquing the human sciences, Wynter articulates a Black Studies project that calls for rescripting humanity as a site of ideological and ontological possibility by calling attention to ways the Western order of knowledge materializes as the dominant way of knowing.

Central to Wynter's thesis is a commitment to deconstructing the idea of "Man." Wynter is concerned with disentangling the idea Man from the notion of human, believing that to do so frees up the (Black) subject to exist beyond the tentacles of Western bourgeois domains and "invent hitherto unavailable genres of the human" (Weheliye, 2014, p. 24). Importantly, Wynter's' project, intent on recasting the human, and thus, redirecting the focus from identity (for example, race, gender, class) to *genre*, should not be read as poststructural evasion, which is to think in purely in deconstructive terms; rather she notes the compounding identity struggles that ensnare, for instance, Black women, is not gender, but genre, or how the Black and woman are already conceptually linked to the Western Man. On this premise, breaking with Western bourgeois conceptions of gender would still leave *genre* in place and attached to the notion of human, and thus, incapable of achieving substantive transformation. Put simply, for Wynter, this issue of *genre* is the fulcrum for what is understood as the "isms."

All our present struggles with respect to race, class, gender, sexual orientation, ethnicity, struggles over the environment, global warming, severe climate change, the sharply unequal distribution of the earth resources (20 percent of the world's peoples own 80 percent of its resources, consume two-thirds of its food, and are responsible for 75 percent of its ongoing pollution, with this leading to two billion of earth's peoples living relatively affluent lives while four billion still live on the edge of hunger and immiseration—these are all differing facets of the central ethnoclass Man vs. Human struggle. (Wynter, 2003, pp. 260–61)

Therefore, to deploy Audre Lorde's much-used heuristic, Wynter proposed a project centered on a critique of racialization and coloniality to say that "the master's tools (a universal notion of gender) cannot dismantle the master's house (Man)" (Weheliye, 2014, p. 23). Under these terms, if a feminist project, or any other critical theoretical framing for that matter, does not endeavor to create an alternative mode of human, then it is only partial in nature, working at the level of the map and not the territory (Wynter, 1990, 2003, 2006). More broadly, Wynter's thinking demands that researchers and practitioners consider how different forms of domination engender forums of possibility and ways of knowing to delineate who can be regarded as human, and ultimately, what can never be.

Defining the human, conceptually, Wynter (1989) began with religious formations of the self. She noted "the self-representation of the two secular models of the human: that of Rational Man and, at the end of the eighteenth century, that of Man as a selected being and natural organism as the universal human, 'man as man'" (p. 645). The symbolic Other in both instances, among others, was the Negro/Black people. The consequence of these formulations was the elevation of liberal humanist models as reasoned and objectively true, a basis that would be reified as scientific and discursive truth. The idea of Man resulting from these productions was demarcating itself as the universal human.

Since coloniality (Maldonado-Torres, 2007), the ongoing aftermath of colonial policies and discourse are typically racialized, the colonial subject does not experience their nonbeing outside of the discourse of Man as human, a relationship framed by Fanon (1952) as follows: "not only must the Black man be Black; [they] must be Black in relation to the [White] man" (p. 90). Coloniality functions to structure the social and political lives of Black people and ensures that they experience the world as nonhuman/not-quite-human in the hierarchical order of humanity. This structuring is what makes the seeming facticity of "Black Lives Matter" a complicated statement in the United States.

To be clear, the statement, particularly in liberal humanist registers, makes sense. Black people living should matter, namely, hold value part of citizenship's apportionments. According to Wynter, however, as *the Black* does not belong to the same definition of humanity, and for all intents and purposes, is regarded as nonhuman/not-quite-human in the equation of Man-as-human, life and mattering are elusive and improbable terms. In a 1994 letter, *No Humans Involved: An Open Letter to My Colleagues*, Wynter names and critiques knowledge disciplines for their role in the reproduction of social hierarchies that engender and legitimate the range of violence on Black living and mattering. To illustrate this point, Wynter pointed to the Los Angeles Police Department and their use of the moniker *no humans involved*, to describe incidents that involved Black people, among others. This logic exemplified the placelessness of Blackness in the social hierarchy and became the essential code for nonhuman (that is, no humans involved), articulating how the order of knowledge, rooted, and propagated by coloniality, transatlantic enslavement, and the convergences of Western conquest, generated a representation of the human as a bio-evolutionarily selected organism. In this order, conceptions of who fits within its bounds and those who do not (nonhuman/not-quite-human) (Wynter, 1994, 2003, 2006) are erected, exacting the conditions for the current order of knowledge.

On the current order of knowledge, fulfilled by conquest, coloniality, and enslavement, Wynter explained that European representation of human as naturally selected "can be induced to see all those outside of our present 'sanctified universe of obligation' whether as racial or Jobless Other, as having been placed in their interiorized status . . . by the extra-human ordering of bio-evolutionary Natural Selection" (Wynter, 1994, p. 54). On these terms, where white (in a biological sense) was human, Black ascendant people would become referent for inferiority: "all of these as the ostensible embodiment of the non-evolved backward Others—to varying degrees and as such the negation of the generic 'normal humanness' ostensibly expressed by and embodied in peoples of the West" (Wynter, 2003, p. 260).

Accordingly, the rationale that allowed for the public assault of Rodney King in 1992, which grounds her letter, was and is part of the same hierarchical apparatus that permitted the in/explicable deaths of Trayvon Martin, Michael Brown, and Breonna Taylor; the apparatus justifies a Rittenhouse not guilty verdict and a Capitol building insurrection; and incessantly regards Black folks as deserving of violence and punishment, or, "The Negro is an animal, the Negro is bad, the Negro is wicked, the Negro is ugly" (Fanon, 1952, p. 92). Though the moment changes, the colonial order of knowledge (Wynter, 2003) remains steady, consistent with her thesis that "the present ethnoclass (that is, Western bourgeois) conception of the human, Man," overrepresents itself "as if it were the human itself, and that of securing the well-being, and therefore the full cognitive and behavioral autonomy of the human species itself/ourselves" (Wynter, 2003, p. 260).

The making of nonhuman/not-quite-human can be understood as anti-Blackness. The term, *anti-Blackness*, as it will be used throughout this text, references a range of violent technologies—epistemic, ideological, material, spiritual, psychological—that threaten Black livability. Anti-Blackness is mediated by the persistent vilification of Blackness bonded to Black bodies, experiences, and ways of knowing (Dancy et al., 2018; Dumas & ross, 2016). The idea, for Sharpe (2016), is similar to the weather in its pervasiveness. Where weather, in its changeability and improvisation, produces and gives way to new ecologies, Black being in the wake is transformed. Here, normative categorizations for Black folks lose their force as the Black (Dumas, 2014) becomes the carrier of history's sociopolitical grasp, "terrors embodiment" (Sharpe, 2016, p. 15), in what Saidiya Hartman (2007) articulated as the afterlife of slavery: "If slavery persists as an issue in the political life of black America, it is not because of an antiquarian obsession with bygone days or the burden of a too-long memory, but because black lives are still imperiled and devalued by a racial calculus and a political arithmetic that were entrenched centuries ago" (p. 6). In a United States context, "slavery is imagined as a singular event even as it changed overtime and even as its duration expands into supposed emancipation and beyond" (Sharpe, 2016, p. 106). To live in the afterlife of slavery is to inherit the status of nonbeing and nonstatus, a condition marked by singularity, or a routine climactic phenomenon that occurs in perpetuity. For Spillers (1987), "even though the captive flesh/body has been 'liberated,' and no one need pretend that even the quotation marks do not matter, dominant symbolic activity, the ruling episteme that releases the dynamics of naming and valuation, remains grounded in the originating metaphors of captivity and mutilation so that it is as if neither time nor history, nor historiography and its topics, shows movement, as the human subject is 'murdered' over and again" (p. 67). In this genealogy of thought, Sharpe (2016) puts forth what she terms *the wake*. For Sharpe (2016), to follow the (non)placement of Black subjects in the United States society to its reasoned and logical conclusion is to recognize Black death "as a predictable and constitutive aspect of democracy . . . that very notion of justice . . . produces or requires Black exclusion and death as normative" (Costa Vargas & James, 2012, p. 193). This theorization demands that the "imagination, mechanics, and reproduction of ordinary [society] rely on the exclusion of ordinary Blacks and their availability for violent aggression and/or premature death or disappearance" (Costa Vargas & James, 2012, p. 194). These are the tangled grounds that [we] walk on, and I believe a way of rethinking relations in and against this requirement of death and dying. The question, "what happens when we proceed as if we know this, anti-Blackness, to be the ground on which we stand, the ground from which we attempt to speak?" (Sharpe, 2016, p. 7), invokes a sense of normalcy and knowing that is Black existence in the wake. In the afterlife of slavery, "living in the wake means living the history of terror, from slavery to the present, as the ground of our everyday Black existence" (p. 15). Moreover, to live in the wake is "to live in the no's, to live in the no-space that the law is not bound to respect, to live in no citizenship, to live in the long time of Dred and Harriet Scott" (p. 16), where laws and rights do not easily, if at all, relate to Black existence. After Rankine (2015), the United States progressive imagination, and for the purposes of this text, student/early-adult development theory, do not have the historical commitment (Okello & Duran, 2021) to grappling with the no's of Black living that state.

> There really is no mode of empathy that can replicate the daily strain of knowing that as a black person you can be killed for simply being black no hands in your pockets, no playing music, no sudden movements, no driving your car, no walking at night, no walking in the day, no turning onto this street, no entering this building, no standing your ground, no standing here, no standing there, no talking back, no playing with toy guns, no living while black. (Rankine, 2015, para. 2)

If then, there has been an insidious configuration, a racial calculus and political arithmetic, that overdetermines Black existence, what "blackened knowledge" (Sharpe, 2016, p. 13) so to speak, is made possible? Amid the haunting of death and the fact of Black liveliness that, daily, traverses death's longing, how do we make room for the figurations of death to spirit, psyche, body, and sociality, while also living into the fullness of Black existence? I am drawn all the more to Sharpe's theorizations, and the likes of Hartman, Patterson, Dionne Brand, Frank Wilderson, and others because of how they refuse to avert their backward-looking gaze. They refuse the simplifying assumptions of liberal progressivism and inclusion discourses that would otherwise sidestep the difficulty, and perhaps, terror, of sitting in the room with history (Brand, 2001). The door of no return, as Brand (2001) teaches, marked a transformation of people into bodies that were systematically emptied of human characteristics, "bodies of emptied self-interpretation, in which new interpretations could be placed" (p. 25). Theorizing a Black humanity in the wake, the attempt to ethically encounter and attend to Black living, is to look beyond disciplinary solutions to "Blackness's ongoing abjection" (Sharpe, 2016, p. 33) that ultimately function to maintain the wake. It, perhaps, means making meaning of and in the shifting grounds. Where the weather of anti-Blackness holds our feet to these waters, I am attempting to think about Blackened methodological tools against environmental tensions (read: anti-Blackness) that push and pull under, always toward Black death. I believe there is knowledge available, a rutter—instructions made of tides and constellations "for finding one's way at sea" (p. 212)—that there are tools, Blackened knowledge, made of Black flesh.

Spillers (1987) called the flesh "that zero degree of social conceptualization that does not escape concealment under the brush of discourse, of the reflexes of iconography" (p. 67), adding, "If we think of the 'flesh' as a primary narrative, then we mean its seared, divided, ripped-apartness, riveted to the ships hole, fallen, or 'escaped' overboard" (p. 67). This narrative, fundamentally, cannot attach itself to "flesh" and produce a "body," and, as such, Black lives are invariably stripped of personhood, they exist outside of normative categories of community and citizenship. Is it precisely this positioning, however, this "scene of unprotected female flesh—of female flesh 'ungendered'—[which] offers a praxis and a theory; a text for living"[6] (p. 68). The invocation of praxis and theory, made in, and of Black flesh, propels my desire in the text to theorize from the place Blackness. Before discussing Black flesh as a portal into Black ontological possibility, I consider how Black rebellious activities[7] created an archive for my thought process.

Black Rebellious Activities or Enunciations of Liveliness

According to Wynter (n.d.), reinventing conceptions of the human necessitates rebellious activities. She documents a spectrum of such activities throughout her scholarly and creative praxis, including written and shared literary work, marronages, and engagement in music-making and listening. In doing so, she avoids simply rehearsing racialized scripts that reject Black humanity. Instead, "every line is sutured to Black life" (McKittrick, 2021, p. 157). Moreover, Wynter (1994) invoked the Black Aesthetic/Black Arts movements as a series of rebellious activities and sites of possibility. In like manner, this book draws from the well of Black rebellious activities, as self-definition (Okello, 2018) emerged from a rigorous tracing of writers/artists of the Black Aesthetic/Black Arts movements—particularly in the life and labor of James Baldwin and Audre Lorde (see chapter 3). Black world-making, as it has been taken up by artists, scholars, and writers (Du Bois, 1903; Hartman, 2019; Lorde, 1984; Quashie, 2021) has been necessary in so far as Black humanity has been and continues to be systemically exempt from ethical regard in the United States sociopolitical imaginary. Society's lack of imagination on, for, and about Black being, delimits the possibilities for accurate and accountable educational theorizing about Black folks. To imagine self-defining praxis (Okello, 2018), against an anti-Black world, is to begin from an elsewhere, or as Amiri Baraka (1996) yearned, "We want a Black poem. And a Black World. Let the world be a Black Poem" (p. 219). Whereas, Blackness tied to bodies is unlovable and unfit for conventional citizenship, Black rebellious activities wielded in the sovereignty of the Black imagination (Scott, 2002), which engenders otherwise possibilities (that is, self-definition), is not a comportment of the Man-as-human assumption that overdetermines educational theorizing. Black worlds recognize the indisputability of anti-Blackness and, instead of attempting to resolve negation, desire to locate living in and beyond the terribleness (Coles, 2023, 2024). Black specificity, here, is a purposeful intervention in higher education and student/early-development discourse, because Black Studies' intellectual project "wants to reject the world of anti-Blackness and too organize, instead, ideologies of and for a world that could embrace Blackness" (Quashie, 2021, p. 5), metabolized by the parallel Black Arts/Studies/Aesthetic/Power movements, which labored to define Blackness outside the limits of anti-Black regard.

These movements were largely concerned with curating modalities of freedom that were not indexed to the Western Man and liberal humanist constructions of progress or freedom, which points to the critical question, how do I live free in this Black body, or as I have written elsewhere, how do I exist in this Black body in this historical moment and into future? (Okello, 2018). Where there is no end to the afterlife of slavery and coloniality, where "violence precedes and exceeds" (Wilderson, 2010, p. 76) Black folks, Black living is and can be made.

The Potentialities of Flesh

Interrogating Black histories and knowledge-making traditions affirms Moten's (2003) meditation that, "the history of Blackness is a testament to the fact the objects can and do resist" (p. 1). Moten continued, "Blackness—the extended movement of a specific upheaval, an ongoing irruption that anarranges every line—is a strain that pressures the assumption of the equivalence of personhood and subjectivity" (p. 1). Blackness as bonded to Black bodies, thus, is at odds with a society that has structured it as a problem. On these terms, seemingly, it would be of little value to theorize emancipatory Black possibility in and through Black bodies (read: spirit, psyche, materiality, emotionality). Spillers (2007), like Wynter and others, through various modalities, intervened on those terms and curated a grammar that could attend to the subjectivity of Black folks, while simultaneously theorizing about what it means to be human in the wake of anti-Blackness. When developing this grammar, Spillers noted that she was attempting to interrupt the routinization of Black people and their treatment in theoretical conversations, and "black people being treated as a kind of raw material. . . . The history of black people was something you could use as a note of inspiration," but when it came to Black folks, that inspiration was "never about you" (p. 300). She continued, "you could never use it to explain something in theoretical terms. There was no discourse that it generated" (p. 300), critiquing the human and social sciences, and for the purposes of this text, development discourses.

Returning to the position of the Black in Western society, Black flesh, in essence, assisted in structuring the position of theory, or plainly put, the Western Man needs/needed Blackness to constitute itself. Theoretically speaking, where Blackness is the line of delineation between human and nonhuman/not-quite-human, Black flesh could not, and cannot, be recognized as having theoretical import because of its role as abjection. Therefore, Spillers's called for revisiting the logic that defined canonical theory.

Whereas, again, the body outlined official personhood and the possibility of self-possession, a set of principles that formally dislodges/dislodged Black folks from citizenship consideration, the flesh designated dimensions of human life. The flesh is not a biological marker, so to speak, though it does represent atemporal fixations, or what Spillers renders as a "hieroglyphics of the flesh," wherein lies "the calculated work of iron, whips, chains, knives, the canine patrol, the bullet" (Spillers, 1987, p. 67). The markings of the flesh "transfer" (p. 67) across generations and into the present, even now, on those who might legally have been liberated in a United States context. Those "hieroglyphics of the flesh" do not disappear because of legality, as Blackness maintains its force as an organizational principle in the contemporary, the afterlife of slavery. So, "in the absence of kin, family, gender, belonging, language, personhood . . . what remains in the flesh . . . the ether that holds together" (Weheliye, 2014, p. 40) Man-as-human, forms a site of possibility. In absence, the flesh does not (cannot) rely on Western constructions of Man-as-human. Spillers reconciled that in the flesh, between the body overdetermined by the genre of Man-as-human, vitality exists in excess, if we would but read for it. This rendering should not be read as an attempt to sidestep the perpetuity of the wake, the afterlife of slavery and coloniality; rather, I am interested in the material "how" of Black living, even as we live subjection, knowing that "we [do] not simply or only live in subjection and as the subjected" (Sharpe, 2016, p. 4). Williamson (2016) articulates a similar idea, noting Black existence as "not reducible to the terror that calls it into existence, but is the rich remainder. . . . it is the multifaceted artifact of Black communal resistance and resilience that is expressed in Black idioms, cultural forms, traditions" (p. 9).

Flesh, and what I understand to be its potential to condition possibility, offers an ontological intervention on the reliance of Western humanism in student/early-adult development and its continuance. Such an intervention may assist in redefining the terms of Black existence in anti-Black worlds. Flesh imbibes, and perhaps more accurately, works in excess of the psychosocial theorizations on and about Black people in the student/early adult development canon, and in doing so, does not embrace liberal humanist and political ontologies (that is, emancipatory laws and discourses that would affix full personhood to Black people) that are structurally out of reach for [most] Black people. Or, in the flesh, as Moten conjures above, Black people persist. In Moten's work, the flesh comes to the fore as Black sociality, distinct from political ontology that defines the world of Man. In that register, Blackness is and can be a site of radical possibility, mysticism, indomitability, and transcendence, and existential revision. Sexton (2011) words are useful in clarifying this point.

> Black optimism is not the negation of the negation that is afro-pessimism, just as black social life does not negate black social death by inhabiting it and vitalizing it. A living death is as much a death as it is a living. Nothing in afro-pessimism suggests that there is no black (social) life, only that black life is not social life in the universe formed by the codes of state and civil society, of citizen and subject, of nation and culture, of people and place, of history and heritage, of all the things that colonial society has in common with the colonized, of all that capital has in common with labor—the modern world system. (p. 28)

Owunna's *Infinite Essence* exhibition privileges this line of sight, and this text, too, is interested in locating Black ontological possibility in excess of anti-Black enclosures. I am drawn to grammars of possibility and praxis like Owunna, and Lucille Clifton's world making poem bent on becoming, always toward the work of being alive. Issuing her position on living, she wrote, "won't you celebrate with me." Here, Clifton brilliantly situated the self—Black women, first-person speaker—as a site of knowing in and against the "tried to kill" that threatens Black living in the afterlife of slavery and results in the miracle of Black survival (Quashie, 2021). The poem can be read in multiple registers, and though the opening line is framed as a question, it is perhaps better understood as a declaration of opposition. This angle is appropriate as a response to anti-Blackness; to see the poem as an extension of Black flesh, however, is to behold what the speaker makes possible, which among things, as stated, is the Black woman as capacious knower.

The audacity of regard in the poem that dares to imagine a flesh deserving of celebration puts forth Black ontological possibility that exists outside of reason, for as Clifton notes, "I had no model." The limitations of student/early-adult development theory are pronounced in such a statement as Black being is incompatible with the psychosocial renderings that assume humanness as attached to the Western Man. Where humanism undergirds student/early-adult development, the etiology of Blackness, which emerges as an object of economic, political, and scientific rationalization, troubles the notion of identity and generalizations/universalization. The speaker, in lieu of a model, in the wake of "Babylon" and the violence of anti-Blackness, "made it up," as in precedes and exceeds rational orientations, signaling the possibility of Black flesh to conjure living (Quashie, 2021) in proximity to death in its multiple forms.

Fleshing the "Self" in Self-Definition

To be clear, self, as I use it now and throughout this text is not akin to individuality, or the notion that Black flesh should commit to independence, autonomous being, and self-reliance. The idea of individualism that is curated out of Eurocentric rational discourses and circulates in the United States social, political, and educational imaginary prioritizes a social subject consistent with the general status quo in United States society. Blackness troubles the quintessential adult citizen that is imagined as the product of higher education. Conceptually, thus, the idea is incompatible with the figurations of self-definition that I am proposing here. Further, in a settler-colonial and anti-Black world, the notion of individualism is not possible where "Blackness is not only a collective designation but a collective indictment" (Quashie, 2021, p. 32). In this context, too, the idea of an autonomous, self-reliant, and individually oriented subject is necessary to advance capitalistic goals. I do recognize the lure of "self" to be one that infers a sense of singleness that rejects relationality and notions of community, and yet what I feel and read in the texts of Black writers and thinkers who meditate on Black flesh is the principle of *we*. This axiomatic "we" is present in the idea of self, believing that even in the absence of expressed communal emphasis, to be present—to speak, to live—is to testify to a relational self or selves. This instantiation is not without contestation.

Again, where Black subjects were owned, there was no sense that they could own themselves, reproductively or otherwise. Ruptured in this instance are notions of relationality, ownership, community, and genealogy in a conventional sense for Black folks. McKittrick (2006) explained the relationship of Blackness to ownership as a "reward system repetitively returns us to the body, black subjecthood, and the where of blackness" (p. 3). At this impasse, Black flesh holds open possibility as it delineates what is irreducibly social about Black flesh as distinct from political death. Following, Moten (2013), as the flesh is social, differentiated from political death, it refuses anti-Black enclosures that would, among other things, have it to exist as a rational Self. Thinking with Spillers, Moten draws attention to the way transatlantic slavery disrupted the possibility of Black relationality and possession. Self-ownership or self-possession, it would seem for Spillers, can be understood in the distinction that is the flesh and body. The flesh, for Moten, is that which is "unowned or unowed by a self" (1:01:06). Furthermore, the flesh is unowned by one who would claim it and simultaneously forms the grounds of resistance for the enslaved [woman] against those who would own [her]. Importantly, this position of resistance cannot be taken by an individual self (as the owned could not own the self), and thus, it is a position that can only occur relationally. Reflecting on Baby Suggs's sermon in the clearing where she resoundingly calls on her congregation to love their flesh; "To love your flesh," as Baby Suggs demanded, "is a given as a communal imperative" (1:02:11). Another way of reading this is that the condition of possibility is not wrapped up in possession, strictly speaking, the conceptual model of self-ownership is not conducive to care and protection as it relates to Black living. Or, the conceptual model of 'self' will fail to bring about practices of care and protection. The flesh, thus, traces what Wynter (1990) calls a *demonic ground*, what I recognize as a site of Black ontological possibility.

On Love and Specificity

Aiming to trace the relationship to the contours of Afro-pessimism, Moten (2013) noted, "I have thought long and hard . . . about whether blackness could be loved; there seems to be a growing consensus that analytic precision does not allow for such a flight of fancy" (pp. 737–38). The condition of Blackness as bonded to bodies, to be sure, does raise pressing questions about the potentialities of something as transcendent, opaque, difficult to pin and yet, deeply yearned for, as love. The thinking about, and the question of whether it is possible to love Blackness and, as such, Black people, has been raised before: June Jordan (2003), asked, "here, in this extreme, inviolable coincidence . . . my status as someone twice stigmatized, my status as a Black woman who is twice kin to the despised majority of all the human life that there is, . . . it is here, in this extremity, that I ask, of myself, and of anyone who would call me sister, Where is the love?" (pp. 270–71). I take Jordan's and Moten's querying to be in search of a conception of love beyond the confines of valuation and toward a love politic that grapples with the urgency of Patricia Hill

Collins (2004) contention, that "Loving Black people . . . in a society that is so dependent on hating Blackness constitutes a highly rebellious act" (Collins, 2004, p. 50). Moreover, being Black in an anti-Black world is a metaphysical dilemma that demands a different orientation to love where it relates to Black people. Love, here, for Black people, must be a site of deep knowledge that is both tool and reprieve from the intensities of anti-Blackness.

The movement toward a conceptual model of love that accounts for the particularities of Black living, constitutes the sort of analytic precision that Moten deems urgent. Thus, I invite the reader to ask, what does it mean to love Blackness? For Dei (2017), "Loving Blackness is an act of psychological and political decolonization, a process that challenges the dehumanization of Black and Brown subjects in their contact with white supremacy. Moreover, loving Blackness as a discourse of anti-racism moves beyond racial dehumanization of Blackness to reclaim Black life" (p. 53). On what love requires, Fanon (1952) wrote, "the fact remains nevertheless that true love, real love—that is, wishing for others what one postulates for oneself when this postulate integrates the permanent values of human reality—requires the mobilization of psychological agencies liberated from unconscious tensions" (p. 28). Fanon's conception of love dovetails nicely with Nash's (2013, 2018) commitment to love politics, which are anchored in second-wave Black feminisms, and "call for ordering the self and transcending the self, a strategy for remaking the self and for moving beyond the limitations of selfhood" (Nash, 2013, p. 3). I am particularly drawn to this thinking because of the insistence on engendering affective political communities. The orientation to affective politics and economies (see Ahmed, 2004) enables an understanding of love as existing beyond identity politics and toward a figuration of "how bodies are organized around intensities, longings, desires, temporalities, repulsions, curiosities, fatigues, optimism, and how these affects produce political movements or sometimes inertias" (Nash, 2013, p. 3). My goal, thus, is not to produce or add complexity to myriad formations of Black racial identity (for example, Cross, 1971, 1991). While important, I agree with Wynter (2003, 2006) that the intersectional projects that attend specifically to identity categories constitute a focus on the map, not the territory (see preliminary vocabulary). The territory, so far as I wrestle with it in this text, is the ontological dilemma of Blackness as mediated by the overdetermined construct of Man-as-human, and how that emphasis

superseding analyses about how the Western Man-as-human is constructed as the only version of human being (Wynter, 2003). The territory exceeds full knowability/mappability (King, 2019). It might be understood as "the liminal precincts of the current governing configurations of the human as Man in order to abolish this figuration and create other forms of life" (Weheliye, 2014, p. 21). Wynter's (1990) intervention called for moving beyond representational, identity discourses, and toward demonic ground, "outside of our present governing system of meaning, or theory/ontology" (p. 356), and "outside the consolidated field" of "being/feeling/knowing" (p. 364). Wynter asked, "in effect, rather than only voicing the 'native' woman's hitherto silenced voice, we shall ask: What is the systemic function of her own silencing, as both woman and, more totally, as 'native' woman?" (p. 365). In like manner, the task before this text is to offer a critique of Western humanism, and its figurations for normative being, particularly as it relates to the ontological conditions of Blackness in the United States.

Importantly, I have chosen a particular archive: photographs, essays, books, and media. I, like other interdisciplinary scholars, assume a responsibility, to the extent that it is possible, to struggle against representational imperatives (Quashie, 2021) as that which definitely constitutes *Black life*, because those logics too often constrain Black ontological possibility. Otherwise stated, I am interested in disrupting the discursive limitations of the proper Black subject, methodologically put in place by representational politics (for example, interviews, focus groups, etc.). For these reasons, I pull away from the use of Black "life" as something that can be apprehended, and toward *liveliness and living* as modes of praxis. In that way, this book is an ethics project that aims to reaffirm the consequence, and necessity, of attending to the abstracting, sensational, affective, ontological breath of Black liveliness and living.

With the map and territory (Wynter, 2006) as my theoretical point of departure, I think with a range of Black reading practices toward two interdependent goals for locating ontological possibility, Black living: to annotate and to redact (see Sharpe, 2016). In its literary use, annotations represent those processes of adding data or explanation to a text or image in order to supplement messaging. If and when, for example, one may need more information to make sense of what they are seeing or reading, annotations bring additional information. Annotations in this way exceed and at times provide a critical explanatory summary valuation of a text or image. Annotations perform an important naming—otherwise stated, a citing about the violent arithmetics that encamp Black living while informing present and future formations (McKittrick, 2014). Returning to Owunna, his photographic practice brought that which was otherwise not visible into sharper relief. The fluorescent paint and shutter settings, as annotations, generated an alternative view of Black living. Similarly, redactions are a form of editing, and most especially, a process of bringing back, recalling, or reducing. Redactions create a particular line of sight by concealing or keeping something from view. For Owunna, it could be said that the intention of "total darkness" was a form of redaction. I read his objective as a belief in the specificity of Blackness. By creating Blackened worlds, one can see the cosmological essence of Blackness. Each of the reading practices used in this text (for example, literary criticism, chokehold, annotations and redactions, listening to images, plot, and plantation) are part of the long practice of Black Studies citing, siting, and sighting, to consider the nuance of Black ontological possibility—multiple meanings of abjection through inhabitation—against the violence that confronts it (Campt, 2017; Hartman, 2007; McKittrick, 2014; Sharpe, 2016). On this premise, I understand otherwise ways of being as imagined and materialized through Black flesh. By no means exhaustively or prescriptively, the various reading practices I deploy are intended as a guide for illuminating the complexity of Black liveliness and living, as a primary rationale for this book is to offer tools for theory, policy, and practice.

A Beginning

Infinite essence materializes Black creative intellectual departure, the type of world-making that self-definition strives to annotate. Loving Black flesh, Black specificity, is attunement, an ethics project, and a way reading in excess (for example, embodied formations, images, scripts, society, etc.) to both understand the workings of anti-Black logic, but more fervently, trace Black liveliness—past, present, and future. Furthermore, this text intends to shift the reference point in human development and knowledge production discourses, and educational theorizing writ large, to avoid the trap of mistaking the map for the territory (Wynter, 2003), of attempting to represent (Black) *being* through Western humanistic frames that are uninhabitable for most.

August,

Deep breath in, 1 . . . 2 . . . 3 . . . 4; exhale, 1 . . . 2 . . . 3 . . . 4. I try to remind myself of this process in the moments when I am most tense, uncertain, and afraid; when my muscles tighten, and eyes begin to well. The understanding that I cannot protect you from the world, from people, from absences and violence, at all times, is my focus and clarity, it keeps me writing, it compels and choreographs my dreams.
It also instructs my time with you. To be clear, fear is not my motivation for how I spend time with you—I refuse to parent from a place of fear. Fear, as deployed by the wake of anti-Black regard, are the grounds we walk on every day. These grounds are unsteady, broken, and always threatening to pull you under, to cause your foot to stumble. But it, this structure of the world, is not your universe. These are not the grounds you inhabit. You do not belong to it, to this place. It will not have you. I decided very early that I would teach you how to fly. Rocking you to sleep, or lifting you into the morning, I would recount that there once was a world that loved Black children—planned for, celebrated, lifted, and took joy in them. In this world, where they love Black children, all Black children are brilliant and have superpowers. In that Black world, children can scale the cosmos—that have resolved physics and upended gravity, re-membered sciences, and mathematics for flight long since forgotten. *Asé*. Those are words they uttered when children intended to leap. To levitate. To fly. Asé. Asé. Asé. I want you to fly, August. Beyond this place. Call it into being. You are of flight. Asé.

2

Breathing, Being, and Human Development

Figure 2.1. Alawuala is the Earth Goddess in Igbo cosmology, and Her name translates literally as "the land which is the ultimate earth." She incarnates the spiritual principles of the primordial Igbo High God Eke-Nnechukwu. With Her connection to the primordial feminine, Alawuala prescribes the universal laws of existence that transcend all life, Nso Ala (Laws of the Earth Goddess), and transmits them to humanity in the blackness of Her womb. Her layered waist beads speak to Her fecundity and control of fertility in all dimensions of life. Her sinuous pose prefigures Her zoomorphic terrestrial form as Eke-Nwe-Ohia, the sacred Igbo python. *Source*: *Alawuala* by Mikael Owunna. Used with permission of the artist.

> The fact of breathing is not, and ought not to be evidence of life, sociality, or citizenship
>
> —Ashon Crawley

How *Alawuala* Inspires This Chapter

Breath and breathing. I am thinking about the labor of breath over and against labored breathing, whereas Black breathing is beauty, living practice, and method; it is inhalation and emergence. *Alawuala* reminds me that the site and sight, à la Katherine McKittrick, of Blackness is of potency and abundance. Blackness is fruitfulness; it has, in its essence, a readiness for productiveness. The image, Alawuala, stages the rich capacity for Blackness to bear otherwise ways of thinking, doing, and understanding—growth. In this chapter, I inhale the potentialities of Blackness, and exhale conceptual possibilities.

∼

Black Study is not about the study of Black people. Black Study as otherwise possibility, more closely aligns with what Da Silva (2013) called "at once a kind of knowing and doing; it is a praxis, one that unsettles what has come before but offers no guidance for what has yet to become" (p. 44). As an approach, it confronts iterations of the question, *what are the experiences of Black people in education?* which, in many cases, serves as the point of intervention concerning Black people's experiences in educative spaces. This line of thinking, if not handled carefully and critically, may function to fulfill an order of knowledge that leaves the overrepresentation of Man-as-human (Wynter, 1994, 2003) unquestioned. Explorations of Black life tend to depend on assumptions of the human subject that do not account for the ways Blackness is refused from the category, or the belief in Blackness as a social, traditioned, source of pleasure, joy, love, and being. Hartman (2019) might say, "[social reformers] always take pictures of the same stuff, . . . failing to discern the beauty and they see only the disorder, missing all the ways Black folks create life and make bare need into an arena of elaboration" (p. 4). Hartman (2019), in reference to Du Bois (1899), offered a pertinent example.

> "What's the object of this investigation?" the woman asked, eyeing him suspiciously.

"Simply to get at the truth," he answered.

"Do you propose to do anything after you get the facts?" she inquired.

"We simply collect the facts," he replied. "Others may use them as they will."

"Then you are trying only to get the facts and not to better things," she said

"Yes," he answered.

"Humph," she replied and then refused to tell him anything. (Hartman, 2019, p. 100)

Du Bois entered Philadelphia as an observer to understand the Negro problem. He posed survey questions and listened intently to the stories of Black people. As a university-trained researcher, Du Bois held tightly to his objectivist training requirement and patiently collected 835 hours of anecdotes, hope, striving, and despair. The line of questioning was important if not a necessary intervention on the deliberate absence of unbiased research of Black people and communities. As it was for Du Bois, documenting Black people's narratives against the force of anti-Black regard that shapes the social curriculum for Black people and how they are rendered in society, is significant work. Notwithstanding, though the interview protocol could detail their circumstances and conditions, Black existence could not be reduced to demographic data points—years of education, job(s), and so on. The fullness of Black existence, or what I elaborate on in this chapter as breathing (or the desire for unrestricted breathing), often exceeds the survey instrument and systematic observation prioritized in the social sciences. Alternatively, Black Study, which departs from the routinization of social science, can produce otherwise possibilities of being—alternative modes, alternative strategies, alternative ways of life in a response to the principle question, what does it mean to be human?

Human development theorizing presumes humanity to be consistent, shared, and accessible (Okello, 2018). When considering self-authorship, three interrelated dimensions of humanity are explored: epistemology, the intrapersonal, and interpersonal. These dimensions are anchored in a line of questioning that attempts to chronicle the varied ways participants respond to the questions of who am I? how do I know? and what are my relationships with others? (Baxter Magolda, 2001, 2008, 2009). Organizations (see Association of American Colleges and Universities [2006] statement on Academic Freedom and Educational Responsibility) have touted the development of self-authorship as the goal of twenty-first-century learning, thereby legitimating the guiding assumptions of the human that conceptually frame the idea. Centrally, I ask, how might Black specificity reconstitute student development theorizing? In what follows, I consider the evolution of self-authorship before placing the construct in conversation with Black Studies.

While valuable to the work of representation, questions predicated on principles of constructivist qualitative inquiry that privilege Western constructions of Man-as-human, do little in the way of explicating the fullness of Black liveliness. In what follows, I trace the epistemological thought that functioned to legitimate self-authorship. Thereafter, I discuss the ways Blackness complicates the dimensions of self-authorship by which the constructivist approach is buoyed.

A Brief Review of Student Development

The history of student development theory is one of waves (see Jones, 2019), progressing from a first-wave moment that emphasized growth development engendered by dissonance, assimilation, and accommodation as a result of their collegiate experiences, to a second wave that shifted the focus to social identities and systems of oppression. Here, the second wave interrogated multiple dimensions of identity and how they might otherwise converge and inform one another. For example, discussing psychosocial and cognitive development, researchers began exploring what is understood as holistic development, particularly investigations on how interpersonal, intrapersonal, and cognitive structures functioned together. Holistic development is anchored in the work of developmental psychologist Robert Kegan (1994), who established the subject-object relationship, in which what was once subject—"elements of our knowing or organizing that we are identified with, tied to, fused with, or embedded in" (Kegan, 1994, p. 32)—becomes object, that which we can actively reflect on and make sense of in the moment. In other words, the subject represents an unawareness that cannot be held unless or until one complicates their knowing. Central to this subject-object relationship is that as individuals develop, they do so in cognitive, interpersonal, and intrapersonal manners. Research on holistic development builds on this foundational work (see Baxter Magolda, 2001, 2008).

Assessment of Self-Authorship

Generally, there has been an interest in designing higher-education learning in ways that promote the advancement of holistic development, and self-authorship has been the construct that educators and researchers employ to reach those aims (see AACU, 2006; Keeling 2004). As learning advocates identified themes such as cognitive complexity, and interpersonal and intrapersonal competence (Baxter Magolda, 2008), self-authorship emerged as a lens for understanding development along three dimensions, which could effectively help adults navigate complex roles and responsibilities.

Kegan (1994) described self-authorship as internal identity that can "coordinate, integrate, act upon, or invent values, beliefs, convictions, generalizations, ideals, abstractions, interpersonal loyalties, and intrapersonal states. It is no longer authored by them; it authors them and thereby achieves a personal authority" (p. 185). Studies have affirmed the capacity to author one's thinking, feeling, and social relating as a key component to adult life and the achievement of collegiate learning outcomes (Baxter Magolda, 2001). As noted above, self-authorship integrates three dimensions of development: epistemological, intrapersonal, and interpersonal. The epistemological, or cognitive dimension, references the ways people know what they know, and the limits and certainties of knowledge in deciding what they believe (Perry, 1970). Here, there is an active construction of meaning dictated by one's internal belief system (Baxter Magolda, 2001; Kegan, 1994). The intrapersonal dimension, similarly, requires the integration of multiple assumptions and disparate understandings in the formation of a coherent identity. The emergent coherence reflects enduring, chosen values, as opposed to those imposed by external forces. Where it relates to the interpersonal dimension, self-authored people have the meaning making capacity to be interdependent such that they can recognize and support multiple sets of needs and perspectives and exist in mutually affirming relationships. The achievement of self-authorship, or the evolution of consciousness, by which one's organizing frames are integrated and subsumed into more complex frames, have been further legitimated by assessment processes that are consistent with the constructive development tradition (Kegan, 1982, 1994).

Building on Piaget's (1950) work that situates development as configured by dissonance in one's current structuring that prompts new, more complex structures, the three dimensions of self-authorship are an interwoven structure. Extending this logic, Kegan (1982) wrote that individuals make meaning in the space between their experiences and their reactions to the experiences—"the place where the event is privately composed, made sense of the place where it actually becomes an event for that person" (p. 2). Thus, understanding and assessing epistemological structures has meant that researchers have had to learn "how people made sense of an experience and what constructions of the world, self, and others under gird that interpretation" (Baxter Magolda & King, 2007, p. 495). Specific to self-authorship, assessment has meant uncovering the subject and object components of meaning.

Moreover, Kegan (1994) concluded that there were certain types of content areas that might reveal subject-object information, noting them as anger, anxiety, success, or change. The assumption is that if interviewees are asked sound, probing questions that can interrogate an experience, then they can/will explicate a sense of self. The approach also presumes that the researcher has been trained in constructivist qualitative interviewing techniques, a paradigm that motions for multiple, socially constructed, and context-bound realities, and an interview that is mutually shaped by the interviewer and researcher (Lincoln & Guba, 2000): "The interviewer constructs questions in the context of what the respondent introduces. The interviewer's primary task is to explore how the interviewees construct themselves to yield the interpretations the interviewees share. To achieve this task, the interviewer must listen actively to identify questions that will locate the boundaries of the interviewee's assumptions about knowledge, self, and relationships" (Baxter Magolda & King, 2007, p. 496). Broadly speaking, the belief that free-flowing conversation about the contexts in which participants experienced tension, and how they subsequently handled those tensions, was the basis for clarifying the pathways to self-authorship, the three dimensions, and the contextual factors that promoted the construct. Participants were invited to choose the content for the interview as they shared their thoughts.

Following constructivist underpinnings, researchers have approached the assessment of self-authorship in other ways such as translating the dimensions into measurable skills and tracking how closely participants align with certain statements to track their typical ways of thinking and acting (Pizzolato, 2007). This procedure, according to researchers, was not without dilemma as participants used language and modeled sense-making that did not neatly align with self-authored reasoning.

CRITICAL APPROACHES TO READING SELF-AUTHORSHIP

Researchers have considered how the incorporation of different frameworks might engender a deeper, more complex rendering of student/early-adult development. Hernández (2016) employed critical race theory (CRT) to examine how social forces influenced the journey to self-authorship. Homing in on seven Mexican American undergraduate women, the belief was that the sample would reflect the most complex understanding of their racialized selves and the social forces acting on their lives, thereby parsing out a nuanced meaning-making process. In order to purposefully include race/ethnicity, racism, and power into self-authorship, Hernández revised the dimensions so that social forces could be built into the fabric of the construct, suggesting that the change "called for a recalibration so that slightly different questions are asked in order to recognize the dynamic nature of racism, power, and privilege in the developmental process" (Hernández, 2016, p. 172). The shift in questions also marked a change in the developmental point from the individual to the political and racialized environment. Whereas each dimension of development was associated with a question, critical race theory revised the question. Regarding the cognitive dimension, the guiding question shifted from "how do I know?' to "how do I make meaning of my social world?" thereby allowing for "investigation of the developmental processes needed for an individual to recognize how the environment provides particular experiences and stimuli, and the meaning-making processes that an individual may use to interpret this information" (p. 172). The revised question called on researchers to consider their epistemological assumptions in research design. In addition, it lifted the importance of moving away from constructivism and toward social constructivist epistemology. As a brand of constructivism, social constructivism "has some affinity to theories of symbolic interactionism and ethnomethodology that emphasize the actor's definition of the situation" (Swandt, 2007, p. 39).

Social constructivism emphasizes, to a degree, the presence that culture has on individual actors and how it shapes knowing. Regarding the intrapersonal dimension question, "Who am I?" by which individuals identify their values and make meaning of their identities, the question shifted to "How does my social world shape my sense of self as a racialized being?" Hernández (2016) wrote that the questions "allow for the study of ethnic identity development and the developmental processes of identifying how social norms may affect sense of self" (p. 174). Methodologically, the question insists on the analysis of race and racism "by placing them in historical and contemporary contexts" (p. 176). Considering the interpersonal dimension, the question "What relationships do I want with others?" was reframed as "What relationships do I want with others for the benefit of my social world?" This framing enhanced the scope of the original question to include public and political relationships wherein political actors can recognize their desires for coalition building on social justice more broadly.

If, however, CRT is useful in revising questions that encourage educators and researchers to consider individuals' social worlds, the reframing of CRT-informed questions does not account for the specificity of Blackness (Wynter, 1989), wherein the very idea of Black humanity is irreconcilable with notions of full citizenship. There is no sense of a Black social self that is not already threatened by literal and social death. In sum, a race/ethnicity and racism approach to meaning making that does not attend to the specificity of Blackness (see Dumas & ross, 2016), still assumes a logic of Man-as-human, and, therefore, a self capable of full recognition in society. The conundrum of Black being is that anti-Blackness is endemic and, at its core, anti-Blackness positions Black people in an antagonistic relationship with society and United States sociopolitical renderings of humanity.

Taken together, even when attempting to critically reconsider the foundational questions of holistic student development, the ever-present assumption in social science inquiry remains that a story can be told in full. For his part, as Du Bois (1899) sat with Black people in Philadelphia, he realized that there was more to the stories narrated about them. He understood that there were limitations to positivist and constructivist methods that raise questions like "How can narrative embody life in words and at the same time respect what we cannot know? How does one listen for the groans and cries, the undecipherable? . . . is it possible to construct a story from 'the locus of impossible speech'?" (Hartman, 2008, p. 3). He knew that much of what Black people wanted to convey could not be captured by the survey questions, and earnestly worked to shift the question from "the Negro problem," to racism and its structural effects on the lives of Black people in Philadelphia. Though elusive, educators and researchers committed to Black living, must "respect the limits of what cannot be known" (p. 4) and yet labor "to paint as full a picture of life as possible" (Hartman, 2008, p. 8). This process finds possibility by theorizing Blackness in a critique of epistemological foundations.

Blackness and the Order of Knowledge

Black disregard is held in place by the laden Western epistemological foundations. Plainly, Wynter (1994) asked, "How did they come to conceive of what it means to be both *human* . . . in the *kinds of terms* (that is, to be white, of Euro American culture and descent, middle-class, college-educated and suburban) within whose logic" Black people could "be *perceived*, and *therefore behaved towards*, only as the Lack of the human, the Conceptual Other . . . ?" (p. 43). Her question is one of classificatory logic. More specifically, her question asks, what is possible for those who do not and cannot ascend to human status?

This rendering in *No Humans Involved*, suggests that Blackness directs how institutions engage with Black people, expecting a behavior toward them befitting of their nonhuman status. While Wynter used the Los Angeles police officials' use of the acronym NHI to drive her point, her larger provocation implicated institutions of higher education and, more specifically, researchers, those generally regarded as one's who generate and advance knowledge. She pointedly queried, "What is our responsibility for the making of those 'inner eyes?' Ones in which humanness and North Americanness are always already defined, not only in optimally White terms, but also in optimally middle-class, variants of these terms? What have we had to do, and still have to do, with the putting in place of the classifying logic of that shared mode of 'subjective understanding?'" (Wynter, 1994, p. 44). The current order of knowledge, advanced by social science inquiry, is beholden to logic rooted in conquest, colonization, and capitalization. Such ideas took hold in constructs like Social Darwinism and eugenics, which functioned to build hierarchies based on typologies of race and biology (Zuberi & Bonilla-Silva 2008). These constructs still inform the field of education, subsequently driving recommendations for practice, policy, and pedagogy. Extending Wynter's (1994) thesis, Sharpe (2016), explained the comportment toward methodological conservatism, writing, "to produce legible work in the academy often means adhering to research methods that are drafted into the service of a larger destructive force thereby doing violence to our own capacities to read, think, and imagine otherwise. Despite knowing otherwise, we are often disciplined into thinking through and along lines that reinscribe our own annihilation, reinforcing and reproducing, what Sylvia Wynter calls our 'narratively condemned status.'" (Sharpe, 2016, p. 13). Placing Blackness at the center of knowledge production is to consider the very idea of the human as a site of contestation and struggle, one that must be reckoned with as it is nestled in the tension of necropolitics and biopolitics (Weheliye, 2014). The human, for Wynter (2003) must be the site of struggle because it is where decisions are made about well-being, and thus, "the full cognitive and behavioral autonomy of the human species itself/ourselves" (p. 60).

As our processes (for example, knowledge production, and, here, the ways educators and researchers interpret and understand Black peoples' knowing and being in the world) fail to consider the making of the human in relation to and against Black people, they maintain a colonial hold on ideas of humanity that cannot fully account for Black liveliness and living. For this reason, in the next section, I place the central questions of self-authorship in conversation with Blackness.

Epistemological: Cognitive Dimension

The epistemological dimension constitutes the ways one knows what they know. Here, the subject-object relationship, an extension of Cartesian theorizing and Kantian reason, is the underlying epistemology for the mature, complex knowing adult (Kegan, 1982, 1994), achieved in and through higher education. The constructivist, epistemological/cognitive dimension reflects Western conventions of thinking, which are invested in separations like the mind over the body, reason over emotion, a singular history and/or multiple histories. Black knowing, or the capacity for Black people to be knowers of their own regard, is a contentious claim in an anti-Black world. More pointedly, training and socialization in social science inquiry direct researchers to trace Black knowing as detached from the specificity of Blackness. Where it pertains to Black people, research processes often reduce racialization to the function of empirical questions, which could otherwise be read as the study of subjects who happen to be Black, rather than a social and political matrix that orders knowledge. In this way, research, and theoretical approaches, which routinely understate Blackness as a social-political formation, often fail to understate the presence of coloniality on Black bodies and minds and, subsequently, the potentiality of internalized carceral terror, which reproduces psychological and affective enclosure (Okello, 2022).

Moreover, coloniality often disciplines Black subjects into thinking registers that reinscribe and reinforce their dispossession by disavowing one's holistic self—affective capacities, memory, spatiality, spirituality, cosmology, and sociality. Though scholars have critiqued Western framings of thought and epistemology (see Ani, 1994; Mignolo, 2011), particularly its deemphasis on the spirituality of knowledge, its lack of attention to racism and racialized violence, the denial of knowledge systems and values, and its general pursuit of power and control, research on holistic student development, except for recent third-wave contributions, is still developing.

The general racelessness (Perez, 2019) of the cognitive dimension and the culture of epistemological racism that it augments, speaks to the tendency of researchers to locate ideas like racism at the individual or, perhaps, institutional level. Blackness interrupts this tendency by demanding a longer view of epistemological underpinnings, and, particularly, who can be a knower. As the weight of history and signification—meaning of thing—converge, and revolve on white epistemologies (Wynter, 2003; Zuberi & Bonilla-Silva, 2008), Black people are removed from the possibility of knowing, fulfilling the script of American grammar (Spillers, 1987).

Ontology: Intrapersonal Dimension

The question "who am I?" for self-authorship, central to student development theory, is a question of being. This question presumes an autonomous power to decide who one wants to be in the world. The constructivist capacity to say, "I am" is consistent with Cartesian dualism, namely, the statement, I think, therefore I am. Ontology, or the question of being, is taken up in the statement I am. Beneath I am one can locate "justification for the idea that 'others are not' or do not have being" (Maldonado-Torres, 2007, p. 253). A reading of "I think, therefore I am," as complicated by the specificity of Blackness, animates the historically acute rendering: "I think (others do not think, or do not think properly); therefore, I am (others are-not, lack being, should not exist or are dispensable)" (Maldonado-Torres, 2007, p. 253). Accordingly, Cartesian dualism (read: the subject-object relationship), which privileges a pure, epistemological reason, upholds the coloniality of Being, or the notion that others are not. As coloniality marks Black people as a thing, Blackness enables a way of understanding Black people as carrying no life or humanity worth honoring in the Man-as-human order of knowledge. On the matter, Warren (2017) contends, that "Blackness cannot lay claim to the capacities that constitute human subjectivity in the world because blackness is a commodity. . . . It is the devastating inverse of ontological narcissism—we might call black being 'ontological deprivation' in an anti-black world" (p. 222).

Tracing this point, it was at the moment of enslavement, as Bliss (2015) explained that Blackness was excluded from the Human project: "The historical appearance of the Black qua slave is the ontological condition of possibility for the appearance of the (unequally) free Human subject. In a very precise sense, then, 'antiblackness' is a synonym for Humanity" (Bliss, 2015, p. 89). More to the point, "the human being provides an anchor for the declaration. . . . If the black is a human, the declaration anchors mattering in the human's Being" (Warren, 2018, p. 18). Against this backdrop, Black epistemology must necessarily wrestle with the fact that Western society was established, cohered, and maintained on the inseparability of Blackness as nonhuman (Dumas, 2018; Wilderson, 2010). This ontological reality presumes that Blackness cannot have human standing and that assertions otherwise do so against the force of a world where dispossessed (read: tortured, raped, beaten, torn flesh) Black bodies could not be perceived as having a life. Black people bear the weight of *Black* as historical terror (Hartman, 1997) on the flesh, troubling postmodern (Butler, 1993) conceptions of identity as fluid and rational imbrications that privilege objectivity as consciousness. Furthermore, Kantian philosophy extends this meditation by defining knowing as the aversion of Blackness: "By locating the conditions of possibility of knowledge before and beyond sense perception, postulating that terms such as time, space, substance, totality, and so on are the tools 'pure reason' provides to the understanding, [Kant] establishes that now scientific knowledge could progress independent of subjective (psychological) and purely empirical concerns and without principles derived solely from either of them" (Da Silva, 2007, p. 59). Following Kant, epistemology, as the knowledge of (pure) reason, is accomplished by an aversion to the body (sense and sensual perception), otherwise known as experience. Through aversion, enlightenment epistemology could claim rationalist discourse and its assumption of objects' impenetrability as the foundation for knowledge. As impenetrability of the object is established, categorical distinction emerges as an order for the complex, thinking adult. Western epistemology assumes categorical distinction as producing thought that "abstracts the concept of origin from Blackness that precedes it. In other words, the concept of origin is the consequence of abstraction from Blackness" (Crawley, 2017, p. 142). If then, Black people exist outside the realm of human, and symbiotically, of a life, how does theory, as Lorde (1980) argued, "integrate death into living, neither ignoring it nor giving in to it" (p. xx)?

Relationality: Interpersonal Dimension

The third dimension of self-authorship advances the question of relationship, namely, "what relationships do I want with others?" (Baxter Magolda, 2001). This dimension stresses the importance of interdependence and the ability to negotiate mutually substantive relationships (Kegan, 1994). Interdependence, in this way, is the byproduct of a social reality that is accepting of mature, complex citizens aspiring to belong. Kinship, on these terms, is a basic need that is available to each citizen. Blackness, however, troubles conceptions of citizenship, and, therefore, conceptions of interdependence as proposed by constructivist framings and self-authorship. Following, Patterson's (1982) conception of slavery as social death, slavery denied enslaved people kinship through natal alienation. Here, Black people were "alienated from all 'rights' or claims of birth, he ceased to belong in his own right to any legitimate social order" (p. 5). If Black people exist in the afterlife of slavery (Hartman, 1997), as the embodiment of slavery's terror, then that which was denied to the enslaved is juridically and extrajudicially denied to Black people in the contemporary, including the claims and obligations to one's parents, blood relations, ancestors, and descendants. Alienation philosophically and materially was intended to close off Black people (again, consider a closed system that is self-referential—making reference to itself as the authority—and recursive) from ancestral experiences and the possibility of integrating community memory into their understandings of social reality. Thus, if part of how self-possessed individuals (that is, full citizens) understand the self is in and through relationships, Black people were understood as those who do not belong, and, therefore, were prohibited from the possibility of being human (à la Wynter).

Natal alienation as a conundrum of Blackness establishes itself by aspiring to the heteronormative, rationalist discourse of enlightenment logic undergirding the premise of choice, that is, what relationships do I want with others? what relationships do I want to the benefit of my social world? Belonging in this sense is predicated on enclosure, or that which can be exacted, and, thus, available to some and closed to others. A deeper meditation on Blackness probes this history of kinship as an attempt to account for a fuller rendering of Black people's social existence and realities.

Moreover, where the interpersonal dimension has been expanded to consider one's public and political presence as representative of a community and organization, constructions of Blackness in the Western imaginary render the relational and representational capacity of oneness a conceptual impossibility. The conceptual impossibility exists because a normative notion of ethics tends to conflate ethical action with white propertied value systems, ideas like economic success, ownership, and self-reliance. Additionally, this normative sense of ethics assumes, again, that a subject is unencumbered and is able to experience reality with a wide range of choices (Okello, 2018). In the Western imaginary, imagining oneself representing the agenda of others, political or otherwise, ought to be questioned. Furthermore, whereas the interpersonal dimensions enable individuals to identify their own needs and the concerns of others, the transatlantic calculation that produces the idea of Blackness as nonbeing, defined by the ungendering—dissociating Black people from categories of Man or full humans—of the enslaved subject (Fuentes, 2016; Spillers, 1987), rendered Black people as fungible, and, therefore, able to be traded, mobilized for labor, cargo, and never able to participate in the exchange of ideas, knowledge, or goods. This is to say, critical frames—liberal humanism frames, feminist, queer, or otherwise—that are unspecific to Black(ness) regard, do little to upset the order of knowledge that privileges Man-as-human, and where that order remains unattended, theory, and the practice and policy they inform, do less to account for how Black people experience relations.

Taken together, the presence of Blackness in conversation with first- and second-wave student development theory, is incompatible. Importantly, the third wave of student development motions for critical and poststructural theories in student development theorizing. The strength of this wave is the explicit devotion to advancing social change by calling for a critical analysis of compounding domains of power and structures that frame development. To that end, Blackness, as a critique of psychosocial sciences that normalize Man-as-human, pushes this idea further. Beginning with Blackness challenges normative ideals of control and objectivity that mimic white logic. Rather than leading to pessimism or despair, Black specificity "must be embraced as the impossibility that conditions our knowledge of the past and animates our desire for a liberated future" (Hartman, 2008, p. 13). Wynter's (2006) delineation of the map and the territory is one framework within Black Study that may nudge this shift. Where student/early-adult development theory has largely been concerned with the map, or symptoms (for example, categories and identities), a Black Study turn squarely considers the territory, or the epistemic roots that facilitate the current conditions of Black being in higher education and society.

Space to Breathe:
On the Map and Territory as Theoretical Grounds

Mapping, understood here as the notion of (identity) development itself, is the point of contention. The idea that development can speak to, describe, and account for the worlds of Black people is overdetermined by constructions of the Man-as-human, or biocentric conception of the Western Man, which should be understood as a white, cisgender, heterosexual, middle-class male subject. This note is not new to researchers, as this assumption largely grounded the establishment of the second- and third-theory waves.

However, the general corrective tendency for addressing this framing has relied on framings of what (identity) development cannot do, thereby justifying a more extensive treatment of diverse experiences through critical and poststructural theories that emphasize expressions of identity and representation. Indeed, expanding who can be seen and represented in theory is essential, as the efforts reflected in the second-wave (and early-third-wave) theorizing explicate. The emancipatory potential of critical and poststructural ideas, however, while helpful, are partial, or as Wynter (2006) contended, "this emancipation had been effected at the level of the map, rather than at the level of the territory" (p. 116). The limitation in attempting to attend to identity, or the contours of identity (for example, agency, authenticity, dissonance, resilience) interventions that propose eliminating or reforming race, appealing to humanity and liberal humanist ideals like freedom, lie in the presumption of the rhetorically overdetermined Man, upheld by Eurocentric, hegemonic ways of thinking and doing, as a stand-in for the human species itself. Wynter (1995) wrote: "Human beings are magical . . . Words made flesh, muscle and bone animated by hope and desire, belief materialized in deeds, deeds which crystallize our actualities. 'It is man who brings society into being'" (p. 35). On this premise, the work of theorizing is not about invalidating generalizations or the universalism of white constructs, nor is it to refute deficit-oriented theories that sustain anti-Blackness in the world such that multiple identities may be more fully included in the canon's parameters.

As noted, Wynter's project, and the potential of a Black Study turn, is to reimagine understandings of the human, to create new modes of being, or genres of being (Wynter, 2003) that will, in effect, show the inapplicability of Western thought and how the conceptualization of human as Man is incongruent with ways to explain Black liveliness. In short, notwithstanding its emerging commitments to projects of criticality and poststructuralism (for example, CRT, queer theory, intersectionality), recurricularlizing (Baszile, 2019) must ask how has, and does, student/early-development theory and the pedagogies, practices, and policy that it informs, understand and frame Black subjects as objects of white, Western thought? Stated differently, how does a rejection of what it has meant to be Black (that is, theorizing Blackness) manifest in theory, practice, and policy? Namely, centering Blackness has resulted in conceptualizations of Black liveliness as consistent with the study of Black experiences, histories, and politics. At the level of the map, these agendas are useful and contribute to an important charting of information on and about Black educative experiences. Yet desires to understand the experiences of Black people devoid of discussion on how constructions of Blackness position Black people in the world, and, subsequently, what Blackness might engender, open, or create, reifies white logics (Zuberi & Bonilla-Silva, 2008), Man-as-human, as the ideological frame for understanding Black people, and what constitutes Black personhood, and Black freedom projects.

The inability to attend to Black being, emerges from the undertheorized presumption threaded through social science inquiry, that there are no humans involved (Wynter, 1994), translated as the overrepresentation of white logics when trying to understand the lives and livings, speaking, feeling, and doing of Black people. The map redrafts these lines, moves things around, and, perhaps, includes those pushed to the margins, whereas Black specificity is to divest from these logics in ways that reimagine toward otherwise genres of being.

The "How" of Black Study

In the open letter mentioned above, Wynter (1994) offered a model for responding to the map (that is, the racial violence committed against Rodney King's body) and the territory (that is, routine use of the acronym NHI [no humans involved] regarding Black people). In student development literature, there has been an explicit focus on various identity categories. To consider the territory, however, would require a commitment to theorizing differently from the start. Following Wynter's (1994, 2006) lead, Black Study may offer one such grounding. Wynter invokes the Black Studies and Black Arts movements: "The emergence of the Black Studies Movement in its original thrust, before its later cooption into the mainstream of the exact order of knowledge whose 'truth' in 'some abstract universal sense' it had arisen to contest, was inseparable from the parallel emergence of the Black Aesthetic and the Black Arts movements and the central reinforcing relationship that had come to exist between them" (Wynter, 2006, p. 109). Explicitly political, Wynter cites Black methods, aesthetics, and traditions as a point of departure from conceptions of Man and Western human and social sciences. Theorizing with Wynter's appellation offers considerations for rewriting the human. In doing so, it theorizes how we know and how we come to know through Black specificity. In what follows, I offer one example on the potential of Black specificity to shift epistemology.

Inhaling Blackness, Exhaling White Logic: On the Potential of Black Research Approaches

The course was new to the program. It was an attempt to facilitate the transdisciplinary commitment that education studies call for, and that higher education demands such that educators and researchers might be able to grapple with the complexity of harm and potentialities of life. The assumptions that led to the course's formation were steeped in the notion that higher education, and, more specifically, knowledge production and student/early-adult development theorizing have a framing problem, which I would clarify as onto-epistemological problems of thought, practice, and policy. Without frames that are capacious in their reach and depth, which aim not for examinations of "what do we have, and how do we make it better?" and instead toward a repurposed ethical line of questioning that would account for, "how do we be/exist?" and "what world do we want?" then efforts to understand "how to do life" in the wake of anti-Blackness become partial at best, and circular at worst. The theorizing tools that preoccupy knowledge production, and more specifically, higher-education research on or about Black being and living, are anchored in enlightenment rationality. If, and when the discourse coheres to generate what counts as good, rigorous research, often through containment, protection, and priority (Stewart, 2022), not only is a more complex rendering disappeared, but processes of knowledge production are also further enclosed by the exorbitant violence of anti-Blackness, enforced by methodological training. Or, one's capacity to understand and frame Black subjects is legitimated insofar as renderings are reached in compliance with patterns of Western empiricism. The course was interested in accounting for and bringing into view Black aliveness (Quashie, 2021), or what I reckon with as the capacity for Black breath and breathing, ways of knowing and being that are not possible in and through Western thought.

> I think number one because the way that I think about research in general, because of its academic connotation is I like ascribe a level of legitimacy to it that this article completely. . . . I'm like we can't trust, nobody. . . . It just reminded me that the

> lens through which qualitative inquiry has come to be is stained with the genocide and mistreatment and unethical . . . all this list of things right, that has shaped the way that we think about inquiry into areas unknown and, it, you know, it just feels like . . . there's blood on the lens. (Dionne)

Dionne was a student in the course; her reflections on inquiry hearken back to a history of unethical and violent practice, perhaps, most aptly rendered in her comment, "there's blood on the lens." Traditional research processes in social science and educational research, for Dionne, sterilize the effect of coloniality and transatlantic enslavement, and, too, the life-making (Bishop, 2017; Tichavakunda, 2021) of Black people in the wake of anti-Blackness. To imagine this possibility, I invited students in the course to respond to a series of ungraded reflection questions. The questions were presented as a final reflection assignment that, broadly, considered how they might be approaching inquiry at the completion of the course.

The focus of the course was on how researchers enter and interrogate Black archives, with the aim of demonstrating how an ethos of Black archival practice could help testify to the complexity of how Black liveliness is lived, documented, and remembered. In doing so, we grappled with a range of questions related to ethics, reflexivity, and positionality. Regarding learning objectives, the course aimed to critically engage theoretical and methodological approaches through close reading and discussion; compare and contrast different theoretical approaches; apply insights from theorists to educational contexts; and design and carry out an independent praxis/research project that addressed a question related to our central course themes. Perhaps, most importantly, the course prioritized Black aliveness as guided by a Black methodological frame for study and research. Whereas Black Study is concerned with the rigorous and reflexive attendance to the Black condition, the guiding frame was developed through Black Study, by Black educators attempting Black specificity in literacy discourse.

BLACK STUDIES CONCEPTUAL CATEGORIES

The course drew on a Black Study frame developed by the Philadelphia Freedom Schools (Carr, 2020), addressing five areas of thought and praxis annotated as: *social structure*; *ways of knowing*; *science and technology*; *governance*; and *movement and memory*. The *social structure* asked, who are Black/Africana people in the [educational and] public sphere at any moment in time and space? This question dialectically dances with the *governance structure*, which asked, who are Black/Africana people to each other? The presumption here is that there is a way that Black people are understood in the United States social imaginary that is different from the ways they are in a relationship with each other. The governance question is not indicative of an essentialist Black experience; rather, it is an effort to understand the philosophies, methods, ethics, and institutions of self-governance that Black people and communities employ. *Ways of knowing* considered how do Black/Africana people think about themselves and the world? How do Black/Africana people create knowledge? And how do Black/Africana people think about the construction of, and nature of reality? *Science and technology* queried, what ways of interacting with the physical world do Black/Africana people create, contribute to, or adapt to meet their needs? What music, art, cultural texts, and practices did Black/Africana people create to mark their time and place in the world? Finally, *movement and memory* meditated on *how* Black/Africana people pass on their ideas/what they have experienced to future generations. Final reflexive questions were directed by this methodology. Additionally, this theme pondered, how do Black/Africana people think about past generations? Moreover, the course engaged interdisciplinary readings in an effort to consider how Black specificity could be taken up in the field of education (for example, C. D. Dillard [2012], *Learning to (Re)member the Things We've Learned to Forget: Endarkened Feminisms, Spirituality, & the Sacred Nature of Research & Teaching*, Peter Lang) and in Black Studies (for example, S. Hartman [2019], *Wayward Lives, Beautiful Experiments: Intimate Histories of Riotous Black Girls, Troublesome Women, and Queer Radicals*, W. W. Norton).

Black Breathing Practices: An Analysis

At the completion of the course, students were asked to reflect on their experience and sense-making in the course. My interest here was in annotating how students were responding to the learning; I wanted to know if there was a difference in their breathing—what they were taking in and what they were expelling. Reflexive questions were directed by the Black Studies conceptual categories that guided course discussions throughout the term (for example, governance, ways of knowing, etc.), asking for example, *what was the feeling of reading Black research approaches? In other words, how did it feel to engage Black research approaches (consider your emotional, psychic, communal, and spiritual selves)? What imaginings does a focus on Blackness provoke for you? In other words, what does Blackness open up for you?* It should be noted that while the course focused explicitly on Black research approaches, the study and learning therein still took place in a white institution, which has a code of ethics regarding Black liveliness and living, namely, understanding both as unthought (see Hartman & Wilderson, 2003) and out of place in the Western order of knowledge. This note is important so that breathing practice is not mistaken as the sum of Black existence and doesn't lean too heavily on the belief that white institutions can be refashioned to account for Black breathing, let alone liveliness and living. That said, an analysis of Black students' reflections from a course on Black research approaches revealed several considerations on the potentialities of Black specificity in student/early-adult development theorizing, and knowledge production, writ large. Specifically, analysis of the students' reflections gave way to what I discuss as Black breathing practices, or the creative impulse to affirm the ranging intensities of Black being through various modalities. Breath and breathing have, and continue to be a site of radical politics, as it enables one to acknowledge both the material repercussions of anti-Blackness, and, too, bring into view strategies for living in precarity. I outline some of those modalities in what follows, acronymized as DEEP Breathing Practices, inclusive of *dignity, endarkenment, exceeding,* and *pace*. In what follows, I review each of these terms and discuss how they might inform student/early-adult development theorizing.

Dignity

On the matter of dignity, Black students in the course discussed their experience as one that validated who they were as African-ascendant people in the world. There appeared to be a felt sense of affirmation, of seeing the self and one's community, as they read and engaged with course material. One student, Brit, noted, "On an emotional side, the more I dug into the coursework, the more I felt validated and seen as a Black woman in the context of my professional and academic life." That she invokes the language of emotionality to discuss her experience is noteworthy, as it disrupts notions of study and knowledge production that demand an objective, distant rendering, followed by logics that mirror the scientific method to ensure rigor and goodness. This invocation names Blackness, and the pursuit of Black knowledge production, as a medium by which one has the capacity to think, feel, and be seen. This instantiation also presumes that dignity, is more than a thought project as enlightenment sensibilities might proffer; rather, dignity is a felt state, thereby, perhaps, suggesting that dignity does not belong exclusively to white institutions and discourses. Dignity is not something achieved through, and controlled by, white theorizing metrics. Alternatively, there exist versions of dignity beyond the entrapment of the Western Man—dignity can be informed by Black ways of knowing and being. Dionne, a student in the course, underscored this point, writing: "I felt seen honestly. I felt dignified or a sense of dignity. It feels like those [Black] research approaches honor a legitimacy in the Black experience that is not always done so in traditional research methods." For Dionne, if Black approaches represented a condition of being seen, then it should be concluded that traditional social science approaches exact epistemic violence concerning Black people (Okello, 2022). On these terms, traditional approaches fail to meaningfully consider Black liveliness unbound from white logic (Zuberi & Bonilla-Silva, 2008).

Moreover, Orlando, another student in the course, noted that Black Study evoked a sense of pride "Focusing on Blackness has always provoked a sense of pride, that I've always wanted to share. But unfortunately, when viewing our culture through someone else's eyes also elicits pain." Interestingly, he puts pride experienced from Black Study in dialogic relationship with what he calls "someone else's eyes," and the consequence of that viewing. I read Orlando to be referencing the workings of Western humanism and, in particular, the orientations that direct white viewings of Black liveliness. The tendency, as stated by Orlando, hearkens back to the limitations of social science inquiry to account for the fullness of Black liveliness, instead reading it mostly as a site of pain and in need of reform. The sense here is that studying Blackness offered him a return of sorts to a core space that he has long valued, but perhaps did not have the opportunity to pursue in his training. Dignity, in this way, was taken up by reconnecting to former sensibilities and ways of knowing that are often reconciled away from Black people as they negotiate white institutions and discourses. Taken together, as Black students inhaled Black approaches, they were able to simultaneously exhale white logics.

Endarkenment: Black Specificity

Inhaling Black approaches, as noted above, marked a return to core ways of knowing and being for Black students in the course, and, in doing so, provoked a different set of responsibilities for them as they negotiated knowledge production. Specifically, they were invited to darken their ideas and imaginations of research, which is to endarken their viewing practices as they dislodged themselves from the workings of enlightenment. Thinking with Dillard (2000), the language of endarken aligns with "the historical roots of Black feminist thought, embodying a distinguishable difference in cultural standpoint, located in the intersection/overlap of the culturally constructed socializations of race, gender, and other identities, and historical and contemporary contexts of oppressions and resistance" (p. 662). On this point, Dillard is clear in her priority to locate epistemic, ontological, and spiritual-cosmological value in the traditions of African-ascendant people. Furthermore, endarkened moves to disrupt oppressive ideologies and logics that are deployed to understand the social, epistemic, spiritual, and intellectual lives of dark people in various contexts. The use of *endarkened*, here, and in the literature, is in contrasting relationship with enlightenment that references a new knowledge and insight.

Endarkening as a breathing practice, "necessitates" (Dillard, 2000, p. 663) a different relationship between the researched and the researcher, between what ones knows and the production of knowledge. Thus, endarkening across the course encouraged Black students to get beyond the individual and elevate the larger communities of African-ascendant people in research and theorizing. As Black students took up the work of endarkenment (Black specificity), they assumed a sense of responsibility that is largely absent in traditional framings of social science inquiry. Brit, reflected this point, writing,

> responsibility became an important element of my research pursuits and the choices made to carry it out. "For whom am I responsible to . . ." This question has guided my research development, and this is a re-direction from how I entered the class. I initially thought that my responsibility was to expose some truth. . . . This sense of responsibility shifted to be for those who I am in community with . . . it became more about communal elevation and empowerment.

There was a felt sense of obligation for Black students to specificity, which demanded that they scrutinize the epistemic and political foundations for doing research. Dionne postulated, "We recognize that there are some serious deficits in the way that we think about qualitative inquiry when it comes specifically to Black folks. And so, what is our sense of mobilization or response kind of moving forward?" She continued this line of thinking, writing, "It (Black specificity) will always cause me to question, through whose sense of typical or normalcy am I reading this? It will always cause me to be critical of not only the author and the perspectives, the methodological choices, who's been included in the research and who's been excluded, and who's been included to fit certain narratives and that sort of thing." Endarkened theorizing, thus, should be understood as a political work and invitation to specificity that might erect qualities of aliveness that are pushed out in traditional approaches to theorizing.

Excess

Anchoring the call to responsibility, Black students expressed an ethic of care that asked that they assume knowledge in spaces where social science inquiry otherwise would not think to look. This is to say that the traditional approaches place value on knowledge that is produced by white logic—notions of objectivity and control—as noted above, and are not constructed to acknowledge, or see otherwise. Black approaches, however, purposefully sought knowledge in ways that exceeded the lens, as in there is knowledge in excess of what is cataloged by social structure approaches that spills out and over from the templates enforced by white logic. Brit wrote about revelations that opened up to her as she grappled with the breadth of Black excess, saying, Black Study "revealed truths about how dominant narratives are pervasive in research praxis and how power informs who/how stories get told, the colonization of research." She continued, writing, "A major realization for my research was to try to push beyond status quo research that embraces deficit and dysfunctional ways of experiencing the world." Dionne discussed similar feelings of excess, likening Blackness to an iceberg: "There's so much more that's under the surface. There's so much more that's untapped potential. And that piece about possibilities and options . . . there's so many pieces of Blackness of the Black experience that we're not pulling into our research. We're not getting all of those stories. We're not getting all of that narrative to really re-situate Black folks in our understandings of time and space." The untapped potential suggests, first, that there is depth beyond the shallow readings and cursory reviews that would deploy Black thought as ornamental. Moreover, as depth, one should read Black liveliness as complex, uneasily situated as a category of analysis or variable to prove a set of hypotheses. Instead, thinking with Blackness demands a range of tools to account for its multiplicity, manifesting across soundscapes, spatial and visual imaginaries, and material outcomes. Where one might be confronted with the limits of an archive, Black thought and method read against those limits, the spirit of which Dionne denoted when she wrote, "where I saw a closed door, I saw an open door. I now see an open door. I see maybe nobody's in a room, but there's more to it." A willingness to imagine possibility in and against foreclosure, suggests that Black thought, as situated in a Black world, evinces life. White logic and methods would have itself be totalizing, "pure, gratuitous violence" (Crawley, 2017, p. 75), and, yet, it has not been achieved. Black thought, as part of the Black world that the course conjured, invited "humanity, community, and culture and the things are integral to the Black" for Brit, and a "desire to branch out to invite those elements into research to create a scholarly work that is expressive, artistic and affirming."

PACE

Accounting for excess, or that which is typically out of focus, sight, and mind necessitates a different breathing pattern for it to become a different way of being in the world. In this way, Black students were cultivating a different relationship with their breath, that is, they were learning to remember their breath in ways that honored pace. This principle encouraged students to sit with and make meaning of the ideas they encountered. Black students discussed coming to Black Study as a set of deliberate movements that, to take up appropriately, would depend on practice. Orlando alluded to this point, writing, "There is a great weight of importance and responsibility to those who choose to use our research to provide a collective mirror that reflects the oppressive society we continue to live in, while providing remedies in the liberation we seek within the society we hope to become." He described involvement with Black Study as an important decision to make that carried within it the responsibility for attending to the weight of anti-Blackness and a commitment to life in spite of it. The presupposition here is that Black theorizing in knowledge production can only be as a good as the Black Study practices that inform it, or what one puts out, is only as good as what one puts in. This practice was reflected in Black students' decisions to tread carefully, noting their immersion as an initial step in the process of cultivating an intentional approach to what they took in and what they put out—learning to breathe anew. The notion of pacing, understood here as a slowing (down) and interruption of practice or training as usual, is illuminated when Dionne noted that (the field of education) should "really start, as a discipline, [to] peel back the layers on Blackness and not even because it's layered in a traditional sense, but there's so much debris and just mess that surrounded, that clouds it." I read Dionne's petition to "discipline" in two ways. First, I understand her to be referring to what it would mean for the field of education, broadly speaking, to meaningfully dialogue with Black Study. The course was her first opportunity to think about the specificity of Blackness and what it could mean for knowledge production and inquiry.

Generally, when it comes to the idea of Black people, they are, however imperfectly, lumped into conversations about race and racism (Dumas & ross, 2016). Or, a focus on Blackness is synonymous with a study on Black experiences. Neither of those approaches takes up Blackness in a meaningful way, such that it could provide a backdrop for the entanglement of Blackness as on organizing element of society. Brit amplified this point: "I appreciated the exposure to works that would have otherwise been unfamiliar to me. . . . Had it not been for this course, I would not have the scope and context for my research." In addition to putting educational research and Black Study in conversation, I understand Dionne to be framing discipline as a practice. To think with and alongside Blackness requires nuance (for example, there is blood on the lens) and the development of practices that would enable the researcher to uncover, rupture, and bring into view Black liveliness and living in a world that refuses it so completely.

Black Study in Theorizing

Blackness has the potential to complicate knowledge production in ways that purposefully consider Black liveliness and living in student development theorizing. As Black students exposed to Black thought instruct, DEEP breathing is possible in theorizing, such that Black dignity is centered, Black worlds become possible, a complexity of Black being is brought to view, and a patient practice of evolution that would allow one to do different is advanced. To be clear, this project in the longer arc of the Black Studies and thought is not new. The emergence of Black Studies as an intellectual and pragmatic site for centering African-ascendant people represents an important course of action in the creation of Black education and spaces.

In this way, the co-optation of Black Studies by the university was inevitable, as the concept has been sanitized to meet the standards of study that are consistent with neoliberal goals of accumulation. As incorporated into the university, Black Studies is too often reduced to content studies, Black history in the objective sense, and, in so doing, one never has to take up its arguments or fervor in practice. DEEP breathing practices, as reviewed above, hearken back to a memory of Black Studies/Aesthetics that sought not the university, or a place in it per se, but the remaking of the university (Wynter, 2003, 2006)—that is, Black institutions.

The Black institution, which cannot be of the university, is beyond the scope of this conversation, but DEEP breathing practices do compel questions about the potentiality of Black thought to direct educational research. This collective exhale of white logic and methods in knowledge production, and theorizing development work, facilitated by Black Study and thought, in part, means asking questions of history, epistemology, ethics, and praxis in educational research. Following the revelations above, researchers ought to ask, is the primary concern making room for Black people in higher education, which in turn opts for integrationist framings of research to guide political, ethical, and conceptual demands, or to center theorizing with scholars like Fanon, Du Bois, and Wynter, for example, to ask new questions of being and construct new concepts that can account for the aliveness of Black people? Relatedly, suppose we are to understand Black Study as a mode of knowledge production that provides critical philosophical and social theories for investigating racialization processes with particular attention to how those investigations shift configurations of Black liveliness. In that case, it will require untethering taken-for-granted discourses from canonical treatments.

As a problem of history, Black Study might ask educators and researchers, how do we understand Blackness (not race and racism) and what has culminated in the disposability of Black people? This question is not easily resolved in a world of research that privileges units of measurement and outcomes-based projects that seek to understand instead of developing a relationship with a phenomenon of investigation. Stated differently, investment in product are always partial, as opposed to sitting with the ways Blackness, for example, was formed and evolves in ways that enclose Black liveliness and living. What happens when we stop attempting to find the resolution to anti-Black disregard, and reckon with its long and unending inundation? Education as a field of practice is not at odds with Black Study, per se. The issue may be in how Education (research and theorizing) understands itself as its pledge to practice, which raises the question of epistemology.

As an epistemic project or order of knowledge, it might ask, how do Black people think of themselves in an anti-Black world? Or, how have Black people endarkened—created Black worlds—sites and practices of knowing, being, memory, spirit, and pleasure that mark their place in their world and support their living into the future? This point draws on the worldmaking sensibilities that Black people have written, spoken, and conjured. Black Study and thought as a decolonial force and method lie in their capacity to engage the realities of Black negation and to construct theories that explain the phenomenon and consider how to negotiate it. In doing so, development theory, and the higher education practice and policy that it informs, may be involved in mapping, but more pressingly, charting new territories untethered from white logics and methods. Black Study and thought as praxis in education is a reconditioning to and of care. Praxis, here, should be read as concentrated, unobstructed inhalations on Black Study and giving oneself over to be changed by its teachings. This process envelopes a new relationship with time and linearity—one allows the liberative thrust of Black thought to direct their living, and then, theorizing.

DEEP Breathing as Praxis: A Conclusion

This chapter is interested in what Blackness allows us to see, what it brings into view, and how knowledge production exceeds the lens. This is not enlightened work; rather, it is decidedly endarkened, committed to "talking and walking around with other people, working, dancing, suffering, some irreducible convergence of all three, held under the name of speculative practice" (Harney & Moten, 2013, p. 110). In the chapters that follow, I attempt to think, tarry, breath DEEP, gesturing toward an otherwise way of knowing and being that could reorder power relations and is incessantly committed to rehearsing practices that take seriously the multiple and compounding identities, knowledge, and method making of Black people. To make a claim for dignity, endarkenment (Black specificity), excess, and pace, is to trouble how we know, the production of knowledge, and how knowledge gets disseminated. Blackness, here, is the clearing, the space for expansive incantations of knowing and being—liveliness and living.

August,

I used to hold my breath when you slept, listening with increased concentration for evidence of your breathing. Some nights, I would watch for the rise of your chest; on others, I placed my ear next to your nostrils. You were still learning how to be, and so I needed to be sure, wanted to help you, because breathing is hard, and so much is contending for your breath; it is not something we should do alone. Learn your lungs, August. I think, no one knows this better than the baby seal. Alexis Gumbs tells the story of the mother Weddell seal, who will push her babies into the water against their will. "She will force her child's head into the water while the baby coughs and sputters and struggles and squirms. [The baby] is new here. She does not know that she can breathe underwater. Until she does. And then everything changes" (p. 23). You are learning to breathe in new and exciting ways, and, even still, there will be moments when you feel out of your depth–coughing and sputtering and squirming. Just breath, is not the fulfillment of your living. Trust your lungs, August. Love to those who will gracefully plunge you into knowing your capacity.

3

"Look a Negro!"

Explicating Self-Definition

Figure 3.1. Following the shattering of the primordial world in the Igbo Odachi Nne Ebere mythical account, the Igbo high god Chukwu finds the martyred body of His feminine double Eke-Nnechukwu and brings Her back to life with His tears. As Eke-Nnechukwu rises from the dead, the cosmos and physical universe are born on Her body as She assumes the form of Komosu. Revived, Komosu takes up residence in Her own cosmic house known as Mkpuke, where She balances the entirety of the physical universe on Her body, Her name being a derivative of Koro-ma-ya-su, Komo-osu/Aru Uso/Ana Uso (body of the goddess). *Source*: *Komosu* by Mikael Owunna. Used with permission of the artist.

Early mornings unfolded as yawning limbs and branches stretching themselves out before the sunrise. On these mornings, before breakfast and the hustle of running showers, I remember how fog draped over the pine trees and dewdrops anointed the grass beneath the leaves. Though I was just waking up, my mother had been awake for hours. Her days never seemed to end. My mother was the last face I saw before bed and the first one to greet me when our worlds started again. "Good morning, my son." Her voice was cool and easy. In a world where Black children did/do not always make it home to see their mothers, "Good morning, my son" was a reminder to a world that would seek to break my spirit, and return my body to her empty and void, that for at least one more day, they had failed. But how did she arrive at this wisdom?

—Wilson Kwamogi Okello

How *Komosu* Inspires This Chapter

As I settle in with Komosu, I wonder what Blackness has had to hold, for how long, and under what conditions. To borrow from Christina Sharpe's ecological turn, anti-Blackness is the weather, and this image, might be gravity, heavy and pervasive and persistently at work on and in the lives of Black people. In this way, my thinking is directed by Western science principles, whereas gravity is the force that draws objects toward its center. As it relates to Blackness and Black people, those objects are often violent. But in the persistence of the weather, new ecologies—ways of being, ways of knowing, organizing principles—emerge. Komosu, then, represents a countergravity,[1] holding Blackness's weightlessness (read: no humanness) and its transcendent possibilities. This chapter attempts one such countergravitational holding.

In *Black Skin, White Masks* (1952), Frantz Fanon gives voice to the contested nature of Blackness: " *'Look! A Negro! . . . Maman, look, a Negro; I'm scared.' 'Laughter had become out of the question. I couldn't take it any longer, for I already know there were legends, stories, history and above all historicity. The Negro is an animal, the Negro is bad, the Negro is wicked, the Negro is ugly. . . . the little white boy runs to his mother's arm'* [emphasis added]" (Fanon, 1952, pp. 90–93). Scholars have termed the vignette above the

Fanonian moment (Ahmed, 2004; Fleetwood, 2011; Kim, 2005; Marriott, 2007). The incident is a meditation on how Frantz Fanon was accosted by a white boy on a train. Publicly, the boy blared to his white mother, *Look, a Negro!* (Fanon, 1952). I highlight this moment as an example of the terror, trauma, unknowability (Cooper, 2017), and inescapability of being marked as Black in a United States context. Juxtaposing the white child's angst with that of my mother's rearing practice sketches disparate anecdotes about the perceived danger children are exposed to in society, in this case a white boy and, me a Black cis man remembering his boyhood. I begin here to demonstrate how these varying moments illustrate some of the competing psycho-affective (Fanon, 1952) messages that Black people may carry in society. The Fanonian moment clarifies the ways anti-Black public spheres can structure Black living, and in response, this chapter examines the complex choreography of Black liveliness and living, self-definition, in and beyond higher-education contexts. The Fanonian moment, also, must be understood as a point of rupture, as Fanon was forced to reckon with these mimetic expectations of the Western Man (read: colonial, middle class, professional), and his existence as outside of those terms (Hartman & Wilderson, 2003; Wynter & McKittrick, 2015). Most immediate to this discussion is that, according to Fanon's mode of thinking, the idea that he was or could imitate Man, that he could subjectively experience the world on those terms, is not trustworthy, and is inconsistent as a means of negotiating one's way in an anti-Black world. On this premise, the centrality of Blackness is my point of departure.

As has been mentioned, anti-Blackness as a framework can be traced to the work of Black existential scholars, particularly the intellectual project of Afro-pessimism (Dumas, 2016; Sharpe, 2016; Wilderson, 2010), which "theorizes that Black people exist in a structurally antagonistic relationship with humanity. That is, the very technologies and imaginations that allow a social recognition of the humanness of others systematically exclude this possibility for the Black" (Dumas, 2016, p. 13). Black people, in this sense, cannot be human, and for all intents and purposes, are something other than human.

Specific to educational contexts, and higher education, in particular, terrains of Blackness, as a social, political, economic assemblage that orders knowledge and relations (Wynter, 1994), are undertheorized. While most educators and practitioners would rightly acknowledge the Fanonian moment as an instance of racism, there has been less dialogue on how histories of US higher-education research, theories, and practices reflect a commitment to the breath of anti-Blackness such that they are enmeshed in the degradation of Black people (Dancy, Edwards, & Davis, 2018; Dumas, 2016; Wilder, 2013).

This framing stretches the antagonistic relationship between Black people and society to that which is beyond racialized identity questions (see Cross, 1971), or the abilities of one to make meaning of expectations and experiences that are racialized (Torres & Hernández, 2007; Hernández, 2016; Pizzolato & Olson, 2016). To exist in a dark body, thus, marks an irreconcilable relationship between Black people and sociopolitical (Okello, 2018) regard. The purpose of theorizing from the hold (Spillers, 1987; Sharpe, 2016; Wilderson, 2010) of anti-Blackness instead of a race and racism approach, is to engender a deeper, more critical understanding of the condition of Black people in a United States context, not to resolve the ubiquity of racism or racial inequality. And, merely documenting racialized violence does not constitute a liberatory method as it upholds the closed and recursive—autopoietic—biocentric system of knowledge that reduces Black people to sites of analysis. Black rebellious activities, as discussed in chapter 1, prompt us to contemplate the essence of liveliness. So, even as Blackness is enmeshed in anti-Black antagonism, it is not entirely defined by it.

On this point, Wynter, following Fanon (1952) asked, "How can we come to know/think/feel/behave and subjectively experience ourselves—doing so for the first time in our human history *consciously* now—in *quite different terms*? How do we *be*, in Fanonian terms, hybridly human?" (Wynter & McKittrick, 2015, p. 45). By "hybrid," Wynter was elaborating on Fanon's notion of sociogeny, or storytelling capacities and the ways humans story themselves over and again. She noted that "the origin of the human [is] a hybridly auto-instituting, languaging cum storytelling species" (Wynter & McKittrick, 2015, p. 25). In other words, again, humans are not merely biological, but script writing beings whose "macro-origin stories are overrepresented as the singular narrative through which the stakes of human freedom are articulated and marked" (p. 11). This logic underwrites developmental discourse and, thus, my intent is toward otherwise ways to locate and construct being: "We need to speak instead of our *genres of being human*. Once you redefine being human in hybrid *mythoi* and *bios* terms, and therefore in terms that draw attention to the relativity and original multiplicity of our *genres* of being human, all of a sudden what you begin to recognize is the central role that our discursive *formations*, aesthetic fields, and systems of knowledge must play in the performative enactment of all such genres of being hybridly human" (Wynter & McKittrick, 2015, p. 31). Whereas narrative scripts are central to being human as praxis, I am interested in how the notion of Blackness fundamentally critiques the ways educators and researchers narrate and define being human (noun), as well as how it demands a deeper, more capacious, and dynamic rendering (Wynter & McKittrick, 2015).

Thus, I lift Blackness as a theoretical intervention on holistic meaning-making theory that has failed to explicitly address the problem of the human, or what it means to be. Specifically, employing literary criticism (Smith, 1979; Wall, 1989), which presumes that Black people have cultivated and recorded survival practices amid anti-Black policies and practices, I analyzed seven full-length books and essays written by James Baldwin and Audre Lorde, asking,

1. How has the Black body been schooled?
2. How do Baldwin and Lorde make meaning of their existence between 1950 and 1992?

I define schooling as the social and conditioning strategies that function to reproduce the status quo. This first question examined how the lives of Baldwin and Lorde were structured by anti-Blackness. The second question, on the premise that anti-Blackness has reverberated across time, exhumed onto-epistemological strategies that might inform Black liveliness and living. For the purposes of this chapter, I focus on the latter question. I offer justification for my choices to emphasize Baldwin and Lorde, and the texts for this analysis, below. I chose this scope of time to bring attention to a Black onto-epistemological canon that was at work alongside the psychological and psychosocial theories of development that became the basis for holistic adult meaning-making theory (Baxter Magolda, 1992, 2008; Kegan, 1982, 1994).

Attending to Black aesthetics, I used creative prose to situate myself in the text by attending to my mother's rearing practices. I accomplished this by incorporating critical autoethnographic (Boylorn & Orbe, 2013) excerpts, like the one above, into the literary analysis. Critical autoethnography allowed me to both narrate and analyze my mother's rearing practice. Consistent with this chapter, I used limbos (James, 1999) as an analytic and homed in on my mother as a way to make visible Black people as theorists. Furthermore, I demonstrate how what I discuss as *self-defining praxis*—invention, intimating, presence, and revision—surfaced in the work of Baldwin and Lorde, and overlaps with the contemporary moment, by visiting the felt world that my mother created in the wake of anti-Blackness. Importantly, as a Black cis man, my thinking is not without tension. I do not claim to fully understand my mother's decisions and own the places where my privileged analysis of Lorde and my mother may falter because of what is inherently unknowable from my standpoint. My appreciation for their meaning-making practices does not absolve me from causing harm; I hope that my sitting at their feet, so to speak, engenders some possibility for lessons learned and advancing an ethical practice of Black Study. Ultimately, I depart from the meaning-making pathways articulated by self-authorship, raised as the necessary developmental outcome for adults (Baxter Magolda & King, 2004; Baxter Magolda, 2008), and point to the possibilities of self-defining praxis for Black students, and Black people more broadly.

In what follows, I examine self-authorship (Baxter Magolda, 2001; 2009), foundational in its regard for adult holistic meaning-making (Kegan, 1982, 1994), and chart the theory's relationship to anti-Blackness. From there, I discuss the urgency of an orientation in support of Black liveliness and living and the advancement of human development and knowledge production discourses in higher-education contexts.

A Review of Self-Authorship

Kegan's (1982, 1994) theory of self-evolution provides an important grounding for holistic early adult development theory. His work animated Baxter Magolda's (2001, 2009) integrated theorizing of self-authorship. For both scholars, there is an emphasis on development as the capacity of one to manage increasingly complex tasks, the movement from external formulas to internal formulas. Baxter Magolda (2001, 2009) detailed the journey toward self-authorship as the movement in and across four positions, shifting from the uncritical acceptance of beliefs, interpersonal loyalties, and intrapersonal states (external formulas) to becoming the coordinator of one's values, identity, and social relations (internal formulas) (Baxter Magolda, 2008).

Learning outcomes such as personal and social responsibility, intercultural competence, and the knowledge production necessary to be an effective citizen, have been said to require self-authorship (Baxter Magolda

& King, 2004; Baxter Magolda, 2008). As a result, self-authorship has been taken up as the goal of twenty-first-century higher education because it represents transformational learning. The shift from subject to object, or adults becoming the coordinators of their values, identity, and relationships, can help them meet the various demands on their lives (Baxter Magolda, 2008; Kegan 1994).

SELF-AUTHORSHIP AND BLACK LIVING

To consider how self-authorship might respond to anti-Blackness, manifested in occurrences like the Fanonian moment above, it is important to begin with three important limitations. First, self-authorship was constructed in a raceless manner. Perez (2019) discussed this as *color-evasive ideology* as a "refusal to address race, and its corollary racism" (Perez, 2019, p. 76). While scholars have taken up the question of race (Torres & Hernández, 2007) and racism (Hernández, 2012; Torres, 2009), with particular attention to the ways racism may come to affect how minoritized students view themselves and their relationships, the evasion of racialization is undertheorized. Race and racism approaches do not consider the construction of the Black as a legible being in the United States social imaginary. Racialization processes could more precisely shift the conversation from race and racism to Blackness and anti-Blackness, the latter of which are absent in holistic renderings of student development, and self-authorship in particular. Addressing racialization processes would mean discussing how being constructed as Black constitutes, on one hand, notions of social death, and, on the other hand, the multiple and varied processes of Black living (or self-definition).

Second, and relatedly, the constructivist methodological underpinnings that led to self-authorship are limited insofar as they reify humanities and social science inquiry that privilege the white, male, middle-class, subject (Wynter, 2003, 2006). This approach means that explorations of the lives of minoritized people broadly, through the lens of self-authorship, are grounded in assumptions of a white male subject, which raises questions about its viability as an outcome of postsecondary education for Black students. Finally, as noted above, Black people exist in a structurally antagonistic relationship with humanity, which systematically excludes the possibility of achieving full regard in society through theories that undermine the historical-made-present condition of Black being. Thus, to appropriately theorize Black possibility requires both unsettling self-authorship and a shift in disciplinary grounding to locate ethical approaches to theorizing. Next, I outline the various components of self-authorship and its theoretical limitations with regard to Black people.

Following External Formulas

Generally, self-authorship presumes that individuals in this phase understand relationships as hierarchal and knowledge as certain. Therefore, a process toward self-authorship in this phase would suggest that individuals hold an uncritical acceptance of anti-Blackness. The sociopolitical culture that sustains, recomposes, and exacts the violence of anti-Blackness, presumably, is met with uncritically. That said, one's identity might prompt a shift from external formulas (Hernández, 2012; Torres, 2009; Pizzolato, 2003). For Latinx students, development along the epistemological dimensions involved a shift from uncritically accepting external formulas such as cultural stereotypes (Hernández, 2012). This understanding follows, that cognitive dissonance must be present to instigate the shift in the self-authorship trajectory. Such an approach, however, can, perhaps unintentionally, put forth that Black people have not thought about, contended with, or made sense of their relationship with external formulas if it has not occurred cognitively. This approach cannot fully account for the capacities of the body as a knowledge-producing site—affective, emotional, material, and spirit selves (Okello et al., 2022). The next section reviews literature on the crossroads, or the process of moving away from external influences.

Transitioning Away from External Influences: Crossroads

According to Torres and Hernández (2007), racism surfaced as a developmental task, specific to the cognitive dimension of self-authorship. For individuals in their study, being able to make meaning of racism enhanced their capacity to accept multiple perspectives and resist internalizing negative images of the self (Torres & Hernández, 2007). Again, progress along the cognitive dimension was necessary as a leading edge for movement in the trajectory of self-authorship. Raising concern about the race-neutral framing of external formulas and individuals' ability to break from them, Perez (2019) noted that while the development occurring in the crossroads toward internal formulas may be useful as a coordinating mechanism, "few scholars acknowledged the potential for differential challenges and rewards among racialized individuals for evaluating external formulas and messages from authority figures" (p. 79). Relatedly, the permanence of the wake (Sharpe, 2016) is understated, which presumes that every individual can break from external formulas, a proposal that anti-Blackness makes impossible (Dumas, 2016; Hartman, 2007; Shahid, 2018; Sharpe, 2016; Wilderson, 2010). On this point, the next section will discuss the process of cultivating an internal voice in the shadow of anti-Blackness.

Developing an Internal Voice

Developing the internal voice is central to the construction of a self-authored system, which is built on three fundamental elements: learning to *trust internal voices, building an internal foundation,* and *securing internal commitments* (Baxter Magolda, 2008).

Learning to Trust Internal Voices

These three elements emerged from interviews, as part of a constructivist study with 30 adults, all of whom were white and in their 30s. Baxter Magolda (2008) called *trusting the internal voice* the phase where individuals begin to make distinctions between reality and one's reaction to it. Furthermore, individuals were coming into the understanding that their reactions could be coordinated by their efforts, even if reality, writ large, could not be controlled. Importantly, reality, as stated above, is discussed across the literature as difficult events that might otherwise cause distress (Baxter Magolda, 2001, 2008, 2009). The larger sociopolitical context, in this case, the wake of anti-Blackness, is not part of the analysis. Pizzolato (2003) and Pizzolato and Olson (2016) discussed the potential impact of power dynamics on meaning-making, suggesting that instead of abandoning external formulas, some individuals repurpose "the use of external formulas by either modifying previously used formulas in a new way to find alternative selves" (p. 423). This finding, while not specific to the wake of anti-Blackness, contests both the possibility and the desire of trusting the internal voice.

Additionally, the achievement of the object-self in this phase (Kegan, 1994) preferences a meaning-making process that privileges the epistemological dimension as a leading edge, ignoring the holistic possibilities of embodiment (Johnson, 2003; Hurtado, 2003; Moraga & Anzaldúa 1981)—considering the body as a mental, emotional, social, spiritual, and spatial construct, always mediated through history. Privileging a leading edge in this way dismisses affective capacities (Ahmed, 2004) that are always and already pressed upon and responding to the wake of anti-Blackness for Black people.

Building an Internal Foundation and Securing Internal Commitments

Regarding the building of an internal foundation, Baxter Magolda (2008) described this phase as individuals trusting their internal voices and the conscious creation of an internal foundation that would coordinate their meaning-making. In this space, individuals "worked to refine their personal, internal authority in determining their beliefs, identity, and relationships" (Baxter Magolda, 2008, p. 280). This phase and its subsequent phase, securing internal commitments, do not explicitly contend with the reality of Black being, which must contend with the realities of anti-Blackness (Sharpe, 2016). One might conclude then, that building an internal foundation and securing commitments treat the internal voice as a stable and enduring place. The wake of anti-Blackness offers no such retreat. The next section details the methodology and methods I employed to examine Black liveliness amid anti-Black realities.

Literary Criticism

The material and conceptual consequences of anti-Blackness have functioned to unrecognize Black onto-epistemologies as viable theory. Yet Black people have always left records of their practice (Smith, 1979). Essays and literary works were a method by which Black people constructed alternative pathways of livability for their communities. Answering Pizzolato and Olson's (2016) call to reconsider what is possible with external formulas and given the historical-made-present manifestation of anti-Blackness (Sharpe, 2016), it was necessary to work with a methodology that could both wrestle with the complexity of history and decipher the intricacies of Black ways of knowing and being. For these reasons, I deployed a literary criticism (Anderson, 2008; Durham, 2014; Smith, 1979; Wall, 1989) to read the ways Black people choreographed living in the wake of anti-Blackness. As reviewed above, Black literary criticism presumes that the livable and survival logics of Black people were, and are, a form of theory. It also maintains that these livable and survival logics were framed in and through cultural mediums like art and literature to ensure ideas were accessible to those outside of academia.

This methodology instructed my analysis to key into themes and strategies theorized through Joy James's (1999) concept of limbos, which considers the various ways Black people progressively move forward despite the vulnerability of their positions. Furthermore, limbo, in its primary usage, references liminal spaces, "oblivion and neglect, or suspension between states" (James, 1999, p. 42). As choreographers of agency, Black folks' conservative or liberal ideologies conduct varying limbos as they negotiate the plurality of its meanings.

Limbos in the Wake

Advancing the use of limbos (James, 1999) as an analytic, this study addressed the ever-shifting conundrum of Black being that must daily choreograph living in the wake of anti-Blackness. To address these tensions, I looked to and translated the limbos of James Baldwin and Audre Lorde by conducting a close reading (Smith, 1979) of seven full-length literary books and essays.

On this note, the Black Aesthetic/Black Arts movements inseparably paralleled the emergence of Black Studies, all of which bear witness to practices of Black being in a Western, United States context. For Wynter (2006), contending with present-day formations of anti-Blackness, could find spirited examples in the Black Aesthetic/Black Arts movements. Thus, I draw on writers/artists of the Black Aesthetic/Black Arts movements as contributors to the well of self-determining rhetoric that was poetry, music, and plays that disrupted the conventionality of Western writing and performance (Baszile, 2015) to meet the needs of Black truth-telling. As such, attention to their work is to move toward Black specificity in constructions of contemporary freedom.

Justification for Baldwin and Lorde

I chose Baldwin and Lorde for five specific reasons: (1) *resistance to temporality and spatiality*—they migrated between realities of their own experience, history/herstory, and the future. Additionally, they both experienced a resident restlessness throughout their lives that spoke both to the parochial toxicity of Western culture and the expansive development of a global imagination; (2) *ability to maneuver in limbo*—they openly grapple with affective, social, historical, physiological, and political conundrums experienced by Black people; (3) *queer sensibilities*—they forgo the elusive embrace of easy definitions for a more complicated accounting of their bodies and history/herstory; (4) *ethical and intellectual imaginations*—they consciously gave language to the incongruence of the United States' values and its actions; and (5) *attention to the interior life*—they emphasized interior scrutiny and radical refashioning required to remake oneself in the wake of anti-Blackness and its interlocking systems of oppression.

Text Selection and Limitations

The literary analysis reviewed the following texts: *Go Tell It on the Mountain* (1953)—a story by Baldwin of history's anguish, internalized racism, and the (ir)reconciliation of those two on one's identity; *Notes of Native Son* (1955)—a collection of essays by Baldwin that include the search for identity in a country, and world, that are unwilling to grapple with history; *The Fire Next Time* (1963)—Baldwin's impassioned testimony in this text educates against the colonizing myths that support whiteness; *The Black Unicorn* (1978)—Lorde sets out to rename herself within an Afrocentric epistemology and spirituality by embracing a Black transnational feminist tradition; *Zami: A New Spelling of My Name* (1982)—in this book by Lorde, Zami, symbolizes a psychic journey toward a reconfigured Third World; *Sister Outsider: Essays & Speeches by Audre Lorde* (1984)—these letters of nonfiction have been formative in the making and remaking of feminist theories broadly, and Black feminism in particular; and *Undersong: Old and New Poems by Audre Lorde* (1992)—within this volume of poems, Lorde takes readers on a journey of metamorphosis; as life experiences shaped and molded her evolving physical and spiritual self, her poetry was also shifting and changing.

Beginning with these texts in the analysis is not intended to dismiss the value of other works across the arc of these theorists' letters. I choose to underscore these particular texts because they each draw out onto-epistemological themes and offer a range of examples that may extend understandings of adult holistic meaning-making.

Analysis

Across the seven full-length works (1,365 pages), I chose sixty-seven passages. For this chapter, I selected eight passages—two from each respective praxis (that is, invention, intimating, presence, and revision). Analysis of each passage was informed by the aforementioned limbo (James, 1999) reading practice/analytic.

Supporting this approach, two research questions guided my data collection and analysis.

1. How has the Black body been schooled?
2. How do Baldwin and Lorde make meaning of their existence between 1950 and 1992?

Related to the purpose of this chapter, the first question examines how anti-Blackness structured living for Baldwin and Lorde. Analogously, with the second question, I sought to exhume epistemological and ontological strategies that Baldwin and Lorde employed to negotiate, make sense of, and choreograph living in the wake of anti-Blackness.

As I read back over the books and passages, I had to make decisions about which passages could best help me to answer the questions levied. I chose passages that I believed closely responded to the research questions and, fulfilling an embodied commitment to the data collection, those that struck a chord with me affectively (Boylorn, 2013; Ohito, 2017). I flagged passages that responded directly to the research questions with Post-it Mini Notes to designate the page and starred (or bracketed) the passages in pencil on the specific page (Saldana, 2009). On some pages, I wrote a note, words, and/or questions to myself in the margins about why or how the passage responded to my guiding questions. Take the following excerpt from Lorde's *Zami: A New Spelling of My Name*: " 'I can't,' I said, knowing full well that what you do with Black crayons is scribble on the wall and get your backass beaten, or color around the edges of pictures, but not write. To write, you needed a pencil. 'I can't,' I said, terrified, and started to cry" (Lorde, 1982, p. 24). On this page of the book, in the margins, I wrote, "This doesn't fit my training/schooling." This note was a signal to me that the passage was an example of schooling in the text. On other pages, I starred words or passages that reflected my reading practice. The following excerpt followed the same practice: "Something happened to their faces and their voices, the rhythm of their bodies, and to the air they breathed" (Baldwin, 1953, p. 13). In response to this excerpt, in the margins, I wrote "embodied politic and embodied knowing/belief." These flagged notes stood out to me in my second read of the texts marshaling a closer look and decision as to whether the passage would move forward into my analysis (Muncey, 2010). Importantly, this analysis looks for precedence and insights in the interpretation of other Black aesthetic art and literature (Smith, 1979), and as such, patterned coding, and analytical memo writing (Saldana, 2009) yielded four praxes: *invention, intimating, presence,* and *revision.*

Self-Defining Praxes

In what follows, I outline invention, intimating, presence, and revision, along with an analysis of selected passages to clarify each concept. In each finding, I break up the natural flow and form with right-justified, single-space passages to distinguish Baldwin's and Lorde's words from my analysis of their words. Additionally, I thread critical autoethnographic excerpts across this section alongside the analyses.

Invention/Inventiveness

Black mothers are dreamers, who know reoccurring nightmares all too well. My mother knew that this world was unsatisfied with her joy, and as it had tried before, would wield every resource available to strip her of it. More than an inkling, she knew that this world was terrified of Black children, à la Fanon (1952), whose testimony from the train is evidence of the anxiety-producing nature of Blackness in public spaces. Or, perhaps she was anticipating the grand jury testimony of Darren Wilson, the officer who indiscriminately shot and killed Michael Brown, referring to Brown as an "it" and "demon" (Grand Jury Testimony, 2014, pp. 224–225). From slavery to the present, anti-Blackness has manifested as the epistemic-ontological grounds of everyday existence for Black people. My mother knew this. History told her so. Partus sequitur ventrem, made to be a priori, has framed Black nonpersonhood since enslavement. The parameters of these laws went about outlining the impossibility of equitable citizenship for Black individuals. Partus sequitur ventrem translates to mean, "that which is brought forth follows the womb" (Sharpe, 2016, p. 15). Born in, and through, Black passage, my ark—my mother's womb—was one that carried with it living memories of a world that has never known the Black body as anything more than property, cargo. The legacies of these parameters survive in studies that show how Black people, though known to be in pain, are thought to feel less, and thereby forced to endure more or, in reports that reflect how Black children as young as nine-years-old are consistently seen as being older than they are. *My mother didn't name each of these references, but "Good morning, my son" was saturated with its memory.*

In her poem *Prologue*, Lorde (1992) recalled the ways she was trained to hold the Western Man as a standard. Years later she lamented, "The color of . . . bleached ambition still forks throughout my words, but I survived, and didn't I survive . . . confirmed" (p. 111). Lorde's recollection is indicative of a larger pattern of narrative construction of the world, whereas "the only life we humans live is our prescriptive representations of what constitutes symbolic life, as well as what constitutes its Lack or mode of symbolic death" (Wynter, 2015, p. 210). These prescriptive representations, or narratives, "always have to be redrawn again, in undared forms" (Wynter, 1995, p. 35), Redrawing as the work of invention then, first implies "calling up again lost memories and overlooked stories" (Durham, 2014, p. 22) that shape our thinking, being, and doing. From there, if, as Wynter explained, humans are storytelling creatures (*homo narrans*), that have constructed narratives of themselves in absolute terms, *inventiveness* assumes a critical agency to create habits of thought, behavior, and doing outside of narrative inscriptions. Inventiveness recognizes socially inscribed narratives as the grounds for narrating nuanced habits of thinking, feeling, and doing.

Baldwin excerpt #1

> The American image of the Negro lives also in the Negro's heart; and when he has surrendered to this image, life has no other possible reality. (Baldwin, 1955, p. 38)

The image of the Negro, according to Baldwin, is the thing that Black people in a Western, United States context work so hard to evade and keep at bay through maladjusted good works. The existence of the Negro image, which should be understood in this passage as a site of thingification (Gordon, 1997), consumes the existence of Black people beyond matters of thought and reason (Baszile, 2015). Black people, and their transformation into things (Gordon, 1997), is the outgrowth of social, political, and epistemic habits, and not merely overcome by acts of will as reasoned by Baldwin when he noted that the image lives "in the Negro's heart." Notably, and with profound purpose, Baldwin delineated the "the American image" of the Negro, from what one could assume is a version of the Negro that is detached from colonial legacies. More pointedly, Baldwin seemed to suggest that embodied struggle must precede ontological re-presentations.

Inventiveness, as Baldwin would have it, must struggle with what "lives in" the body—the epistemic and spiritual violence that dates back to origins of the wake—to fully understand one's reality.

> *Lorde excerpt #1*
>
> My mother knew very well I could follow directions, because she herself had spent a good deal of effort and arm-power making it very painful for me whenever I did not follow directions. And she also believed that a large part of the function of school was to make me learn how to do what I was told to do. (Lorde, 1982, p. 27)

This passage illuminates the myriad ways society deploys schooling apparatus to socialize people into existing epistemic and ontological frameworks. Importantly, Lorde recognized the critical praxis of her mother who both wrestled with the normative expectations of society and made calculated decisions to equip her Black daughter for survival under those expectations. Unruliness, as we might infer from Lorde, offers insight into the body's deliberate attempts at resistance to normative ways of being. By rummaging through memory, I am thinking about what is made visible and possible. In the enormity of structural violence and racialized enclosure that plays out in schools and society, Lorde seemed to be commenting on everyday enunciations of liveliness, asserting that something is and can be invented that rejects normativity, alongside some recognition of the limitations of those practices in the throes of anti-Blackness.

Unchecked, individuals are seduced (Dillard, 2012) into old blueprints as legitimate courses for knowledge accumulation, or what Lorde (1984) called that "piece of the oppressor which is planted deep within each of us, and which knows only the oppressors' tactics," is functionally at work in our knowing and being (p. 123). Part of the work of deconstruction is exposing how one has been taught to meet and reflect the status quo. Invention/inventiveness as praxis allows for this type of historical reading and reckoning, carving out a path for intimating.

INTIMATING

In all of the legal and extralegal ways that the wake of anti-Blackness structured life for Black people, my mother worked at joy. She invented. She brought in rays of the sun that the dusk left over; she manufactured livable moments, created spaces of care and appreciation, taught us how to touch our spirits, and made "homeplace" (hooks, 1990) in the midst of all that was unlivable in the world we lived in. In this sense, "even as we experienced, recognized, and lived subjection, we did not simply or only live in subjection and as the subjected" (Sharpe, 2016, p. 4). With attention to our circumstances and the larger anti-Black world that structured our living, "Good morning, my son" was her way of talking back, of loving Blackness and Black mattering. My mother affirmed what had been deemed socially unlovable. She reminded me that I was somebody's child; I belonged to someone, somewhere. Despite the rolling hills and plains that I would have to climb after breakfast and before I stepped onto the stoop in the evening, my mother saw me, hoped, dreamed, and was waiting for me to return. There was an active awareness, an undeniable certainty within my mother, of how life had been structured for and around us; the medley of peace that saturated her words was a cunning maneuver to coat the ugly truth of emancipation, namely, that it was an unfinished project.

Dillard (2012) explains the notion of remembering as a recognition of the ways minoritized individuals, particularly Black women, have been seduced—trained away—from themselves and must be pieced back together. Filtered through the historically produced subject, intimating here captures the interpretive process of bridging lived experiences with living memories embedded in words, acts, objects, or sounds to generate temporal (site bound) meaning (Durham, 2014). This interpretive process may involve unlearning, such that individuals can reconnect with a core self but are chiefly concerned with resolving the demand(s) they are faced with.

Baldwin excerpt #2

> I could not get over two facts, both equally difficult for the imagination to grasp, and one was that I could have been murdered. But the other was that I had been ready to commit murder. . . . My *real* life, was in danger, and not from anything other people might do but from the hatred I carried in my own heart. (Baldwin, 1955, p. 99)

Though Black people may harbor rage, a reoccurring fever for which no apology is owed, Baldwin persuaded readers of a precarious reality that is full of nuance, contradiction, and carefully weighed decision-making. Missteps for Black people, that include rage as a legitimate response to oppression, can be deemed as threatening behaviors. Baldwin's lamentation keyed readers into the never-ending utility and bout with external formulas. Specifically, intimating is at work in this passage as it incorporates past and present, real and imagined lives into Baldwin's way of knowing and being.

Lorde excerpt #2

> Our poems formulate the implications of ourselves, what we feel within and dare make real (or bring action into accordance with), our fears, our hopes, our most cherished terrors. For within living structures defined by profit, by linear power, by institutional dehumanization, our feelings were not meant to survive. (Lorde, 1984, p. 39)

Here, Lorde discussed poetry as the creative grounds on which one struggles with and against a society driven by rationality for the essence of their humanity. There is a clear recognition of anti-Blackness in this passage as she lamented that "our poems" (the implications of ourselves), or Black interior lives, were never meant to survive in a Western, United States context. Intimating, thus, is contested work; it is the labor of making real one's desires and hopes despite the pressure Black people are under to surrender them. In transforming feeling into language (intimating), however, interiority can become an idea, and then a version of personhood—presence.

Presence/Presencing

In practice, presence is the ability to survive across time and show up in innumerably new ways. It echoes the work of Aimee Meredith Cox (2015), who described how Black women and girls "engage with, confront, challenge, invert, unsettle, and expose the material impact of systemic oppressions" (p. 7) and the normative expectations of Black respectability. As the wake of anti-Blackness structures lives, sociologist Nikki Jones (2010) considered how Black women and girls navigate the violence in their daily lives. She wrote that "[Black] girls' lives seemed to be defined by this everyday struggle to balance the need to protect themselves with the pressure to meet normative expectations associated with their gender, race, and class positions" (Jones, 2010, p. 208). Furthermore, presence constitutes what Hartman (2019) discussed as the tactics, strategies, and mechanisms of refusal that were cultivated to escape constraint. Presence, in this way, is praxis "for how the body interacts with its environment" (Cox, 2015, p. 29). Presencing is acutely insightful, proceeding from a position that recognizes Black people as intimately aware of where their rights and responsibilities are truncated. Further, they are willing to adopt innovative tactics to negotiate those limitations.

Baldwin excerpt #3

Take no one's word for anything, including mine—but trust your experience. Know whence you came. If you know whence you came, there is really no limit to where you can go. The details and symbols of your life have been deliberately constructed to make you believe what white people say about you. (Baldwin, 1985, p. 335)

Baldwin seemed to be advocating for a materialized and felt experience—embodied knowing—as a choreographing (Cox, 2015) approach. Redirecting knowing from the cognitive to that which is embodied, Baldwin situated his nephew's present living in the larger genealogy of Black survival practices, suggesting that future presence is tied up with intimating. Moreover, Baldwin understood that presence represents a conundrum because of society's unwillingness and inability to see Black people as anything more than historically stigmatized images. Keenly, he understood that they have long been the targets of epistemic violence, making their words and bodies illegible (Dotson, 2011); thus, his objection is all the more necessary.

Lorde excerpt #3

We can train ourselves to respect our feelings and to transpose them into a language so they can be shared. And where that language does not yet exist, it is our poetry, which helps to fashion it. Poetry is not only dream and vision; it is the skeleton architecture of our lives. . . . The white fathers told us: I think, therefore I am. The Black mother within each of us—the poet—whispers in our dreams: I feel, therefore I can be free. (Lorde, 1984, pp. 37–38)

In this passage, Lorde is reflecting on the limitations of cognitive capacities, more specifically, the limitations of rationality (Baszile, 2015), an extension of the Eurocentrically mediated Man-as-human. Here, Lorde motioned for embodied knowing, a manifestation of invention and intimating, as fundamental to a survival project for Black people. The body, like poetry, in this passage offers a window into the imaginings of Black people that stretch beyond the expectations of what Black is, isn't, or should be. Moreover, to both theorize and make meaning in the wake of anti-Blackness, one must be careful not to conflate experience with existence. Lorde accepted this point, describing poetry as the "architecture of our lives," taken to mean that Black people maintain a relationship with the public sphere that forces improvisation to be an immutable function of life. *Free*, thus, should be understood as a negative dialectic, a politics of refusal, and tempered affirmation. Furthermore, *free* represented an embrace of disorder and incoherence decidedly committed to creating new presence in perpetuity.

"Good morning, my son" was an expression of presence. Some days I heard it as a reminder, other days it tasted like instruction. It told me before deceit and miseducation could entangle me, that my life was legible, intelligible, and worthy of acknowledgment; that my presence in this world was good. "Good" is not a simple word in the wake, where one lives the history and present of terror in, and on, our bodies. As the realities of that terror are often minimized, if not erased, my mother understood that our bodies and minds are threatened by violence, epistemic and material, in this Western, United States context. Amid this shadow, my mother taught my siblings and me about joy. As revision, her daily prayerful intervention offered an image of otherwise possibilities for living in the wake of anti-Blackness.

Revision

A constant in self-defining practice, revision constitutes the always active and enduring forces of the wake that prompt one to revisit their ways of knowing and being. Lorde (1992) remarked, "The process of revision is, I believe, crucial to the integrity and lasting power of a poem" (p. xiii). In a similar stream of consciousness, Baldwin (1985) wrote, "to do your first works over means to reexamine everything. Go back to where you started, or as far back as you can, examine all of it, travel your road again and tell the truth about it" (p. 36). Determining whether or not one's way of knowing and being structure needs revision appears to be guided by its ongoing utility. The process appeals to the sociopolitical demands one is situated within, or as Lorde denoted, "what was/is the work of the poem"

(p. xiv), as every piece, "has a bedrock of experience(s) within which the poem is anchored" (p. xiv). As it relates to one's way of knowing and being, presence, as elucidated above, is the prism by which those experiences are transformed into ways of knowing and being.

Revision doesn't appear to be a spontaneous gesture. Black living, over and against the enduring forces of the wake (Sharpe, 2016) that prompt one to revisit their ways of knowing, being, and understanding galvanize revision. Additionally, revisions appear to be motivated by images of what could be. Revision, in these ways, constitutes a process by which individuals construct habits of thinking, being, and understanding, as they encounter, relate to, and engage with various settings. To make a critical delineation, the work of invention/inventiveness is to grapple with questions of the human, constructions of how one's life is constructed in relation to the Western Man, and what possibilities exist therein for otherwise narrations, whereas revision is the friction and shifting ground for alternative versions of being human—modes of Black livingness.

Baldwin excerpt #4

> With this cry, and the echoing cries, the tarry service moved from its first stage of steady murmuring, broken by moans and now and again an isolated cry, into that stage of tears and groaning, of calling aloud and singing, which was like the labor of a woman about to be delivered of her child . . . for the rebirth of the soul was perpetual; only rebirth every hour could stay the hand of Satan. (Baldwin, 1953, p. 127)

Likening the threshing floor to that of giving birth, analysis of this passage suggested that self-defining praxis is not a finite experience, but a series of configuring moments that contribute uniquely to an ever-evolving image of personhood. Provocatively, Baldwin walked readers through this experience with close attention to the sensory mechanics of the body. Relatedly, I conclude in this imagery that the body is a site that must be continuously revisited in self-defining praxis.

Lorde excerpt #4

> We learned to appreciate each other's softness behind the lockers, calling it all different kinds of names and games—from

94 | On Blackness, Liveliness, and What It Means to Be Human

> touch tag to how-does-that-feel, to I-can-hit-harder-than-you. Until Gennie said to me one day, "is that the only way you know how to make friends?" and right then and there I began to learn other ways. I learned how to feel first and ask questions afterward. I learned how to cherish first the façade and then the fact of being an outlaw. (Lorde, 1982, p. 86)

This passage captured the possibilities of resemblance revisions by illustrating how the observation of others' modes of knowing and being can convict and call forth revisions in the viewer that were once outside of their purview. Along these lines, self-defining praxes, as images of the possible, allows individuals to touch and observe otherwise possibilities. Additionally, the body, as a site of meaning, is persuasively untangled in this passage as Lorde lifted the importance of affect—"feel first"—and spatiality—"appreciating each other's softness"—as critical to her knowing and being. In this instance, Lorde cherished the idea, morphed that idea into feeling, and embraced the feeling as a revised presence.

Annotations of Black Living: Implications for Educators and Researchers

Student/early adult development writ large, and self-authorship in particular, do not account for the specificity of Blackness. As this analysis reveals, not attending to Blackness—power dynamics and racialization processes therein—is to overlook psycho-affective dilemmas that structure Black liveliness and living. Additionally, student/early adult development theory is the ground by which pedagogy, practice, and policy are developed in higher education. Effectively, thus, learning, the expectations of development, and policy and practice construction reflect society's investment in dominant framings of what it means to be human, that is, all students should commit to meaning-making processes that mirror the Western Man. These findings are an example of not simply decentering the Western Man, but working toward Black specificity, and in doing so, they illustrate a critical frame for constructing pedagogy, practice, and policy. Self-authorship's dedication to interpersonal, intrapersonal, and cognitive dimensions constitutes the meaningful assemblage of holistic patterns in student development theorizing, and thus, marks important learning. Self-authorship, however, may not "make [us] larger, freer, and more loving." As self-definition would have it, responding to the wake of anti-Blackness does not cohere around particular strategies and tropes that favor preferred objective locations, or those forms of knowing and being that accent broader cultural expectations. Rather, they are constructed in and constituted by one's subjectivities. Self-defining praxis is aware of the body as a dynamic entity, highly historicized and contextualized, contingent on period and place, and considers the various other factors that shape an individual's identity. Here, as the findings explained, self-defining praxis accentuates the ways Black people cultivate an interior proposition for living, despite the entanglement of their social positions in a United States context, and globally.

Methodological Interventions

Baxter Magolda (1992, 2001, 2008, 2009) affirmed constructivist developmentalism as a paradigm for gauging adult meaning-making when she asserts, an individual's way(s) of knowing are best understood through the principles of naturalistic inquiry, that is, observing participants in a societal or cultural context. Her work, more than that of others, takes up this logic in a longitudinal methodological framework that thoughtfully follows participants across a set time span. I wonder, however, about the ways in which long and disciplined approaches may recursively place constraints on what can be known; these constraints become legitimized by an assumed sense of rigor. Self-defining praxis, as shown above, works against the disciplining of social science inquiry, and attempts to locate meaning-making in the praxis of Black living. The referential work and consequence of citing Black conceptions of being is about providing clues on not just how to be, but how to live differently.

Annotations

Self-definition, as a theory in the flesh (Moraga & Anzaldúa, 1981), explicitly intends is to annotate and make visible Black living (Sharpe, 2016) in the wake of anti-Blackness. In doing so, Black people are permitted to locate methods of liveliness that allow them to choreograph living in and under the full weight of anti-Black closures. Self-defining praxis complicates how meaning is strived for and attained by situating decision making in the hold of anti-Blackness while also amplifying agency. To teach with and toward self-defining praxis is to suggest that the stakes are high for

Black people in and beyond higher education, who, from the moment they wake, are the target of assaults on their knowing, their being, and understanding. To be clear, this is not a call to sympathy; rather, it is the recognition that Black specificity for Black students means that they are aware and have access to life-sustaining praxis, while simultaneously chipping away at the hostile spaces that enclose them; it is working with them to be freer; it is both loving them and prioritizing opportunities for them to love themselves.

Relationships with Students

As mentioned above, self-defining praxis, as a theory in the flesh (Moraga & Anzaldúa 1981), foregrounds the body and history, reckoning with the two as central to one's knowing, being, and understanding in the world, and as such, has implications for how Black people exist in the world. As a conceptual practice, self-defining praxis anticipates and thus differently prepares for, but is not preoccupied with anti-Blackness. This framing beckons educators and researchers to look carefully and responsibly, without turning away, at the epistemological and ideological histories that construct what it means to be human, and how one might creatively step outside of those logics by attending to an otherwise system of knowledge in support of Black worlds and worldmaking. This does not give educators a license to presume they understand the breadth of Black individuals' experiences; rather, it is an invitation to deeply consider the wake and build one's pedagogy and practice from that vantage point. Concomitantly, it charges educators to imagine pedagogies and curricula that situate Black onto-epistemologies—Black aesthetics, arts, literature, and essays—at the core of their work.

Once more, Black people are not the sum of anti-Blackness, as they are always and already invested in their survival, joy, and healing. Educators and researchers must be ever committed to wrestling with anti-Blackness and the varied ways it manifests, as well as to considering how Black specificity instantiates otherwise ways of being human.

We Who Are Dark: A Conclusion

Following the train incident, Fanon (1952) goes on to write, "In the world through which I travel I am endlessly creating myself" (p. 229).

"Look a Negro!" | 97

We who are dark (Love, 2019) know the haunting of "Look a Negro!" as the grounds for everyday existence, and as this chapter elucidates, are readily engaged in making room for breath in anticipation of the next attempts at asphyxiation. As evidenced by Baldwin, Lorde, and my mother, this haunting is interrupted by a rich tradition of knowledge production in the wake of crisis (Sharpe, 2016). Self-defining praxis, different from self-authorship, thinks about the relationship between history, racialization, and epistemology, illuminating an otherwise approach to meaning- and method-making mediated through the praxes of invention, intimating, presence, and revision. More broadly, these praxes call for a politics of theorizing about Black liveliness and living that normalizes, but is not the sum of anti-Blackness, and in doing so, invites new regard for Black liveliness in and beyond higher-education contexts.

∼

August,

Naming Black children is contested terrain. Naming is both past- and future-oriented work. The act of naming speaks to identity, often defining groups, organizations, and states. To name a thing, or to give a name to someone, is an expression of distinctness and originality, the marker by which someone or something is made different. In this way, perhaps, names are symbolic. Names have the capacity to locate and direct, to pause, and to guide. Names, and the subsequent definitions and meanings attached to them, follow, and tarry, and linger, softly and as fiercely as a raging fire. Naming represents an essential quality of being. I wrote the following, inspired and drawing on Imani Perry, in March 2021, one month before you were born:

　　We don't aspire for you to become a president or captain of industry. There will be no boasting about your famous acquaintances or luxurious cars, and I won't feel ashamed if you lack these. Our practicality has its limits. Our desires for you are basic: to have enough to eat, a roof over your head, leisure time, and freedom from constant struggle. We hope you'll be recognized for your efforts and talents. However, our aspirations for you extend beyond mere prestige. We yearn for a vibrant passion, deep human connections, appreciation of beauty, and the pursuit of excellence. The greatness we envision for you is of a timeless nature, not gauged by prominence but deeply rooted in the realm of imagination—our enduring gift.

Daddy dreamed about you, but your mother prayed for you, in the quiet season, pointed and specific, long before you arrived. In these ways you have the best of us and are the fulfillment of every good and great thing. At the precise moment, when it felt like the world was crumbling, the wells went dry, and the soil turned hard, you taught us about hope, about things that can grow, our faith made flesh. Hope, we are learning, is a discipline, and because we hope, we have a responsibility to commit to the world, even if it feels dire. You are our discipline and hope, and our ability to dream again. And so, we name you fearlessly and specifically. We speak a heavenly joy and ancestral inheritance over you. In a world that contests Black dignity and being, your name commands it. Dignified, noble, of high regard. It is steeped in the Yoruba tradition and means the power to make things happen. Know it. Repeat it. Refuse to shorten or strip it away. It took daddy some time to grow into his name, to shed the opinions of others, but I've made a commitment to speaking it early and often. To honoring your grandparents, and the Acholi people. I don't know what battles you will fight, but there is victory in your blood and power in your voice. We love you, and look forward to growing with you in our community, August. Asé Okello.

Part II
Black Ontological Possibility
The Praxes of Self-Definition

4

Invention

Narrating the Impossibility of Black Ontology

Figure 4.1. According to the Igbo wisdom tradition, our Chi (or Highest Self) resides in the Primordial Androgynous Blackness of Be Chukwu, the Divine Realm of the Creator. Dreaming in perfect harmony with the Creator, our Chi's "super-deep-sleep" gives rise to temporal experience as we know it. Our lives are these dreams, and when we die, our Chi awakes again in Be Chukwu. *Source*: *Be Chukwu* by Mikael Owunna. Used with permission of the artist.

How *Be Chukwu* Inspires This Chapter

In the image of *Be Chukwu*, I am thinking about uninterrupted dreaming, a space of flow and liquidity where ideas are permitted, expected to expand, and take form over and over again. I sense in this image a longing, a will to unfold, to live into one's becoming. *Be Chukwu* opens this chapter as an invitation to consider the worlds the white imagination has constructed around Black being. That seizure (read: history) complicates and works against Black people's rhythm, musicality, and kinetic genius in motion. That history complicates, however, does not foreclose Black ingenuity.

A Note on Scenes of Subjection

Black people are not the sum of violence and disposability. The framing, or grammar of Black living as summarized by terrains of terror tends to depend heavily on re-presentations of cultural narratives and artifacts proposed by social structures—sociopolitical mechanisms of power that discipline ways of seeing and interpreting who can be human in the contempered moment, and historically. The use of history, in its attempts to structure conditions for Black living in the realm of Western humanism, is an already compromised motive. History, as an ideological and political creation, can function to preserve and reify power imbalances that narrate Black folks as outside of humanity. Thus, a central question undergirding this chapter, and all other matters of narrating Black existence, asks, how does one return to and engage with the terror that has frequented Black living, without succumbing to, or reproducing grammars of violence? Here, I draw inspiration from Hartman (2007), and intend to throw into crisis the official story, the "what happened when" (p. 11), as a narrative fiction, formed and supported by Western humanism in order to advance the image of Man. By doing so, I "make visible the production of disposable lives," while attempting to attune with care, to the "mutters and oaths and cries of the commodity" (p. 11) of Black liveliness and living. My concern, again, is with annotating anti-Blackness and creating the conditions to think and produce otherwise knowledge, in excess of Western humanism, as occasioned by Black specificity. Fanon (1952) was instructive on this point when he wrote, "I am not a prisoner of History [l'Histoire]. I should not seek there for the meaning of my destiny. I should constantly remind myself that the real leap [le véritable saut] consists in introducing invention into existence" (p. 229). On this premise, I revisit scenes of subjection to clarify the double meaning of invention, or what I understand as mythmaking, or the historical, social, and political narration about Blackness and Black people that circulates around the notion of Man as human, and *inventiveness* as the vitality of Black living that precedes and exceeds mythmaking—the capacity to create habits of thinking, behavior, and doing outside of prescriptive representations.

∽

Considering that Black being exists beyond the "sanctified universe of (moral) obligation, or that circle of people with reciprocal obligations to protect each other" (Wynter, 1994, p. 44), Black males are "burdened by the threats others perceive them to be. Society's belief that Black males are dangerous and in need of control and criminal sanction nullifies the ability to perceive them as victims of violence" (Curry, 2019, p. 288). Importantly, in this chapter I use the term *male* and not *men* in full recognition of the need to be explicit and clear about sex and gender distinctions, and the ways they are too often conflated. This analysis lifts theories of Blackness and Black feminist theories to grapple with nonpersonhood, and the nihility of Black being mediated through transatlantic slavery (Spillers, 1987). Insomuch as gender convenes and asserts historical social orderings of personhood under the Western Man (Wynter, 1994) a priori, Black (males) are negated from the origin of human (that is, are capable of gender distinction), and, as the analysis will show, viewed by society as nonhuman/nonbeing.

Among the unfortunate reminders of this social disregard in the current sociopolitical context are the numerous cases of police brutality that involved, but are not limited, to the slaying of George Floyd on May 25, 2020. In the harrowing scene, a Black male pleaded for his life—for breath—while a white man held his knee on Floyd's neck. I revisit this murder cautiously in an attempt to ground the context that surrounds Black males' lives and bodies. For more than nine minutes, Floyd went unheard, and perhaps worse, ignored, as officers disregarded the fact that he was slowly dying, though he definitively stated as much. This scene is mimetic of the ways the Western Man disregards Black males as capable of feeling. As campuses have issued statement after statement, largely condemning the virulent incident of Floyd's murder, less has been said about the historical underpinnings—the policies, practices, ideas, that have shaped how society accounts for the bodies of Black males.

These historical underpinnings, as I will show, track into the educational context, demonstrated in this investigation by the scene of alleged sexual violence committed against Black males at the University of Michigan. In this case, Dr. Robert Anderson at the University of Michigan is alleged to have sexually assaulted Black males. The University of Michigan hired Dr. Anderson in 1966, and he held multiple positions (for example, associate physician at University Health Services [UHS], director of UHS, team physician in the Athletic Department, clinical instructor at the University's Medical School, a lecturer in the Department of Medical Care Organization at the School of Public Health) throughout his tenure. Anderson, subsequently, created and sustained a culture of sexual violence that exploited what many Black males came to believe about the university, namely, "that they would be taken care of at Michigan. That [they would] be part of a storied legacy of great men . . . That [they would] be protected" (Tinsley, 2020, para. 15). A 2021 report concluded that "no University personnel took any meaningful action despite the cloud of rumors, jokes, and innuendo that followed Dr. Anderson throughout his career" (Wilmer Hale, 2021, p. 61). I chose to examine this scene to look more closely at the ways power can be used and distributed in educational contexts. The University of Michigan, as a prestigious academic and athletic institution, benefits from the labor of Black males, in what might be understood as an extension of plantation politics (Williams, Squire, & Tuitt, 2021). Against this reality, Black men live.

The challenge here, of mapping the un/believability of Black males' vulnerability to rape and sexual violence in higher education is not an attempt to erase, overstep, or stand in opposition against Black women, Black trans people, and Black nonbinary people who experience inordinate amounts of violence in and beyond higher-education contexts (Crenshaw, 1990; D. C. Hill, 2016; Linder & Harris, 2017); instead, I am demonstrating the ways white supremacy, too, refuses Black males' humanity and the processes of Black livingness called forth by Black males' historicized positionalities. Following James (2013), I believe that "any philosophical aversion, emotional dissonance, political 'shame' toward critiques of racial rape leaves black masculinity theory adrift or disengaged" (p. 126). These analyses intervene on this gap by keying in on Black masculinity's longer histories, and how the realm of affect absented those masculinities, as a lens for understanding the impossibilities of Black males' vulnerabilities in the present. Specifically, I examine historical messages related to Black males and sexual violence as a bridge for reviewing the allegations of sexual violence against Black males at the University of Michigan. Using the chokehold (Butler, 2017) as a theoretical framework to analyze the gendered and sexualized vulnerabilities of Black males, I conducted a critical discourse analysis (Fairclough, 2003; van Dijk, 2003) of media documents, asking how does white supremacy function to both terrorize Black males' bodies and ignore their pain in educational contexts? I follow these analyses with considerations for attending to Black liveliness in educational theory and practice.

Contextualizing Black Males in US Society

When there has been discourse on Black males' minoritized identities, it has tended to revolve around Black males' racialized encounters (for example, Rodney King, Michael Brown, Trayvon Martin) with systems of oppression in the public realm (Crenshaw, 1990; James, 2013; hooks, 2004). History and theory often discuss Black males' vulnerabilities in relation to the lynching event (see K. K. Hill, 2016), which fits the cultural narrative of Black males' bestiality—the weapon that white supremacy deployed to bring them under submission. As a matter of fit, Black men and boys' fear proctored the white social imaginary and steered discipline toward them. James (2013) spoke to this point, writing, the "common perceptions of black suffering became embodied in and represented by male trauma—emanating from the lash, shackle, the brand, convict lease, lynch mob, death row, mass imprisonment, and 'stop-n-frisk'" (p. 126). More theorization is needed, however, to understand the ways gender and violence gets deployed ahistorically (Harris & Linder, 2017) to define the boundaries between human and nonhuman (Curry, 2017), which ultimately affects how collegiate educators work with and theorize about Black males. Lugones (2017) denoted, "under the imposed gender framework [of colonial modernity] the bourgeois white Europeans were civilized; they were fully human. The hierarchical dichotomy as a mark of the human, also became a normative tool to damn the colonized. The behavior of the colonized and their personalities/souls were judged as bestial and thus non-gendered, promiscuous, sexual, and sinful" (p. 1). For these reasons, it should come as no surprise that a lawyer, commenting on the alleged sexual abuse of forty Black males at the University of Michigan, would say, "we have never seen this many African American men abused in any setting" (Greig, 2020, para. 6). Though I revisit this statement later in the chapter, it is important to note upfront that the syntax of disbelief, here and across culture writ large, augments Black males' already impossible notion as susceptible to gendered and sexual violence. Following this logic, I trace the ways Black males have been ejected from the possibility of being victims of gendered violence, and how those perceptions track into higher education, ultimately, affirming the need for this analysis.

History as Invention

To be clear, then, the figure of the Western, European Man, is an invention of Western humanism. On this point, Wynter and Scott (2000) noted the following:

> Now, here is where the conception of the genre of the human and of the governing sociogenic principle [a principle she adapts from *Black Skin, White Masks*] comes in. For it would be the code, the law of the code, the principle, which functions as the ground of the history that will be narrated and existentially lived. So, the ground of our mode of being human will itself be the a priori or ground of the history to which it gives rise. But the paradox here, of course, is that it cannot itself be historicized within the terms of the ethnohistory to which it will give rise: that code/mode must remain, as you say unhistoricizable. As ours now remains for us. (pp. 197–98)

So, Western humanism, manifesting through history, as a discipline, method of articulation, and episteme, encloses Black ontological possibility, Black living. What's more, inventions of history also materialize as, and in the afterlife of slavery, as that which in incommensurable with the work of endless creation (Marriott, 2011). One particular nexus for these occurrences of invention was gender and violence.

Historicizing Gender and Sexual Violence

Black positionality is contested terrain. James (2015), writing on the early philosophers of humanity, noted the "free male as a human theorist, the slave as anti-human nontheorist, and the non-slave female as semi-human, defective, anti-theorist. This natural order of things presented ideology-as-philosophy in which the capacity for theory and freedom are proprietary possessions held against future citizens" (p. 260). This Aristotelian trifurcation of human, antihuman nontheorist, semihuman worked to classify white males as sole holders of the marker human. The notion of "the slave" was more than a discursive, theoretical idea, but a biopolitics formalized and created through acts of terror and enslavement of the human.

According to Warren (2016), the purpose of antebellum biopolitics was "not to manage black 'life,' to make the subject live on and manipulate the conditions of this living, but to expel blacks from the very terms of 'life' and 'death' all together" (p. 108). Within this realm, Black human-beingness becomes a baseless claim. Furthermore, in this state of injury, "it is the ontological violence that preconditions the physical torment of the whip, the canine patrol, the knife, and the gun. This form of violence situates Blacks outside the traditional terms of humanism and into the realm we might describe as the "ontological state of exception" (p. 108). Though there have been shifts in Blackness's recognition in the social imaginary (see *Brown v. Board of Education (1954)*; Civil Rights, 1965), "emancipation through some form of discursive or symbolic intervention is wanting in the face of a subject position that is not a subject position . . . 'an interdiction against subjectivity' . . . an accumulated and fungible object, rather than an exploited and alienated subject" (Moten, 2013, p. 748). This matrix ensures that the idea of Black personhood is vulnerable to the urges of the Western Man and, subsequently, is important to understand in the service of supporting Black men's meaning making.

Situating Black people in the juridical codes of slavery that facilitated their dispossession, "every feature of social and human differentiation disappears" in light of this encounter (Spillers, 1987, p. 78). Theft of the body marked a "willful and violent (and unimaginable from this distance) severing of the captive body from its motive will, its active desire" (Spillers, 1987, p. 67). Among those defining points of differentiation stripped from the captive was the notion of gender and sexuality. Evasive and improbable, in slavery's arrangement, "the female body and the male body become a territory of cultural and political maneuver, not all gender-related, gender-specific" (Spillers, 1987, p. 67). Building on Spillers, Bliss (2015), posited, "gender and sexual differences among the enslaved veil vulnerability to sexual violence within and directed at captive communities. Gender/sexual expression as a 'human' characteristic is possessed by those already empowered as 'human'" (p. 261).

Rightly then, as Sexton (2018) records, "male gender in Black inconsistently mediates structural vulnerability but affords none of the traditional entitlements of the Western Man or maleness. Power in Black is a negative affordance" (p. 7), distinct from the ways the Western Man operates as a domain and power and humanness. Commenting on the issue of power, Spillers et al. (2007) purported that Black males cannot merely be patriarchal, whereas they "appropriate the gender prerogatives of white men because they have a different kind of history" (p. 305). Curry (2017), dislodging the familiar claim that Black masculinity is sufficiently patriarchal, postulated, "gendered power relations are dynamic, unstable and ambiguous, and . . . masculinity does not always legitimize patriarchy" (p. 2). Furthermore, he contends that Black males, generally marked as hypermasculine and violent, are considered and theorized through patriarchy (Curry, 2017). Hence, Black males are "thought to be the exemplifications of white (bourgeois) masculinity's pathological excess. In other words, the toxic abnormality of hegemonic white masculinity becomes the conceptual norm for Black males and boys" (p. 3). Black males, extant, as noted above, in a structural antagonistic relationship with society are always already deemed threatening (Sexton, 2008). Irresolvably linking Black males to hegemonic white masculinity has added to and supplanted violence on and toward Black males as natural and necessary.

Importantly, discussions on the sexual violence toward and against Black males must grapple with the rape and sexual exploitation of Black women (James, 2013, 2015). As explained above, the frame for interpreting Black (men's) victimization and trauma was threaded through public acts of abuse typified by lynching. In this way, acts of sexualized violence toward Black women were inconsequential as they receded from view. According to McKittrick (2006), "ownership of black women during transatlantic slavery was a spatialized, gendered, often public, violence; the black female body was viewed as a naturally submissive, sexually available, public, reproductive technology" (p. 44). Once their bodies were territorialized, it marked them as inhuman, indecipherable, "rape-able," and without place (McKittrick, 2006, p. 45). The geographic expansiveness of slavery, thus, extended Black women's available bodies. Survivors and historians have intensely labored against racialized-sexualized depictions to capture and reflect the experiences of enslaved Black women (see Giddings, 2008; Jacobs, 1987; McGuire, 2010). Though the record is clear, stereotypical depictions persist that function to categorize Black women as hypersexual, inhuman, and, therefore, undeserving of protection (D. C. Hill, 2016).

Sexual Violence Research in Higher Education

Related to higher-education research, white women have been centered in discourse on sexual violence and response efforts (Harris, 2017; Hong,

2017; Linder, 2017). It is during the 1970s that the language of rape culture emerges in public discourse as a term that points to the ways society blames victims and normalizes white patriarchal violence. During the 1970s and '80s, the setting for this particular chapter, conferences, convenings, legislation, publications, and programming like "Take Back the Night" surface in the public sphere. Antirape activism gained some traction in higher education during this time, and with it, some services to support survivors. According to Jessup-Anger (2018), "On some campuses, these services were organized as a partnership between a community-based rape crisis center and a campus women's center. On others, university-based rape crisis centers offered services to both the campus and the community" (p. 9). Erased from early conversations on sexual violence, though present on the margins, was a serious discussion on the intersections of sexual violence and the experiences of minoritized folks as survivors of sexual violence (Jessup-Anger, 2018).

Harris (2017) challenged scholars to consider minoritized students, in particular, women of color, by lifting critical race theory and critical race feminism as analytics to examine women of color's experiences with sexual violence. Illustrating critical race feminisms potential, she noted that the framework places women of color at the center of analysis, critiquing notions of essentialism and calling for an explicit interrogation of interlocking systems of oppression that "contribute to women of color's sexual violence and maintain women's invisibility in the discourse of campus sexual violence" (p. 44). Similarly, pointing to the necessity of an intersectional analysis, she posited that intersectionality allows "for a closer critique of how and why women of color are left out of the discourses, including policies, practices, and programming, surrounding sexual violence" (p. 45). In this way, women of color's experiences, due to color-evasive rhetoric, are absent from campus policies and discussions.

Building an argument for historical approaches, Harris (2017) noted that an intersectional lens "exposes how women of color's bodies have been constructed throughout time, via patriarchal and white supremacist structures, to serve the needs of dominant society" (p. 45). In like manner, she postulated that ahistoricism makes it difficult for college educators to respond and effectively interrogate the contextual influences of sexual violence. Circuitously, ahistorical approaches have contributed to narrow, identity-neutral educational strategies (Linder, 2017). Here, failure to use nongendered language, or not include a broader description of genders as victims in educational programs, "perpetuates the under-interrogated ideal that women are victims and men are perpetrators" (Linder, 2017,

p. 73). Cohen (2014) concluded similarly that "rape is still the most gender-specific of all crimes [where] 'only a man . . . can be the actual perpetrator, only a woman [can be] the victim" (p. 3) in many gendered paradigms on sexual violence.

Where it involves Black males, stigmatized as hypersexual and violent brutes, there is an overwhelming reluctance to unsee their endangerment and the highly sexualized environments that rear them, despite the rates at which they experience statutory rape, sexual coercion, and sexual manipulation (Biello et al., 2013; Cavazos-Rehg et al., 2009; French et al., 2015). Curry and Utley (2018) suggested that the sociopolitical realities of Black males are often ejected from consideration, outlining the ability to theorize them "as invulnerable to sexual coercion, sexual abuse, and statutory rape, despite their intimate proximity to these kinds of violence" (p. 234). Put simply, the failure to interrogate this dominant narrative is to facilitate miseducation in higher-education teaching and programming (Hong, 2017, Linder, 2017). That this abuse occurs within a matrix of domination (James, 2013), as shown in the next section, placed limitations, then and now, on how Black males could respond.

The Chokehold and the Maintenance of Man: A Theoretical Framework

Without respect for the power imbalances formed in and through the master-slave relationship (Scott, 1990), it is difficult to comprehend the negative affordances that Black males are bound by in instances of sexual violence. Historically, sexual violence is constructed through white patriarchal frames of power, which ensured that women, and some men, could be victims of this power. Accounting for Black males requires an understanding of racialized patriarchies that omit, and make impossible, that they would benefit from the hegemonic policies and practices. Further, historically, Black males were, and continue to be, confronted with few self-determining choices within a racialized patriarchy that demands their forced or coerced submission. For these reasons, I employ the chokehold as a theoretical framework for locating the liveliness and living of Black males.

Paul Butler (2017) uses the chokehold metaphor and analytic to capture the complexity of the Blackness. He noted, "A chokehold is a process of coercing submission that is self-reinforcing. A chokehold justifies additional pressure on the body because it does not come into compliance, but the body cannot come into compliance because of the vice grip" (p. 4). Conceptually, the chokehold is useful concerning the existence of Black living broadly, and Black males, in particular, for several reasons. First, the chokehold does not invite a reasoned, individualized response. For one placed in the chokehold, the threat of movement ensures that there can be no compliance because the grip provokes resistance (noncompliance). In this way, the chokehold redistributes one's resistance on the self.

As an imposition upon the self, the hold "not only persists to the extent that it is resisted, but it also tightens" (Sexton, 2018, p. 6). In this state, one cannot comply, and one cannot escape regardless of the tools of mediation. As an anti-Black ontological tool, the chokehold has the same functionality across the racialized and gendered spectrum of Black males. In this way, though the chokehold is most cited in relation to state-sanctioned, official police agencies, its powers extend to include the general public. Stated differently, if state-appointed, law enforcement agencies, as one source of anti-Black power, are permitted to treat Black people with contempt, then the broader public as owners of the Western Man (Harris, 1993), too, own this power to humiliate and harm (Sexton, 2018). Finally, the chokehold, in its essence, ensures that Black males are not threats (Butler, 2017). The terrifying truth attached to this logic is that Black males "are thought to be a threat in their very being, and not for any particular conduct or performance. It is, therefore, as impossible for Black males to follow the required script as it is for them to submit to the chokehold" (Butler, 2017, p. 6). This forced-choice outlines the impossible decisions that construct the realities and vulnerabilities of Black males. Where it relates to the figure of the Western Man, one might understand how the chokehold, as a discursive technology of power, maintains histories of domination (read: Black people as the sum of violence) as the order of knowledge that governs society.

Yet, even as the chokehold attempts to restrict breathing, one must not ignore the evidence of living—refusal—as that which demands otherwise. Or, as Moten (2008) noted, Blackness, among other things, is a constant demand for an "ontology of disorder, an ontology of dehiscence, a para-ontology" (p. 187), such that, as Western humanism encloses, Blackness shouts, kicks, call, yells, shrieks—*invents*. Taking up the chokehold as a frame for not only annotating anti-Blackness, but, also, a practice for destabilizing Western humanism by attending—listening, seeing, feeling—for the exception. Scholars of Black Studies, particularly Paul Gilroy (1993) and M. NourbeSe Philip (2008), have deployed analytics in ways that are akin to my intentions. Philip, for example, employs the slave ship as a conceptual device, enabling readers to contemplate the histories tethered to it and what they illuminate—biocentricity (see chapter 1) and Black social death. Furthermore, by anticipating, the ship prompts us to disrupt recursive logic and to invent otherwise ways of knowing and being. Imbued by Blackness, the chokehold renders a speaking subject "by way of an eruption of phonic substance that cuts and augments meaning with a phonographic, rematerializing inscription" (Moten, 2003, pp. 13–14), in the place of the nonspeaking, inconceivable speaking object. Black people, thus, are not left in the place of object, unheard and impossible in the Western social imaginary. Taken together, against historical *inventions* of and about Blackness, Blackness is a site of *inventiveness*.

Critical Discourse Analysis: An Approach

Responding to the praxis of invention/inventiveness, I took up the work of surfacing the undetectable, bringing the present self back into conversation with forgotten (or ignored and untaught) patterns of knowing, being, seeing, and feeling. Using the chokehold (Butler, 2017) as a theoretical framework to analyze the gendered and sexualized vulnerabilities of Black males, I placed historical records in conversation with the temporal moment, particularly the allegations of sexual violence committed against Black males at the University of Michigan. In doing so, I conducted a critical discourse analysis (Fairclough, 2003; van Dijk, 2003) of media documents, asking how does white supremacy function to both terrorize Black males' bodies and ignore their pain in educational contexts? This framing raised questions of subjectivity amid anti-Black disregard.

Critical discourse analysis "is a type of discourse analytical research that primarily studies the way social power abuse, dominance, and inequality are enacted, reproduced, and resisted by text and talk in the social and political context" (van Dijk, 2003, p. 352). Critical discourse analysis intends to interrogate and expose power relations threaded through the structure of discourse and how these productions function to sustain inequitable policies and practices. Power, as noted above, is discursive and manifests in different forms; critical discourse analysis brings light to these various expressions of power by analyzing the linkage between history and temporal contexts and practices. In addition to making connections across space and time, critical discourse analysis also examines the epistemological nature and relationship of texts to individuals within a particular context. As an interpretive tool of analysis, critical discourse analysis can interrupt hidden or taken-for-granted assumptions, making room for alternative perspectives to surface.

According to van Dijk (2003), critical discourse analysis attunes to "socially shared representations of societal arrangements, groups, and relations, as well as mental operations such as interpretation, thinking and arguing, inferencing and learning" (van Dijk, 1993, p. 257). Describing two levels of analysis, van Dijk (2003) pointed to the micro and the macro. Micro references language, texts, and verbal communications, whereas macro examines powers and relations between social groups. The macro considers how power is used as a form of coercion and mental control through "laws, rules, norms, habits, and even a quiet general consensus" (van Dijk, 2003, p. 355). This approach meant highlighting "instances in which particular voices conveyed perspectives that would either be deemed relevant or dismissed in relation to their legitimacy and credibility" (Patton, 2014, p. 733). Power can be context-specific, granting authority to those who hold particular positions within an organization.

To analyze the allegations of sexual violence toward Black males at this institutional site, I made connections between official documents' language and the larger sociohistorical patterns that follow these incidents. For example, use of the language "Michigan Men" in briefings projected gendered notions of loyalty and strength, which follow long-standing tropes about men's reluctance to experience emotionality and vulnerability. Taking notes throughout my process, I asked questions like, how might this language prevent Black males from expressions of vulnerability? I returned to these types of questions/notes throughout the analysis.

To respond to this chapter's questions, I began by reading through official documents related to the allegations. In the first read, I attempted to get a sense of the intent of the messages, what was being said and unsaid? I considered history, which raised questions such as what does it mean for Black males to believe they will be protected by white institutions? I thought about positionality and the role of power, asking, how are Black males being silenced, or permitted to speak and tell their stories? Will they be believed? Following my initial review, I reread critically to tease out the many interpretations that might exist. Next, I sought to frame the messages through the chokehold lens and against a historical backdrop that carried deeply embedded ideas about Black males' bodies in the white social imaginary.

Critical Discourse Analysis of Allegations

The University of Michigan (Michigan) is a prestigious institution. Arguably, Michigan's football program has been the athletic department's crowning achievement. Through 2015, the football program ranked first in NCAA history in total wins and winning percentage. On April 21, 2020, the headline of an article published by *Mlive.com*, read, "Black males were 'particularly vulnerable' to sexual abuse by late University of Michigan doctor, lawyer says." Among the forty-one articles and reports reviewed about this incident, which included motions, depositions, interviews by former players, and reports on local and national news sites, I key into this article because of its focus on Black males. The article discussed how Dr. Robert E. Anderson, a white man, sexually abused forty Black males during medical exams in his roles at the University Health Service and physician for the football team.

Michigan's profile as a premier institution, responsible for recruiting and producing world-class athletes, many of whom are Black, provides an essential backdrop to this story. During my first review of the article, I was drawn to the attention placed on the experience of Black males. Lawyer Jamie White of White Law PLLC, who also represented survivors in the Michigan State University case that brought charges against the athletic doctor Larry Nassar, discussed the sexual abuse context. Readers learn that Anderson, who died in 2008, had been under investigation since 2018, when a former University of Michigan wrestler, Tad Deluca, sent a letter to the athletic director Warde Manuel, detailing the multiple instances of sexual assault that he endured in the 1970s. According to reports, Anderson performed unnecessary bodily exams. Deluca, a white man, is credited with being the whistleblower in Anderson's case, which has since generated several lawsuits against the university from dozens of former student-athletes. Throughout the article, White intends to bring light to a less reported on phenomena of Black males' vulnerabilities to sexual assault and how the sociocultural environment of universities, and the broader society, might confront these terrors. However, a closer reading of the article raises concerns about the potential of the article and White's legal approach to confronting cultures of sexual violence. White grounds his argument, and seemingly his case for the survivors, in the fact of their vulnerability, stating, "Most, if not all, of these men from the 1970s and 80s, were first-generation college students. They came from depressed socioeconomic backgrounds, and their only lifeline was these athletic scholarships. For those reasons, these men just beared what Anderson would do because, as they will say, there were not any options. They will all unilaterally say that had they not cooperated with these sports physicals, they would have lost their scholarships" (para. 2). White, drawing on his clients' voices, made an important point, suggesting that these Black males endured what they did because they were dependent on university scholarships. This concern is relevant; it finds historical legitimacy in enslavement where the bodies of Black people were the property of owners and could be subjected to dehumanization therein. As property and manifestations of white supremacy, Black women and men could not be raped, and their perceived hypersexuality stripped them of any credibility in reporting. Rape could not be a crime because violations only registered as an offense for those considered human. Again, the colonized and racialized subject, as products of white supremacy, were nongendered (nonhuman), overly sexual, and deviant.

In these instances of sexual violation, white institutional power structures in and through collegiate athletics exploit Black males (Beamon, 2008; Murty et al., 2014). These power structures recruit them to satisfy their institutional needs, promising, in many ways, to elevate them and their families into new opportunities, be it academic or professional. In doing so, institutions are generating millions of dollars off of unpaid Black labor. Between 2014 and 2016, the University of Michigan averaged 127 million dollars in revenue. The performance of Black males, therefore, is beneficial to the university and alumni, with little immediate financial return and the slight possibility of earning wages professionally for Black male athletes themselves.[1] This exploitative relationship creates conditions whereby Black males' bodies are unrecognized beyond their profit, and thus, able to be used and acted on without discretion. Thinking through the chokehold (Butler, 2017) as a technology of white supremacy, Black males, in this scenario, do not have the institutional power to reject the abuse, nor would they have their refutations taken seriously.

Anderson, as a team doctor for the prestigious brand that is the University of Michigan and Michigan football, had the power to assess the fitness and, more precisely, the status, of Black males. His position infused him with chokehold authority, and with it, the power to relegate Black males to an inferior status, both during private sessions, and in the context of the students' ability to play/perform on the field. In the event, for example, that Black males were noncompliant with Anderson's demands, the possibility of Anderson using his authoritative position to make claims/

decisions/diagnoses that could otherwise harm these students cannot be understated. Placing these incidents in a historical context, empowered with the chokehold as a sociopolitical apparatus, it is important to note that sexual violence has little to do with sex; rather, it is an illustration for how "gender violence functions as a tool for racism and colonialism" (Smith, 2005, p. 15). Anderson's acts of sexual violence, therefore, mapped white patriarchal (supremacy) structures onto campus and the lives of Black males. What's more, the behavior reinforced the historical, made present, treatment of bringing Black males, and the many stereotypes they are imbued with, under submission.

THE MICHIGAN MAN

In his attempt to clarify the context of Black males' vulnerabilities, White refuses a more extensive critique of institutional and cultural conditions that accentuate vulnerabilities, which locates the problem of abuse on one person's decisions (that is, Anderson was an abuser) instead of the larger systems that enable the behavior. He exclaimed: "[We have] never seen this many young African American men abused in any setting by the same person, but certainly not in the setting of one of the most prestigious universities in the world" (Marowski, 2020, para. 6). By centralizing Anderson's abusive behavior to the failures of one person, he abdicates the University of Michigan of responsibility, and at best, stations them as the unassuming site of Anderson's aggression. In both cases, the singularity of white supremacy undermines the probable violence and exploitation of Black males.

In the same breath, White engages in the same dangerous hypermasculine rhetoric used to render Black males incapable of pain/assault by amplifying their resilience in the abuse. When recapitulating how Black males were making sense of the violence compared to the survivors of Larry Nassar at Michigan State University, he posited, "They are Michigan men." Further defined, "A *Michigan Man* must be loyal to Michigan. . . . This involves dedication, passion, and leadership. It involves a commitment to academics, loyalty to other *Michigan Men*, and the resolve to accomplish great things in the right legal and ethical manner" (Nicholson, 2010, para. 14). Dedication, passion, and leadership are valuable traits for any institution of education, but an unrelenting loyalty to the institution could function to place property over lives, or what one believes they deserve. This point becomes clear when White reported: "As they come forward and we have these conversations over and over again, the central theme is always consistent: 'I hate what happened, and in hindsight, I feel ashamed. But I love this university and I want to be part of the solution and help them be a leader when it comes to dialogue involving these sorts of issues'" (Marowski, 2020, para. 8). The "but" of the statement moves experiential pain into the shadows in favor of a "loyalty" to the institution. Furthermore, allegiance to the idea of Michigan (read: reputation, prestige, prominence, elitism), and the fixture of "Michigan men" (read: tropes of masculinity) disappears the actuality of rape and sexual violence to an unnamed space denoted as "sorts of issues." Here, one might read that survivors know something happened to them, yet they, perhaps, are owning that the abuse was their fault, notwithstanding the power dynamics at play. Cementing the impossibility of Black males' vulnerabilities, White said, "His clients [do not] want to be involved in a 'burning-at-the-stake mentality' . . . and I find that remarkable" (Marowski, 2020, para. 9). That White would find their resolve "remarkable" lends all the more to the hypermasculine narrative that would rather understand Black males as durable and more resilient than those who could otherwise be culturally vulnerable to racialized patriarchal violence.

Explicating Invention/Inventiveness

The question of self-definition is partially a question of value, wherein that which was invented as no value, is an inventor of value (Moten, 2003), led by the question: how does one exist, in the body that they hold, in this historical moment and into the future? The analysis above pursued a critical intervention on this question as it puts the temporal body into a relationship with the historical caricature. However false they may be, caricatures carry meaning, and thus, the temporal body infuses it with definitions and messages it actively determines and those it assumes merely by existing. Invention as narrative tracing establishes clues for how Blackness, and more specific to this chapter, the narrative degendering (see Fuentes, 2016; Spillers, 1987) that transformed Black people into flesh, has been positioned across time. Here, analyzing allegations of Black males' white supremacist sexualized violence through the lens of the chokehold (Butler, 2017) surfaced three critical inventions that come to bear on student development theory and practice: *the myth that Black people broadly, and Black males, in particular, do not have interior lives worth protecting; the historicized incapability of Black males to experience pain/assault; and sexual violence is ongoing and unremarkable in the lives of Black males.* In what follows, I detail each of these implications.

First, this critical reading points to the notion that institutions and institutional actors find Black interiority illegitimate. The implication explains how the material body is restricted and affective lives are made unintelligible. Moreover, it denotes the historical belief that Black males do not possess affective and emotional capacities worth understanding and defending. Considering the former, succinctly, Ellison (1952) called this material disposition, this way of seeing and understanding Black people, a construction of the "inner eyes, those eyes with which they look through their physical eyes upon reality" (p. 3). These inner eyes connect to a historicity that makes Blackness incoherent with living essences and in this case (see chapter 2), catalyzes the failure of institutions and their actors to conceive of Black males as sentient beings. Where the body is restricted, it is an object of control, subject to the aims of the Western Man (Harris, 1993). Though Ellison intended to make clear the sensibilities of Western humanism to narrative/invent disregard, inventiveness reconstructs the looking process, or how one might see the self in the public sphere.

One of the ways institutions and educators can support inventiveness, is empowering Black males' narrative voice (Harris, 2017). The weight of history and threat of violence can force Black males to internalize raced and gendered mythologies. Creating space on campus, in community, where Black males can name their fear, frustration, and pain, can assist in demystifying the deeply held assumptions that presume Black males do not feel. Building on Delgado and Stefancic (2012), "stories also serve a powerful additional function for minoritized communities. Many victims suffer in silence. . . . Stories can give them a voice and reveal that others have similar experiences" (p. 49). Notably, the writing of this chapter only happened because survivors shared their stories. At its core, this chapter is an attempt to lift their voices in support of others.

The racialized and gendered institutional architecture made it all the more likely that Black males could be indiscriminately exploited, violated, and abused. The case of Michigan clarifies this pattern; as football players, their bodies were recruited and exploited by the engine and reputation of Michigan athletics. Furthermore, the allegations of abuse install a similar imbalance, for as Black people are coerced into the Western Man's parameters, power holders exercise their will over Black bodies as *agreements* that are part of the culture (see biocentricity in chapter 1). Invention expands these instances of power differential as the decisive relationship between Black males, the educational enterprise, and society. For educators and researchers, confronting Black interiors' illegitimacy and opening Black males to sexual abuse will mean choosing to see how institutions and policies rest on or are supported by, white patriarchal beliefs meshed with histories of Black males as hypermasculine and expected rapists.

Institutions and educators were incapable of seeing Black males as experiencing pain/assault in ways that register as human, therefore forfeiting them from realms of freedom, belonging, and acceptance. Bound to stereotypical images of strength and violence, and generalized frameworks that fail to account for their full lives and disregard their stories, Black males cannot be perceived, believed, or perhaps even see themselves as victims of assault. The racialized and gendered framing that discerns Black males as originators and benefactors of sexual violence affects how their realities are understood. This perception lingers as an unwillingness to acknowledge their stories and data as relevant. Or, when the public is made aware of the quantifiable and narrative data (Curry & Utley, 2018; French et al., 2015), it is treated as an outlier to the Western Man's association of Black masculinity as violent and aggressive.

Laced with these stereotypes, Black males are encouraged to live with and in the trauma of sexual violence. Inventiveness here, as an otherwise being and praxis for supporting students in higher education, recognizes that the logic of white institutions does not protect Black males, and in many cases, exist as its nemesis, or the thing that white institutions are trying to (re)solve. From this vantage, one can see how Western humanism, as noted above, can feign commitment to Black males' lives in research and opportunity, and ultimately never see them as fully human or worthy of protection. Supporting Black males would mean broadening the analysis beyond gender, much like Tarana Burke (2018), the founder of the #MeToo movement, has attempted to clarify, "Part of the work of the Me Too Movement is about the restoration of that humanity for survivors because the violence doesn't end with the act. The violence is also the trauma that we hold after the act" (para. 1). Educators and researchers ought to be mindful of the ways trauma survives in the history and bodies of Black males, and that institutions, seeded in white patriarchy, are unable to name, attend to, or treat Black males. A healing project that can grapple with their vulnerabilities and trauma may be a conduit to reconstructing dangerous environments. This reconstructive environment must resist essentialist policies and programs and look to the margins to consider those often erased from the dialogue.

Finally, these implications pose a terrifying reality for theory and practice, which suggests that educators and researchers must grapple with Black males' probable encounter with white supremacist violence as distinct and, equally, unremarkable. The chokehold ensures that Black pain and trauma go unrecognized because it does not allow for the defense of humanity. Reading the allegations of sexual assault at the University of Michigan demonstrates the power of the Western humanism and its epistemological unwillingness to self-correct. Seeing and attending to Black males' liveliness would disrupt ahistorical framings that elide the structural dimensions of sexual violence (Linder & Harris, 2017) as a uniquely gendered issue resulting from patriarchal power. To do this, educators must embrace the use of analytics that center power, racism, and identity intersections (Harris, 2017).

Further, to respond to the humanity of Black males would unsettle the idea that Black males are more than a means of production or things to be controlled; it would undermine the sanctity of the Western Man and the illusion of Black males as dangerous (Curry, 2019). Importantly, the praxis of invention/inventiveness is not benevolence; it is the decency of regard for Black males' perpetual vulnerabilities in a Western, United States context. Accounting for this decency will require critical racialized and gendered frames, expansive in their ability to grapple with anti-Black assumptions that entrap Black people, and nimble enough to untether the truth that white patriarchal analytics confiscate Black males' lives.

Inventiveness

Invention, as a frame for contextualizing Black living, by reading the historical-made-present mythmaking of Western humanism, performs a necessary critique of subjectivity and subjecthood in a United States context. The praxis of invention asks, how, for whom, and for what purpose are Blackness and Black people constructed this way? Troubling the human question of what is taken up as foundation in higher-education theory and practice, thus, is to grapple with the normative narratives, representational politics, and the invention of Man that works to contain and contest. Bound to invention, inventiveness, though it remains situated in the historic, does not abandon the process of infinite, and endless creation; it assumes the bodies' desire for breath, asking, what is the sound, look, and feeling of Black liveliness and living? On the question of inventiveness, a presumption of living, one is attuned to the utterances, sometimes barely perceptible. Here, I am drawn back to the problematic of the "Michigan Man." While I am not interested in restoring the idea, it's worth mentioning that the concept, as an object of desire, was one some survivors felt committed to. Maintaining the integrity of this idea, and seemingly feeling a sense of commitment toward both the idea itself and those with whom they shared it, compelled survivors in their thoughts and behaviors about advocacy. On these terms, one reading of the survivors advocacy in the case can be understood as an injection into narrative incompleteness and absence—invention. Survivors could narrate, step toward, and open up Black ontological possibilities against narrative restraints, historical and temporal.

Rewriting the Human: A Conclusion

This interrogation is not about Anderson so much as it is the ways sociopolitical realities in higher education reject Black males' voices and vulnerabilities to sexual violence, and more broadly, Black as human. The Black males reflected in this case, however, survived. If higher education is to ethically attend to their voices, it will require that they move away from white patriarchal paradigms. Listening, as Harris (2017) put forth, to the experiences of Black male students and inquiring from them about their needs, can help to expose systems of domination. The chokehold (Butler, 2017) as an analytic and theoretical framework can facilitate an intersectional framing of Black males as uniquely raced, gendered, and historicized. This situated response brings a necessary historical, gendered, and sexualized lens to Black knowing and being, and a nuanced reading of white patriarchal modes of domination for institutions and communities that may lead to its eventual rewriting. In this chapter, a version of critical discourse analysis, theorized with the chokehold as an analytic, considered invention—inventiveness as a praxis of and for Black liveliness and living, that takes seriously the force of narration as a constituent element in un/defining the Man-as-human and its potential rewriting.

August,

A few weeks after your passage into this world, I took you to the shoreline. It was one of those places that I couldn't wait for you to see and experience. It's a space that I visit and return to when I need to breathe deeply. The shoreline is a site of communion and assembly, solace, and imagination. It is never the same, always shifting and returning, "looking inward and outward, at once before and after" (Lorde, 1978, p. 31) and taking shape anew. The shoreline, for many, is a point of departure, a boundary that defines what is firm from that which is unstable and fleeting, as if safety can be constructed on that which appears to be steady. Place your ethics and hope elsewhere. What I mean is that there is value to be found in getting beyond the shoreline, to depth, to going deeper. Take a deep breath, and ask yourself what is underneath those decisions—the ones you make, and the ones made for you, beneath those policies, and under those events. There is much in the world to be uncovered and remembered; we can cultivate a practice of depth—in relationships, in our analysis, in our work—by getting beyond "false bottoms" (Gumbs, 2020) and by learning to be specific with our intentions and diligent with our breathing. Keep going, August, and once there, go deeper.

5

Toward an Ontology of Black Intimacy

Figure 5.1. "A powerful Igbo axiom states that "mmadu bu oku na mmiri" ("the enlightened one is a synthesis of fire and water"). Fire and water are both cosmic elements that were born at the origin of the universe. The ancient Igbo divined that the human body incarnated the same fundamental elements found in the stars and that we host quantities of these elements in our physical forms. *Source*: *Oku na Mmiri* by Mikael Owunna. Used with permission of the artist.

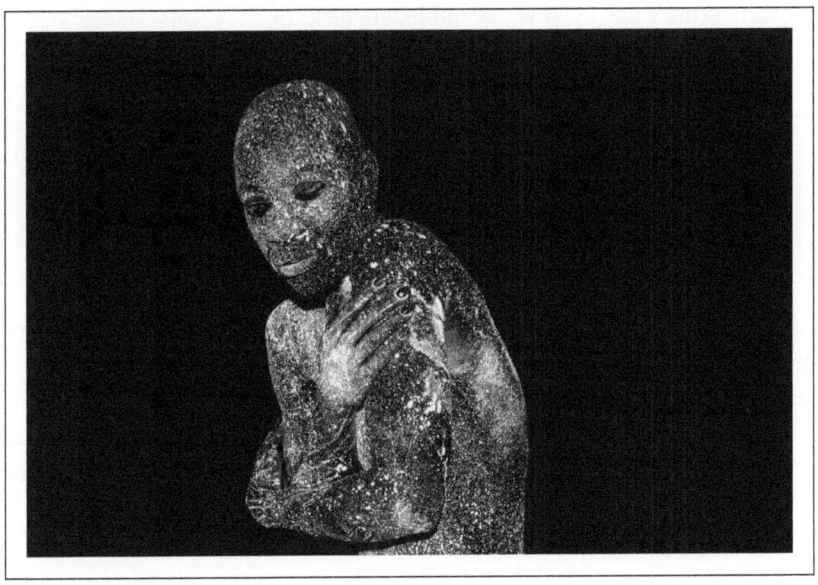

Tenderness might just be a gesture, it might just be a look, a Black look, some regard, relayed between people in peril.

—Christina Sharpe

Shared experiences in the realm of the social do not necessarily index shared positions in the realm of the structural.

—Frank Wilderson

How *Oku na Mmiri* Inspires This Chapter

I am drawn to the tenderness of *Oku na Mmiri*, tenderness as gentleness and kindness; tenderness as sympathetic, and warm, and soft; tenderness as grace and full of regard; tenderness as care. It is a tenderness that evokes feelings of devotion and affection, love, fondness, and compassionate care. In this photo, I sense fulfillment in intimacy, in recognizing and celebrating the life-sustaining qualities within oneself/the collective relational *I*. In addition, the photo is tenderly instructive, and it enunciates the potential of worldmaking and possibility. Within us/we then, is worldmaking capacity, if we would listen, feel, touch it. This chapter opens with the image of Oku na Mmiri, providing an opportunity to witness the worldmaking dimensionality of intimacy. In line with the overarching theme of this book, the image, and subsequent chapter, emphasize that intimacy is not something that requires proof, but rather something that inherently exists in the context of Black livingness.

∽

He knew things, and his presence at the back of the room was forward leaning, as if to say, "What you are sharing is serviceable, but I have a different set of questions for you." We connected following the keynote and shared contact information. Our follow-up exchange over email was the flashpoint in my theorizing on and with Blackness. It began as follows:

Hi Mr. Okello!

I wanted to ask you another question. How do you feel about being black in this country? *Let me explain what exactly I mean. I am extremely proud of my heritage.* ███████

████████████████████████████████
████████████████████████████████
████████████████████████████████
████████████████████████████████
████████████████████████████████
████████████████████████████████
████████████████

But, at the same time, I'm scared. ███████

████████████████████████████████
████████████████████████████████
████████████████████████████████
████████████████████████████████
████████████████████████████████
████████████████████████████████
████████████████████████████████
████████████████████████████████
████████████████████████████████
████

Sincerely,

Winston

The redactions above are purposeful and intend to raise questions for policy and practice that ask, do white institutions and frameworks have the capacity to account for, and meditate on, the fullness of Black existence? Reading white institutions and frameworks as the continuance of enslavement, insofar as they regulate Black bodies and minds, the redactions are the conceivable blockage that allows for just air enough to preserve a degree of life[1] and not the vitality of Black aliveness (Quashie, 2021). On this premise, what are the pathways to Black liveliness and living for

Black students in, through, and against white institutions and frameworks? Sovereignty and self-possession as conditioned by the Western Man do not exist for Black students. Accordingly, educators, counselors, and all those working with Black students must grapple with this impossibility as the afterlife of slavery (Hartman, 1997) and consider what it means for Black students to choreograph a critical way of knowing, being, and understanding in response to these conditions.

To that end, this chapter is about what liberalism masks and leaves behind; it grapples with the felt sense of captivity and asks, how do Black folks exist in their bodies, in this historical moment and into the future? To address this question, I trouble the oversimplification of Black subjectivity in the social sphere and shed light on the ways researchers may come into a wider, more expansive viewing of Blackness and the implications for Black knowing and being therein, by exposing neoliberal seeing patterns rooted in anti-Blackness [Black fungibility], and their impact on knowledge production. Further, I am interested in how educators might understand and support Black ways of knowing and being. Black students are knowers and are deeply aware that their flesh is unprotected. The work, and, indeed, the dilemma for educators must be to name that place, where Black people exist as "carriers of terror, terror's embodiment," and, yet refuse to foreclose "living in the wake" (Sharpe, 2016, p. 15). In what follows, I build on racialized socialization practices such as *the talk* (Anderson & Stevenson, 2019) to propose the *Black intimate*, a conceptual frame for reading Black interior practices in and against anti-Black logics. Here, I take up the tradition of the Black essay, in the form of two letters (Baldwin's letter to his nephew, and a personal letter from a student to me), in order to theorize the Black intimate.

Letters embody praxis; as the textual embodiment of material lives, epistolary texts key into the richness of interiority, advancing the richness of autobiographical and autoethnographic methods. I am particularly interested in how the Black intimate, rooted in Black oral and spiritual traditions, is an example of a praxis of Black livingness that edges toward Black specificity, believing that the messages Black students receive about how to manage their body/mind/spirit, directly or through classroom instruction, can influence how they move through the world and reconcile their lives as already threatened by anti-Blackness in ways that make room for joy. In the next section, I turn my attention to the ways logics of liberalism train educators and researchers into sterile analyses that foreclose the fullness of Black existence.

On Being Gifted

The letter arrived in unremarkable fashion, courtesy of Youngstown City Schools. "To the parents of Wilson Okello," the envelope announced. In my third-grade mind, mail to the house, about me, was always good news. Performing in school was my job, and to that point, I had done okay—a shelf of certificates and report cards scattered with the opening letters of the English alphabet usually meant praise or a "keep up the good work." Excellence was my parents' expectation, not their request, with the hopes that a dutiful laboring in the language of goodness might accomplish what Blackness wrapped on Black students bodies could not. It must be that social science research, and the researchers who studied [us], had proven as much. While somehow controlling for race and class in a high-poverty, low-performing school district, research determined that some Black kids were academically advanced, more talented, and therefore, had earned/ were deserving of a different set of opportunities than the pathological underperformer; that classrooms absent the distraction, volatility, and anguish of structurally determined vices could produce better life options.

It would be a similar set of studies, perhaps, that concluded that a second-class caste, primarily determined by race and gender, could be solidified, and industrialized by examining the "progress" of Black and Latinx students in the third grade. The stakes, masked as the opportunity to learn differently, albeit in the same district, in a different setting, with new teachers and other similarly motivated students, felt high, the stakes are always high for Black students and the ones who raise, lift, and love them. Notwithstanding, so far as I could tell, this is what "keep up the good work" was all about, moments like this that could usher in new possibilities, options, for me, us. "Do you want to go?" my mother queried, which felt like an odd question given her and my father's insistence on academic performance, that ultimately, the decision was theirs on whether or not I could attend the program. Sensing her slight trepidation, I followed suit: "I guess so," I muttered, unsure of what I was agreeing to, but feeling like the invitation was more than what I should reasonably pass up.

On the Significance of the Hold: An Interlude

The hold was the place beneath the deck of the slave ship where the storage/cargo (read: Black people) was kept and guarded for the length of a sea voyage; it is a material cell and prison; a placemaking apparatus where humans are made fungible, currency; it is ideological and intimate, and material and regulatory. The moniker of gifted was no different. Conceptually, the idea that gifted as akin to high-achieving students is the outgrowth of social science research. As a hold in and of itself, to be seen as gifted is to adopt a violent viewing practice—auction block, everyday, mundane surveillance of Black expression—that expects Black students to acquire Western Eurocentric postures of being. In these ways, the hold of the ship repeats (Sharpe, 2016; Philip, 2008), such that no matter where one encounters Black students in educational sites, Western Eurocentric postures hold.[2]

An Orientation to Holding

We were split off into groups of four to five. There were few instructions to follow, and in front of us lay an assortment of bright-colored tracks and a few marbles. The activity was simple, if not altogether stressful. Our parents and siblings circled around us and were instructed to watch and observe our genius in action, while we, the gifted kids, were given five minutes to build a structure that would carry a marble across a series of obstacles. I don't remember what we built or if the marble ever made it from point A to point B. What is vivid in my memory was that I was being given permission to play, in front of my parents no less. There was an assumption about my creativity and there seemed to be specially designed activities to help nurture it along. "In what world do Black kids have an opportunity to express their creativity through play?" and "Is this what they do in a gifted program?" were the sorts of questions that were being asked, I'm sure, between parents and child alike that evening. The orientation affirmed what the letter had attempted to spell out—the general belief that I and my new peers met some criteria for giftedness that (Black) normal students did not.

The demarcation was drawn and reinforced in subtle and deliberate ways. Even if we, the chosen, never said as much, the distribution of resources and opportunities meant that our "normal" peers should come to terms with their plight as part of an unconquerable social order, and that we should accept ours as a privilege reserved for the few. The lesson of social science (and educational) research that was taking shape, as it pertains to Black bodies and minds, was that some exceptional Black students were worthy of engagement insofar as they were able to be reformed, fixed, or pulled out of their (self-)destructive dispositions. If students were exposed to ideas revolving around creativity and play, and kept away from rational, carceral logics—such as those that would teach Black students to monitor and police themselves psychologically—then some Black students could adapt, however imperfectly, a posture worthy of human regard.

Admittance into the "gifted program" marked my entry into and introduction into social science research with Black students, only it wasn't my research. Effectively, I systemized into the well-worn conclusion that tracking students because of how they model particular types of achievement is good for them and society. In an effort to mitigate disproportionate outcomes for Black students and families, relocating the "brightest," exceptional Black students into a separate space specially designed to meet my/their unique talents could build the proverbial bridge out of poverty, and challenge us/them in ways that exceeded teachers' capacities in "normal" classroom sites. Black students don't need a lesson in social science research. They know about living in the afterlife of slavery, that there are innumerable resources committed to resolving their being because they interrupt the natural order of things. They have been and continue to exist as the subjects, tests, and sites of experimentation for scholars, cultural critics, scientists, Black, and non-Black, those who care about them, and those who just build their careers on their backs. Though no one would ever come out and say it, there is an unwritten expectation, connected to and extending beyond research, of regulating Black bodies and minds.

Though the symbolic affordances of freedom bestowed postemancipation rights discourse to Black people, social science research converted Black people into integers, data, and the source of national investigation. On full display, though tucked neatly in the pages of Black (respectable) performative expectation, the white envelope "To the parents of Wilson Okello" was a way out, and into the recognition that not all Black people can make it, but the ones that do, the special, gifted among you, should be acknowledged as such, and perhaps, when ready, you can return and save the others. My experience of being researched was a lesson in how research on Black students can be geared toward saving some of them. Research on Black students, as it happened to me, was a lesson in saving some—the well-behaved, respectable Negro, based on unexamined premises of liberalism. The assumptions directing these frameworks portend that once "freed" from legal slavery, Black folks were conferred with all the rights of Man (Wynter, 2003), and as such, access to power, status, and humanity. Muted by this discourse, however, was the double-binded nature of freedom.

The message, that didn't translate then, but that etches into view, even as I fork through these memories and words, is, and was, that social science research can control for, resolve, explain away, settle, or disentangle Blackness and ways it has been constructed over time. Social science research often neglects to engage with this process of deciphering altogether, operating under the assumption that Black living lacks the intricacy and complexity worthy of investigation. Instead, it tends to treat Black existence as a static object subject to evaluation. Too, research with and about Black people has primarily homed in on understandings of racism and the compounding nature of structural oppressions. However, questions of Black subjectivity demand a different set of tools to read and think through power, agency, and knowing in the afterlife of slavery.

Imitations of Freedom

The creation of categories of "normal" and "gifted" among structurally oppressed people is particularly insidious, given the truth it works to conceal. The clearer through line of deficit orientations that would treat Black students as broken, is, perhaps, more legible in its unoriginality with respect to flawed social science. The less distinguishable motivations, shaded beneath the goodwill of benevolent white institutions, are the declarations they make about the limitations of [Black] social death. Social science research pushes past the extant question of emancipation that asks if emancipatory figurations of Blackness are at all possible—is it possible "to unleash freedom from the history of property that secured it?" (Hartman, 1997, p. 119).

Since Reconstruction, "the antagonistic production of abstract equality and Black subjugation has rested upon contending and incompatible predications of the freed-as sovereign, indivisible, and self-possessed" (Hartman, 1997, p. 117). The advent of freedom, tethered to liberalism's conceptions of the universality of citizenship, created what Hartman (1997) discusses as the burdened individuality of freedom, which references "the liberal individual, rights bearer and raced subject as equal yet inferior, independent yet servile, freed yet bound by duty, reckless yet responsible, blithe yet broken-hearted" (p. 121). The reality "marked the transition from the pained and minimally sensate existence of the slave to the burdened individuality of the responsible and encumbered freed person" (pp. 116-17). These sets of assumptions are projected onto Black students, helping to mediate and direct social science research, often, about them. It is these unfounded sets of presumptive attributions—Black people as fully autonomous beings, capable of achieving and fulfilling the entitlements of the Western Man—that were extended to me, internalized, and, thus, taken on as an early researcher.

At no point, during the orientation or thereafter, was there discussion about what it meant for us, mostly Black kids, to be siphoned out of our home, neighborhood schools and seated in the instruction of gifted learning. I do remember, however, being reminded of what a "privilege" it was to be considered and selected, and the gratitude I should have for being part of it. And there, on the metonym of privilege, a metamorphosis occurs like that of "'chattel into man' and the strategies of individuation constitutive of the liberal individual and the rights bearing subject" and all the expectations of a precarious autonomy (Hartman, 1997, p. 116). More specifically, my childhood immersion into the politics of self-improvement was a type of disciplining that inched me toward a politics of being, which was overly concerned with transitioning Black students into neoliberal postures of citizenship and respectable versions of Blackness that might earn them currency in the educational and social order.

I offer this framing to say that there exists a politics of inundation that promotes a form of self-policing that may reify (our) narratively condemned status. Where it relates to Black scholars, Dillard (2012) would discuss the inundation, susceptibility, and reification as a form of seduction that entices Black scholars away from themselves. In this instance, the "themselves" could otherwise be read as a way of unseeing one's connection to, or the ways one is implicated in the larger community of African-ascendant people, and in the matrix of Blackness more specifically. Hartman (1997) wrote it this way: "The displacement of the whip can be discerned in the emphasis on self-discipline and policing. The whip was not to be abandoned; rather, it was to be internalized. The emphasis on correct training, proper spirit, and bent backs illuminated the invasive forms of discipline idealized as the self-fashioning of the moral and rational subject" (p. 140). This internalization plays out in destructive ways when it comes to research with Black students. As a politic that is valued (read: funded and a popular topic of grants and fellowships) by neoliberal frameworks and research constituencies, it teaches us, effectively, to decenter the import of Blackness and its sociopolitical contours, in favor of a thinner framing that focuses on experiences of Black [students] and, when there is racialized analysis, the emphasis is on race and racism (and perhaps intersecting systems of oppression). Additionally, I aim to highlight the limitations of emancipation, or what notions of freedom mean for Black people, particularly, to critique routine presumptions about what constitutes Blackness in the social imaginary and research processes. The message in the white envelope, the belief that some were of worthy of a gifted opportunity, and others were not, are products of the same logics that cannot recognize late liberalisms—an extension of Enlightenment liberal practices that justified colonialism and transatlantic slavery—uneven social, political, and economic arrangements, an anti-Black structuring episteme, that overdetermine the life chances of Black students. This episteme fits squarely into Wynter's (2003) human/not-quite/nonhuman paradigm.

While it might be tempting to read Black students, elevated to positions of distinction, achieving by standards outlined as gifted and talented, and those who are not afforded the same distinctions as the natural outcome of educational opportunity, an examination of these distinctions on the premise of burdened individuality, narrows what and how we should understand freedom to be, particularly as the "double bind of emancipation—the onerous responsibilities of freedom with the enjoyment of few of its entitlements, the collusion of the disembodied equality of liberal individuality with the dominated, regulated, and disciplined embodiment of Blackness, the entanglements of sovereignty and subjection" (Hartman, 1997, p. 121). For Wynter, it might be said that neither the gifted, nor the "non-gifted" students implicated in this social divide should be viewed as a recognizable humanity, as the two distinctions rely on and inform one another, and both exist under the dominion of progressive political projects that track students into social pathways. Where Blackness is constructed over and against the Western human, Black students, gifted or not, are locked in regulated futures in the United States social imaginary. For this analysis, gifted may also point to not-quite-human, which misinterprets the force of Blackness and how it shapes Black liveliness and living. In light of this premise, constructs of liberalism as guides for research are insufficient for understanding Black liveliness and living. More precisely, research ought to consider the relationship between Blackness and the Man-as-human, the order of knowledge that undergirds processes of racialized domination in the United States and globally.

Liberalism and the Hold

Taking up the Man-as-human thesis means educators and researchers must grapple with the varied and multiple expressions of Western humanism in the contemporary. Whereas much research *on* Black students has long been wrapped up in liberalist tendencies to reform or to hold, and make Black people respectable, by celebrating progressive policies, decisions, and institutions that rely on selectivity and experimentation (for example, charter schools, magnet schools, etc.), the maneuver often overshadows what Black people are expected to take on and internalize into social life as part of their agreements. Plainly, notions of freedom in the United States imaginary did not, and do not, resolve the regulatory confinements of the hold. Rather, the logic extends enslavement's deliberate impositions onto Black people in ways that function beyond the physical hold and the proverbial whip. Elsewhere, I have termed these logics internalized carcerality (see Okello, 2022).

Returning to the hold as an anti-Black tool of racialized surveillance, with *just air enough*, the prospect of overcoming the weight of anti-Blackness, not as a historical project, but, rather, as permanent antagonism on Black knowing and being, is not a rational or developmental task. The pervasiveness of Black subjection is normative and necessary in society. Following Baldwin (2011), "The American triumph—in which the American tragedy has always been implicit—was to make Black people despise themselves" (p. 257). Under the terms of self-despisal, "the only orientation possible is either acquiescence to being wrong or antagonism to the hypothesis of wrongness" (Quashie, 2021, p. 108). The presumption here is that the question of "how do [we] exist" (Okello, 2018) is not a question at all, as it has already been answered by a world that says what Black people are situated within the structural hold, or we are entangled in the work of refusing that imposition (the internalized hold). And the hold repeats. The terror of this predicament is that in both instances, Black folks are "turned away from rather than *into*" the self—the interior space where one might be able to engender an alternative rendering (Quashie, 2021, p. 108). Simply put, the question of Black self-definition, "how to exist, how do we be" cannot be answered by terms dictated by the anti-Blackness of universal ideas like human value and worth that stress proximity, if not complete acquiescence, to Western humanism. Foregrounding the inescapability of history's sociopolitical grasp, theorizing from the hold, thus, must consider an otherwise world, an endarkened space, to acknowledge, take up, and love Black flesh in educational contexts.

Black Intimate and Intimating

As noted above, research with Black students has long been preoccupied with conformity on the presumption that liberties must be earned. On the recognition that liberalism, and progressive practice insofar as it concerns Black folks, rests on integrative and redemptive assumptions, Black worldmaking must grapple with the range of political and cognitive schema that produce and legitimate Black exceptionality and, where possible, constitute and inspire a heterogeneity of Black being. In the hold, where the only certainty is the climate of anti-Blackness (Sharpe, 2016), persistent antagonism generates a critical form of knowing that has enabled Black folks to pass over and through these environments. Thus, while the weather transforms Black being, those held in its clutches are always imagining anew. Conceptually, Black intimating may facilitate such a practice.

Black intimating builds on notions of *the talk*, a socialization and coping strategy deployed by family members, mentors, guardians, and the like to buffer traumatic stress that results from racism and environmental stressors that exceed individual and collective coping resources and may threaten well-being (Anderson & Stevenson, 2019). The talk intends to heighten one's awareness about the particularities of existing in a racialized body, as it encourages skill development and strategies to grapple with the commonplace of anti-Blackness in society. This type of racial socialization has been defined as the "verbal and nonverbal racial communication between families and students about racialized experiences" (p. 65). On the belief that anti-Blackness is endemic, such that there is no conceivable end to its variance, the talk, both historically and in the contemporary, provide Black students with "verbal and/or behavioral messages of four primary content types: cultural socialization (cultural pride), preparation for bias (discriminatory preparation), promotion of mistrust (wariness regarding interracial encounters), and egalitarianism-silence about race" (Anderson & Stevenson, 2019, p. 65). These charges tend to emphasize protective and affirmational capacities such that Black students can come, in some ways, to normalize, and thus, anticipate the potentialities of threat and, yet emphasize, that being Black students is not the problem; rather, their Blackness has been framed as such. In some instances, the talk embraces a legacy approach (Stevenson, 2014), wherein messages are ideological and historical in nature. As an epistemic and historical project, intergenerational, collective memory is an essential meaning making tool.

Building on these conceptualizations, there is an otherwise world created by the talk that I propose as the Black intimate. The Black intimate is a site and habitat of Black aliveness (Quashie, 2021) that sits with the question of this text—how to be, or more fully, how do Black people exist, in the bodies that they hold, in this historical moment and into the future? As a metaphor, in conversation with the Black interior, it is "life and creativity beyond the public face of stereotype and limited imagination" (Alexander, 2004, p. x). In taking up the language of intimate, I draw on its double meaning as, first, descriptive of closeness; indwelling; interior, private, and trusted. Intimate, or intimacy, is akin to something felt and personal; one is privy to, or of something. Intimate is given to acquaintance; it is a state of inwardness and communion; intimate signals relationality, a quality of being seen and known; intimate is affecting, inlying, and sensual, a product of the senses; visceral. Intimate as a verb or *intimating*, regards a communicative process of proclamation; to make formally and publicly known; it regards something implied, hinted, or insinuated; it is an act of referencing or referring to. Together, these two meanings conjoin to declare a sensuous, interior space. I use the meanings interchangeably to point to the ways they inform one another. In a world that has normalized anti-Blackness, Black folks are, in essence, believed to be nonrelational (see Spillers, 1987), which, is to say, they do not possess an interior space that resembles human relations.

Furthermore, in an anti-Black world, the hold, "there is no ethical possibility for the one who is Black: there is no figuring through one's humanity because one's humanity is figured already as marginal, subjected, diminished" (Quashie, 2021, p. 108). The latter point exemplifies the potential of the Black intimate because it gestures away from versions of being contingent with overdetermined radical subjectivity or resistance; instead, it focuses on the integrity of the thoughts, feelings, desires, and ambitions (Quashie, 2009). One particular method that approximates the work of intimacy and intimating, is what might be understood as the Black essay. Before expounding on the themes of what I put forth as a Black intimate praxis, I discuss the particularities of the Black essay.

Black Essay

If, as has been noted, part of the function of anti-Blackness is categorial alienation from what constitutes the human, it is also psychic, emotional, and conceptual narrative distortion (Wa Thiong'o, 1986; Woodson, 1933).

Breaking open these distortions, and getting away from the predominance of European epistemological framings, I comprehend the Black essay's contribution within the context of diaspora literacies (Clark, 1991), a legacy intricately tied to the ongoing journey toward Black emancipation. Recognizing the potential of the aesthetic, and more precisely, understanding artist/writer/essayist intent, can serve as a catalyst for healing and fostering self-esteem (Clark, 1991; King, 1992). While broadly speaking, the Black essay does not advance "respectability or fidelity to community" (Quashie, 2021, p. 82), and even less a recovery to the category of the Western human, it is a call for specificity, and homing in on the particularity of Blackness. Therein, the essay does invite a certain type of intellectual freedom, "the freedom to work around, with, and through an idea" (Wall, 2018, p. 1), there has been a political imperative for Black literary writers and authors to use the essay form to grapple with the force of anti-Blackness. For Wall (2018), the essay, under the pen of Black writers, is a mechanism for sociopolitical intervention on debates on such topics as slavery, abolitionism, and civil rights. The dialogic approach to the essay represents, for me, an exemplar of Black intimating, gesturing toward intimate living. Intimating can be as open-ended or sharp and complex as an issue might demand. The Black essayist, historically, has had a penchant for deferring conclusions and gesturing toward the possible (Costas Vargas & James, 2012; Wall, 2018). This approach presumes that the dialogue is unending, and their contribution is but one to a larger discourse. If there has been a topical subject that has demanded the Black essayist's attention, it is the shifting and ever-elusive idea of Black ontology, how to be—how do I exist, in the body that I hold, in this historical moment and into the future? Essayists have grappled with and contemplated enslavement, and for the purposes of this text, the limitations of legalized freedom. Regarding the latter, as the primary method for Black acceptance in the social imaginary of the United States is through integration and redemption—both of which require Black folks to be non-Black (human) or mimic the Man-as-human formulation—which is impossible. Given the construction of a society that relies on the exclusion, premature death, and disappearance of Black folks from society, Black flesh, the excess, and elsewhere of the Man-as-human, makes room for Black aliveness.

Baldwin's Love for Black Flesh

Of the many variations and examples of Black essays that may constitute Black intimating, I focus on Baldwin's (1963) letter to his nephew James as an exemplar. His nephew, a teenager at the time of writing, could just as well be Winston, could just as well be Trayvon, Tamir, Dejerra Becton, and painfully, the list continues. Baldwin wrote the following:

> This innocent country set you down in a ghetto in which, in fact, it intended that you should perish. . . . You were born where you were born and faced the future that you faced because you were black and for no other reason. The limits of your ambition were, thus, expected to be set forever. You were born into a society which spelled out with brutal clarity, and in as many ways as possible, that you were a worthless human being. You were not expected to aspire to excellence: you were expected to make peace with mediocrity. Wherever you have turned, James, in your short time on this earth, you have been told where to go and what you could do (and how you could do it). . . . The details and symbols of your life have been deliberately constructed to make you believe what white people say about you. Please try to remember that what they believe, as well as what they do and cause you to endure, does not testify to your inferiority but to their inhumanity and fear. Please try to be clear . . . about the reality which lies behind the words *acceptance* and *integration*. (pp. 7–8)

Baldwin enters the complexity of Black beingness with caution. Annotating, or bringing into a view the social imaginary that ensnares James's existence, Baldwin does not mince words as they relate to the contextual predicament. Baldwin confirms the anti-Black immanence of death nestled in their social arrangements, in effect, socializing James with a sense of normalcy and preparedness. Moreover, there is a purposeful critique of the progressive politics that the 1960s advanced, specifically around the notion of acceptance and integration. This context, with respect to where the letter goes and how it concludes, is critical so as not to oversimplify Baldwin's love politic that may seem to depart from or overcome the reality of his anti-Black assessment. Loving Black flesh does not advance political desire or autonomy where it does not exist, and as such, I do not read Baldwin's invocation to love to be one that is possible in the constraints of a United States social imaginary. Instead, through the framing of the intimate, Baldwin leans into Black flesh, which, as opposed to negating or reducing the afterlife of slavery, aspires otherwise (Crawley, 2016; Moten, 2013; Sharpe, 2016) to a place the presumes Black being in excess of White humanism (Man).

Winston and the Liberal Redaction

The letter in the white envelope addressed to my parents was a lesson on disappearance and a utopian future that refused victimization through Black integration, or the construction of Black cyborgs. Following Costa Vargas and James (2012): "many stories of redemption from white racism or colonization announce a Black cyborg: a modified, improved human whose increased ethical, spiritual, and physical capabilities generate unusual strength, omniscience, and boundless love" (p. 198). In contrast to Baldwin and other Black essayists, the Black cyborg is preoccupied with progressive logic that believed it possible to salvage, to reform some Black bodies and minds, and discard all others. And, if one is to be rescued, it is the body—resembling the citizen incumbent in the dominant social imaginary—that would be retained, not the (Black) flesh. Black intimating, as a praxis of "how do [we] exist" how to be, is a material happening that is expansive, impulsive, creative, articulate, and chaotic; it is a site of being (Black intimate) in the world, and "the locus at which self-interrogation takes place. It is not an arrival but a departure, not a goal but a process, and it conduces toward neither an answer nor a 'cure,' because it is not engendered in formulae and prescription" (Spillers, 1996, p. 84); it is a form that makes a world of being (Black intimating). Intimating, as a question of "how" is interrogative and more open than questions of who and what one is in the world. How is a question indicative of conditions and means, existentially asking, "what am I feeling, what resources do I have, what do I need, what can I do, what might be its impact" (p. 109)? The question "how?" also serves as a statement, reflecting not only actions taken but also creations formed (Da Silva, 2019). Intimating is a an enfleshed practice, that understands that Black being cannot be ethically reasoned in an anti-Black world as Black existence confronts social, psychological, and spiritual violence without reprieve.

Returning to Winston, the student who reached out to me, and his email above, redaction reduces Winston to his injuries—soul, spirit, and psyche. These lacerations, though indecipherable in the legality of redress discourse, leave their mark, becoming a hieroglyphic of the flesh (Spillers, 1987). Intimating intervenes on another plane of existence, more specifically, it calls attention to affective capacities to communicate the indecipherable and articulate the ineffable condition(s) of being. In the place of Black flesh, as I have discussed, there is opening, and where there is opening, there can be "a nexus between inside/outside, self/other, and

Toward an Ontology of Black Intimacy | 139

individual/community" (Warren, 2016, p. 40). Black intimating, in this way, reconfigures the hold as a beholding habitat. Black intimating is a seeing, observing, keeping, regarding, and choosing to look (Okello, et al., 2021) that works beyond normative power relations, however temporary. It is a practice of regard, reckoning, and relationality.

To read the unredacted letter from Winston is to understand his sense of things as an astute rendering and profoundly perceptive—the globe, according to Costa Vargas and James (2012), "shares a phobic response to Blackness. . . . Black [people], including the preborn and the deceased, have no vulnerability which the polis need to respect" (p. 195). Redactions as they are deployed in the opening of this chapter, follow a history of Black living that is made invisible as those experiences are purposefully annotated or blotted out, subtended by anti-Black and colonial architectures. I am not interested in rescuing Black people to fit the category of human, nor am I interested in that which is salvaged by educational interventions. Rather, I am after a way of knowing, seeing, and being in excess of what has counted as progressive logic. I am attempting to "carve away the accretions of deceit . . . so that other kinds of perceptions" might come into view (Morrison, 1998, p. 7). Black intimating animates a beholding that desires to hear and see Winston against the versions of events as dictated by progressive liberalism. White institutions and frameworks do not, and should not be expected to possess the ethical commitment to account for, and meditate on, the fullness of Black existence. Intimating is operationalized on these grounds:

Hi Mr. Okello!

I was the kid that you gave the business card to at the Honors College talk. My name is Winston, and I just wanted to follow up with you. After all, I did say that I was gonna email you tonight.
    I wanted to ask you another question. How do you feel about being Back in this country?
    Let me explain what exactly I mean. I am extremely proud of my heritage. My parents are hardworking immigrants that came from Haiti, a country that had many problems. Despite their challenges, they were able to carve a path for themselves, and have successful careers. I have learned that many of my ancestors, both from the US and Haiti, had to stand up against

terrible things such as slavery, Jim Crow, and other forms of racial discrimination. And they prevailed, and made it better for the next generation. I am honestly proud to be Black.

But, at the same time, I'm scared. Ever since Trayvon Martin's death, I've been scared. Whenever I walk alone in the street, I shy away from others, and try to look as nice as possible, just in hopes that something like that won't happen to me. Now, I might be overreacting, and my fears and solutions to combatting them might be a little misguided, but no one has been able to abate my fears. I can only pray that God protects me, and I get home safe and sound. Sometimes, I feel like that being Black might just be the thing that puts me in danger, and I'm afraid of that.

I don't usually voice my concerns to anyone outside my family, but after our short discussion, I feel like I can get some valuable insight from you. . . .

Sorry for the long email, and thank you in advance for your answer.

Sincerely,

Winston

Whereas the United States social imaginary positions the Black subject as autonomous, infused with the social political power to participate as a full citizen, the Black essay as a body of writings troubles these instantiations, providing a nuanced reading of Black aliveness in the world. Through annotations and redaction alternative lines of sight are possible that probe the precarious condition of Black existence in the afterlife of slavery—liberalism's solution to Black conduct and behavior. Baldwin, engaged in a Black intimating, illuminates a heterogeneous project that may lead to various expressions of Black living. For the purposes of this chapter, I highlight the three components of Black intimating praxis annotated from Baldwin's (1963) letter to his nephew, James, beginning with the letter's inclination to Black relationality.

The Black intimate materializes first and foremost from personal experience. It is helpful to think with Williams (1992) about the notion of experience as a movement away from objective truth to experience as the always rhetorical event, so as to resist the too-easy oversimplification of Blackness with experience. Moreover, the text or verbal exchange that is intimating does not proclaim or proximate authority, but as a compilation of experiences, confirms a phenomenological being and becoming. The Black intimates' relationality is in its capaciousness, which allows it to be both subject and object, the one who is telling and the subject of the telling; it is a mobilization of empathy that is found in the "intimacy of a single voice speaking across time and space" (Quashie, 2021, p. 96)

If every story is itself a form of travel and traversal, "a spatial practice" it becomes all the more possible to understand the Black essay as a Black intimating praxis, and thus, a site of worldmaking. While it is possible to analyze the Black essay for its refutation of anti-Black regard, I am most interested in what its form embodies. The Black essay, as Black intimate and intimating, thus, emerges as a Black world. Baldwin, here, is not so much interested in critiquing the Western Man or advancing a politics that affirms Black worth/value per se (Quashie, 2021); rather, the intimate world of affect created is one that has regard for and makes room for Black (feeling) beings, whereas emotions are, themselves, a form of worldmaking. The experience created is one that can inspire other future forms of affective encounter. The Black essay and contents therein, as intimating, constitute otherwise possibilities for reckoning. Reckon, as I use it here, is a dynamic conception that infers movement and motion against the demands of anti-Black world. The assumption here is that Black knowing and being are unrecognizable in many ways for educators and researchers (read: redacted, erased, made invisible), due to white logics that have not accounted for the thrust of Blackness in the classroom or research. In this sense, reckoning references the laboring capacities of a subject to direct their actions and movements in the making and remaking of the self. The inspiration to reckoning responds to the unfreedom of progressive logics and regards the processes by which those systemically unfree persist toward becoming something other than unfree.

Reckoning as intimate practice is and can be circulated and shared as habits/resources of knowing and being. Baldwin's intimating approach here can be seen in the ways he contends with the psychological imprisonment of anti-Black logic that would have James believe what "white people say." Inspiring reckoning in this instance, Baldwin urges, "What they do and cause you to endure, does not testify to your inferiority." On this premise, intimating offers a form of care and regard that explicates the project of anti-Blackness, and, seemingly, intimates a laboring beyond the moment. The statement works against the ethical dilemma of anti-Blackness to assert that Black people are inherently worthy and of value, and that humans are supposed to actualize their worth, "to believe it, to act of its accord, to negotiate its parameters" (Quashie, 2021, p. 108). Reckoning with being thus is intimate work, unbound to progressive discourse.

Affirming the Black Interior: A Conclusion

Taken together, while liberal redactions emphasize resolutions of anti-Blackness, of greater import with intimating, is a world where, however briefly, Winston can emote, speak the unspeakable, and feel freely, unredacted and uninhibited. Educational discourses, theorization, and research have conflated the emancipated Black subject with a fuller version of Black existence or at least one that is redeemable into respectable versions of society. Concealed beneath the benevolent narrative of liberalism are fuller and longer realities of Black existence, and wrapped up in it, questions of being, (un)safety, and purpose, oft unspoken and absent in the general discourse of higher education (Stewart, 2019). Intimating, as praxis, intervenes as a form of being that can legitimate beingness through experiential tellings, while simultaneously creating the conditions for those experiences to land and take flight toward an elsewhere place of being in the world.

∾

> August,
>
> There was a season of your life, where, admittedly, if I turned my back from you and quickly turned back around, you would still be there. I remember hearing that those moments wouldn't last–that a time was coming when your curiosity would fuse with your imagination and you would be off, above, away from this place. In all the ways this world will pull at you–your time, your body, your mind, your spirit–there is intimacy to be found in presence and the permission you take to just be. I know what it means to make meaning in

movement, and, August, I love to see your movements in the world. You are Black aesthetic illumination with every breath. I appreciate, too, the worlds our elders and ancestors constructed such that we would not forget. Some of it is in text, some in story, and some in the presence of art, mural, and sky. Some of it is felt in the ways your family holds, or the long and loving stare they share with you when you enter a room. Worlds are not always of things built by hands, but in sounds, scents, and touch. Where there is motion, make time for slowness. Gift yourself pause such that you might find intimacy, inspiration, constellations of breath in and outside of you.

6

Presence

Black Ontology as Image-Making and Imagination amid the "Uninhabitable"

Figure 6.1. Chukwu, the masculine polarity of the Igbo primordial androgynous deity, never fully recovers from the traumatic shock of the death and resurrection of His feminine counterpart Eke-Nnechukwu. Discerning the inevitable shortcomings from the new existential state that arrives after the shattering of the First World, Chukwu decides to leave the physical universe behind, return to His solitary pillared chamber (Ozi-Obi-Chukwu), and lock the Door of Mercy (Uzo Ogo) behind Himself. *Source: Chukwu's Retreat from the World* by Mikael Owunna. Used with permission of the artist.

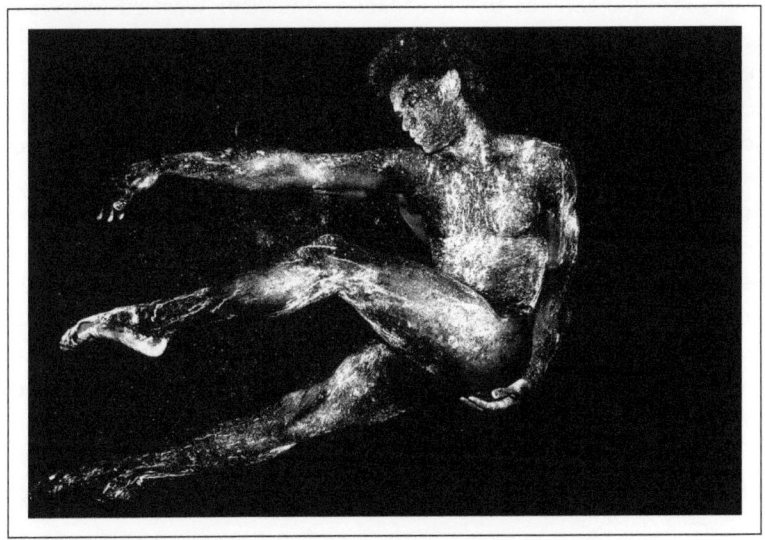

How *Chukwu's Retreat from the World* Inspires This Chapter

I am thinking about the choreography of Black being. A sense of refusal overwhelms me as I witness *Chukwu's Retreat from the World*. By refusal, I mean that a line has been drawn and a decision made to say no, to turn down; refusal pulses through this body on the premise that what is, is not all that there is, that there is more than the catastrophe of anti-Black regard that compounds. The photo represents an inclination to and for liberatory gestures, assemblages, and arrangements that might animate, incite, and sustain liveliness and living. As such, *Chukwu's Retreat from the World* supports this chapter's aim to affirm the imagination and materiality of Black worlds.

∾

The influence of humanities and social science disciplines has shaped limited notions of how Black people can exist within the U S social imaginary (Wynter, 1992, 1994). Despite these constraints, there exists a realm of Black ontological possibilities that extend both within and beyond established geographic boundaries. Ralph Ellison (1964), addressing the problematic nature of conventional foundations, emphasized the pervasive challenge faced by Black individuals in resisting categorization and noted, "I learned that nothing could go unchallenged especially that feverish industry dedicated to telling Negroes who and what they are" (p. xx). Ellison's critique extends to the broader context of Western universities, asserting that they play a significant role in socializing students to conform to societal norms. Ellison's perspective serves as a critique of how academic disciplines have historically defined the parameters of existence, limiting who is deemed acceptable and dictating how individuals are allowed to navigate their identities. This hierarchical arrangement, evident in social, curricular, and epistemological regulations, perpetuates the marginalization of nonnormative individuals and social formations—those outside the Western Man-as-human standard. Moreover, following Ferguson (2004), canonical formations outline trajectories for ethical subject formation, "they specify what it means to be human, a citizen, and moral being" (p. 66). Here, though Blackness is not inherently problematic, it is encamped in an American grammar[1] (see chapter 1) that understands it as a problem.

In this context, American grammar operates to mold Blackness into conformity with societal standards that are racialized and heteropatriarchal, asserting that aligning with normative tendencies can garner the highest societal regard, epitomized by Western Man. Upon entering higher education, some Black students anticipate gaining recognition, normalcy, freedom, and agency (Ferguson, 2004; Okello & White, 2019). The underlying assumption is that proximity to Western Man can disentangle individuals from the complexities detailed by Spillers as grammatical, representing an "other" deemed irreparable.

Following this line of reasoning, Black individuals and organizations historically adopted practices to curtail behavior, showcasing compliance with societal standards to remedy perceived cultural pathologies and exemplify an ascent. A notable example from the peak of the 1960s civil rights movement emphasizes a commitment to American citizenship, a desire to contribute to a new societal order, and a pledge to refrain from disruptive behavior (Ferguson, 2004, pp. 75-76). Nevertheless, reminders persist about the fallacies of self-discipline based on white epistemological foundations. The Blackened figure remains incompatible with the Western imagination, rendering it improbable for them to attain moral and ethical citizenship through submission to racialized and heteronormative regulations (Ferguson, 2004). Ellison (1952) echoes this sentiment, describing the desperate need to convince oneself of existence in the real world and the futility of efforts to gain recognition. To be sure, it is crucial to acknowledge that the Black experience within and beyond educational settings, seeking recognition in the face of anti-Blackness, is marked by intricate layers of complexity and tension.

Notwithstanding, in the teeth of ordinary anti-Blackness, Black people insist on breath and breathing space; they continue to breathe and engage in living amid precarity. Thinking with Wynter (1995), I am interested in the ways that theorizing the flesh allows us to imagine Blackness and Black folks as more than the complexity of identity differences, toward the nexus of "space, place, and poetics" (McKittrick, 2006, p. 122), or what I understand as the poetics of presence, which is the ability to survive across time and show up in innumerable new ways. Presence is praxis for how the flesh interacts with its environment, and, acutely insightful, a method of positioning that recognizes Black beings as intimately aware of where their rights and responsibilities extend and are delimited in the United States social imaginary. I understand presence/presencing as both a spatial, spatializing project, as well as meditation on affective space. Presencing can be fleshed as ontological (for example, physiological, emotional, spiritual), inhabitation (an act done), and doing (verb—a practice). Also, it is a manner of effectively locating emotions, staging them in the now, or future, and, *as necessary*, adopting innovative tactics to negotiate living.

Whereas Black ontological possibility is a spatial project, presence is best understood as an aesthetic practice, a fleshed form of geographic knowledge that questions existing geographic behaviors; it is an insurgent space, demonic ground, already at work in living in the uninhabitable (Wynter, 1995). Therefore, this chapter examines Black liveliness as it has occurred in and through photographic images, asking how does the flesh function as a rebellious site of meaning and being against the enclosures of anti-Blackness? To accomplish this, I employ Tina Campt's (2017) listening methodology to conduct a critical analysis of two recurring images in the narrative of Black people in the United States in and beyond educational contexts: (1) the Black Power fist and (2) two hands elevated and open, commonly, and henceforth referred to as *hands up, don't shoot*. A close tracing of these embodied gestures can help map the onto-epistemological work of presence for Black people as they compete with normative standards.

On the Matter of Presence

Theorizing presence, thus, must grapple with what Weheliye (2014) discussed as a "theoretical register about what it means to be human during and in the aftermath of the transatlantic slave trade, and the imagination of liberation in the future anterior sense of now" (p. 39).[2] More precisely, the question of how to be for Black people is onto-epistemological, forcing theorists and educators to sit with the indivisibly holistic nature of Black being (Okello, 2018; Schalk, 2018). The reasoning that pins the notion of complexity on one's cognitive reasoning minimizes Blackness, and subsequently, Black being as a knowledge-producing site, mainly since the rational brain is the last portion of the brain to make meaning of bodily messages (Menakem, 2017).

Accordingly, Cartesian dualism (see chapter 2) hides the mandates of anti-Blackness that mark Black people as imminently, and recursively chained to biocentricity. Here, the Black as a fungible state of property is never questioned, much less theorized or meaningfully engaged. Echoing this point, Hartman (1997) noted, "The fungibility of the commodity makes the captive body an abstract and empty vessel vulnerable to the projection of others' feelings, ideas, desires, and values" (p. 21). Plainly, Black people as fungible is thus normalized, coterminous with Black enslaved people who are to be controlled and arranged as necessary and for infinite use (Harris, 1993). In this place, where nonhumanness is never explicitly questioned, attuning to methods of Black livingness can open toward otherwise ways of being by instigating grammatic interventions that, as the next section shows, interrogate terms and ideas, and their purposes.

Attunement to Black Possibility

Following King (2016), the register of Black fungibility—exchangeable property, the defining feature of chattel slavery—holds capacity for an otherwise knowing in relation to the social death octaves that often accompany its definitions. As the work of Spillers (1987) and Hartman (1997) has shown, Black fungibility, too, existed as "territories of cultural and political maneuver" (Spillers, 1987, p. 67) that could make and remake themselves infinitely across spaces. This spatial and geographic tradition thus "denotes and connotes pure flux, process, and potential" (King, 2016, p. 1024) in and against the expectations of transatlantic slavery that mark Black people as conquered spatial and geographic territories (read: presences). As McKittrick (2006) stated, "This category not only visually and socially represented a particular kind of servitude, but it was also embedded in the landscape" (p. xvii). The educational landscape mimics social dimensions that call for Black suffering and servitude (Dumas, 2014) and demands that they live with the retentions of enslavement, and yet Black people live and should be read as shifting, moving, and unruly entities that are refusing capture.

On these terms, King (2016) objects to Black people as singularly products of labor, insisting on a reading of their laboring as otherwise ways of "living in, through, and beyond abjection, they both enable a glimpse of Black people (and ideas of Blackness) as suspended states of boundary—lessness, gender ambiguity, and intercessory spaces" (p. 1030). Black flesh as countersites can be places of possibility, futurity. For Campt (2017), Black futurity "moves beyond the simple definition of the future as what will be in the future. It moves beyond the future perfect tense of that which will have happened prior to a reference point in the future. It strives for the future real conditional or that which will have had to happen" (p. 17). It is a conjuring of the future that has not occurred, but for the sake of a fully realized Black humanity, must happen. A tense of "future real conditional" points to a politics of "prefiguration" (Campt,

2017, p. 17), or presence that motions for "living in the future now," performed through acts and or action.

The Invention of Man and Alterable Geographies

Following Wynter (1995), McKittrick (2006) postulated, "If Man is an overrepresentation of humans, Man's human geographies are an extension of this conception" (p. 128). There is a geographic dimension to achieving a future real conditional representation of the more-than-human that must contend with the ways Man underwrites what is inhabitable, and ultimately, what is not. Man's geographic imagination stories geographic arrangements, and the limitations therein. Or, Man's geographic sense of place in educational sites is naturalized and normal, which makes clear how space is socially constructed. Geographic spaces, however, as dictated by notions of what was perceived to be uninhabitable, are incomplete. McKittrick (2006), building on Wynter's (1995) thesis on the invention of Man, where the Man-as-human is deployed as classificatory logic for constituting normal, posited that "living" was occurring in the imagined place of terra nullius/nonexistence/no life (p. 130). The uninhabitable spatializes alternative genres of being (see preliminary vocabulary), wherein the uninhabitable was not so much unlivable, as it was a site acted on by Western colonial sensibilities. Blackness is always already unnatural and out of place, and, thus, unrecognizable, not present. And, yet again, Black people live, clarifying that otherwise genres of the human exist as the site and sight (McKittrick, 2006) of Black liveliness and living.

Continuing this point, Alexander (2004) posited that "understanding the violence that has in large part characterized our history and underscored our vulnerability opens an avenue to get at what is articulate, resistant, and powerful" (p. 201). This sentiment suggests that to privilege the flesh, its sensations, and knowings is a first step to transcending contorted expectations projected onto Black people and a gesture toward otherwise possibilities. For Moten (2003), Black being is already outside of the category of human, and therefore, is a disobedient object. As disobedient objects—defined, interpreted, and theorized as an analytic failure—Black flesh exists in opposition (Ferguson, 2004) to normative disciplining. Thus, Black people exist in the "breakdown of the breakdown" (Moten, 2003, p. 140). These rebellious movements, as those who pass over and beyond the various psychological, spiritual, emotional, social, physical, and spatial assaults on the flesh, are indicative of what it means to imagine otherwise, to theorize from the elsewhere "by way of a kind of recapitulative improvisation lingering in the iconic break of this double breakdown" (Moten, 2003, p. 140). From that otherwise space, in the break, one can improvise the cramped spaces (Jacobs, 1897; Okello, 2024) of Western canonicity; to listen, read, annotate, and embody in Black (Moten, 2003). To live in and of Black being, thus, is to enunciate Black liveliness. Therefore, I theorize instantiations of Black liveliness as presence, as image-making activities, through the idea of marronage.

ON MARRONAGE

Rebellious activities announce, index, and honor Black liveliness and living (McKittrick, 2021). Following Wynter (n.d.), rebellions were simultaneously praxis and "theoretical activity," where theory was inextricably tied to praxis (p. 387). On these terms, rebellions functioned as a breach of the established and normalized belief system that objectified Black people. Here, Wynter annotated the ways that Black refusal—creativity in the face of negation—called forth practices of otherwise being. Indeed, the making of culture as rituals, performances, and array of artistic expressions functioned to invent and enunciate Black liveliness. This chapter examines the notion of presence by employing the rebellious idea of marronage. Maroons were those African and American Indigenous folks who "escaped conditions of enslavement" (Crawley, 2017, p. 88). Theorizing marronage, Crawley (2017) called it the aesthetic practice of "picking up your stuff and leaving where you are not wanted, making something with a radical potentiality and critical edge" (p. 88). To be clear, marronage is not a theory of the margins or the borderlands, for each of these places lays claim to an imagined position. Rather, maroon bespeaks an outside of the outside; it is a "subversion of the axiomatic culture and the axiomatic psyche" (Wynter, n.d., p. 387); it is where exile captures the capacity to be violated, to be acted on violently (Crawley, 2017). Despite being tucked away, in marronage, there is an always "existing aesthetics practice of joy and enjoyment, pleasure and the pleasurable, even with the knowledge that the world could befall and produce terror because of the fugitive nature of their world making" (Crawley, 2017, p. 89). Marronage was a process through which individuals devised ways of interacting with human and nonhuman forces to resist the social order. Building with Wynter (2006), I am interested in reading Black people as territorial (read: onto-epistemological) sites of exile in educational spaces.

The conditions of marronage and the enactment of a maroon flesh, made presence, are scenes of affect—joy, love, desire—improvisational, and nuanced with each performance, and they cannot be assessed by normative standards of Western Man and its constraints for what it means to be human. Maroons created modes of vitality nestled in the swamps, and there, outside of the proverbial outside of the plantation, established and maintained modes of vitality. These patterns of behaviors epitomized a wayward and experimental livelihood (Hartman, 2019) that sought to produce otherwise possibilities while situated in dispossession, all the while remaining watchful for signs of capture. Thus, each movement or posture taken could symbolize otherwise possibilities or advanced preparation, antagonize or affirm one's affinity, retreat, or demonstrate an act of refusal. In what follows, I theorize two postures that Black people in educational spaces have taken up as exemplars of presence.

Listening to Images

Bodies are the curriculum of culture and policies. Spillers (1987) called this transmission a "hieroglyphics of the flesh," which have not vanished in the afterlife of proper personhood. Thus, understandings of Black being are historical and affected by the sociopolitical contexts in which one is situated. In this way, "qualitative studies cannot simply operate at the level of the linguistic. We must begin to examine the inherent links between perception, embodied experiences, particular spaces, and habitual practices" (Kuntz, 2009, p. 150). As a way of reading beyond the lines, and listening in the break (Moten, 2003), it becomes necessary to engage nondiscursive registers that move beyond the linguistic to lift the resonances beneath. To do this, in this chapter, I employ the notion of stasis (Campt, 2017) to attend to Black people's material lives in and beyond educational contexts.

Thinking with Campt (2017), I theorize stasis as a form of haptic sensory contact and an "inherently embodied process that registers at multiple levels of the human sensorium" (p. 6). Intervening on constructivist epistemological principles that depend on the resolution of dissonance and reduce complexity to the reasoned reflections of participants, stasis suggests that Black liveliness and living exists in a complex state of tensions, or "tensions produced by holding a complex set of forces in suspension . . . unvisible motion held in tense suspension or temporary equilibrium" (Campt, 2017, p. 51). Stasis recognizes that to be legible in the afterlife of slavery means mirroring the hegemonic order and making oneself readable in a social context while not relinquishing one's essence. Engaging Black bodies and minds as depictions of stasis reveals an "effortful equilibrium achieved through a labored balancing of opposing forces and flow" (Campt, 2017, p. 52), whereas they are actively resisting attempts to arrest their subjectivity through reflective objectivity. Stasis demands that we attend to the muscular tension and the complex forces that surround and produce reflexive moments. Theorizing with Fanon, Scott (2010) called muscular tension a powerfulness amid debility and "resistance expressed through a refusal to accept or acquiesce to defeat" (p. 39). Building on this idea, Scott stated that Fanon summons the trope of muscle tension to describe a state of arrested activity, as a "trembling, held back by a restraint, on the edge of a new consciousness—and which might also be defined as a form of consciousness that readies itself to direct the body in activity. I think it is possible to delineate aspects of this state that can be called powerful" (p. 64). This framing requires that one read muscular tension as a performance of stillness (objective positions), a form of stillness in motion, never completely ceding to motionlessness or movement. What changes when the modes of inquiry move beyond the binaries of subjectivity and objectivity to engage Black liveliness through the lens of quiet frequencies and stasis?

Embodied knowing rests in the tense relationship between "identity, belonging, and self-fashioning" (Campt, 2017, p. 159), and as such, this chapter keys into ontological possibility by listening to registers beneath two central images in the lives of Black people in and beyond educational contexts: *the Black Power fist* and *hands up, don't shoot*. At a minimum, these actions are the difference between open and closed fists, yet, as these analyses demonstrate, they represent hope, frustration, and desire. I explore these images on and off campus, at or near their public emergence in the United States imaginary. I chose two photos of each gesture and juxtaposed their meaning as paired symbols. The selected photos were popularized by media outlets and distributed across various official and social media platforms; each photo was within three years of Black public movements for equity and justice. I chose images beyond the campus grounds to evince the ways the sociopolitical is part and parcel of the educational context, always and already affecting students and impacting culture. Additionally, this chapter intends to consider Black people beyond the educational context as invaluable contributors to Black ways of knowing and being and, thus, should be accounted for in scholarly work.

Freedom Movements

One tracing of Black freedom movements leads back to the emergence of Black Power during the 1960s. Following the shooting of James Meredith in Mississippi, Kwame Ture (formerly known as Stokely Carmichael) declared to a crowd, "We have been saying freedom for six years. . . . What we are going to start saying now is 'Black Power'" (Editors, 2019, para. 9). Conceptually, according to Ture and Hamilton (1967), Black Power rejected notions of assimilation with society, as to do so was to embrace the goals of the Western Man over the lives and decisions of Black people. Thus, centrally, Black Power emphasized self-determination, that is, "full participation in the decision-making processes affecting the lives of black people, and recognition of the virtues in themselves as black people" (p. 44). Black Power believed in a consolidated Black base in support of Black people. Moreover, as Ture and Hamilton (1967) wrote, "It is a call for black people in this country to unite, to recognize their heritage, to build a sense of community. It is a call for black people to define their own goals, lead their own organizations, and support those organizations. It is a call to reject the racist institutions and values of this society" (p. 42). At the time of this writing, Ture was a chairman of the Student Nonviolent Coordinating Committee (SNCC), and as such, had the ear of young adults, particularly college students, across the nation. Materially, Black Power came to represent the desire for Black dignity and personhood amid the rational apportionments of civil rights legislation (see Civil Rights Act of 1964, Voting Rights Act of 1965). Further, Black students called for a sense of place in and beyond the college campus (Biondi, 2012; Rojas 2007). If homing in on SNCC and Black Power's work during the 1960s fulfills an organizing framing for the images, the Black Power movement provides the twinning psychological and political agenda. In a speech at the University of California Berkeley, Ture asked, "How can black people inside of this country move? And then how can white people who say they're not a part of those institutions begin to move? And how then do we begin to clear away the obstacles that we have in this society, that make us live like human beings? How can we begin to build institutions that will allow people to relate with each other as human beings?" (para. 5). The focus on the idea of movement is more than just a turn of phrase. Instead, it folds into Black Power's sentiment that Western humanism has oversurveilled and -controlled the mobilities of Black people in the United States.

Brief History of Black Power Salute

Historically, the Black Power clenched fist is most readily associated with Tommie Smith and John Carlos at the 1968 Mexico City Olympics. To openly contest Black people's relationship to the United States and, specifically, the allegiance that a national anthem performs for the visual sphere, Smith and Carlos decided to wear black gloves and raise their fists in the air. Black Power, as noted above, was a burgeoning concept, and the raised clenched fist became its symbol.

Brief History of Hands Up, Don't Shoot

Following the death of Michael Brown in 2014, eyewitnesses to the murder noted that Brown had his hands up when he was shot and killed by Officer Darren Wilson (Corley, 2015). Though there is contention on the veracity of the claim, the notion that unarmed Black people can be murdered resonates with those who live in the aftermath of police and state-sanctioned violence on Black people. Since 2014, the open-handed posture has functioned as an indefensible claim to Black mattering.

Analysis of Black Power Salute

To analyze the Black Power salute, I employ stasis as articulated by Campt (2017). The Black Power salute visualizes rigid grammar and a complex set of tensions. At once, it is an act of proud defiance that dares to agitate white normativity while simultaneously engaging in a vulnerable posture and presentation. The muscular tensions that must be deployed to embody the posture illuminate the capacity of Black people to enact power with limited resources available to them. The tension "constitutes a state of Black powerfulness amid debility, a form of resistance expressed through a refusal to accept or acquiesce to defeat" (Campt, 2017, p. 50). Stasis describes the "tensions produced by holding a complex set of forces in suspension and invisible motion held in tense suspension or temporary equilibrium" (p. 51). Against this backdrop, listening to the images required that I see more than stilled photos in time; rather, these images reflect Black people's laboring against systemic oppression that encamps the historical moment and setting. Stasis charged that I "listen to the infrasonic frequencies of images that register through feeling rather than vision or audible sound" (p. 52) in attending to the tensions.

Yale Cheerleaders, November 2, 1968

The first image feels familiar, inspired by Tommie Smith and John Carlos's generation-defining portraiture two weeks earlier. Yale cheerleaders, Greg Parker and Bill Brown, reflect the Olympians' pose during the national anthem at a football game between Yale and Dartmouth. Before reading the photo, I immediately notice the striking similarities between Parker and Brown and Smith and Carlos. First, the imaging takes place during the national anthem. I can hear "Star-Spangled Banner" playing in the background, and I can see the invisible question that it raised for Parker, Brown, and Black people more broadly. The first stanza of the national anthem, written by amateur poet Francis Scott Key, ends with a question mark, "O'er the land of the free and the home of the brave?" (*The Lyrics*, n.d., para. 1). This punctuation is curious, given the affirmative tone that the song attempts to communicate. It would seem, as performed, that there would be no question of freedom or bravery as the tune often ends in a declarative fashion. Therefore, the writing's significance is critiqued by Parker and Brown with their pose and timing. They seem to be saying that the anthem, and perhaps what it represents as a banner for Black people, is laced in falsity. Their heads bowed, refusing to look at the flag (though not visible in this photo), furthers their point.

Though viewers cannot tell if their eyes are open or closed, it appears that they are in another place, perhaps, in meditation with the tune of the Black national anthem, "Lift Every Voice and Sing," composed by James Weldon Johnson. I am struck by the potentialities of the Black national anthem, given the positioning of Parker and Brown. With raised arms and clenched fists, the two men stand at the front of their assembly, seemingly as leaders in a predominantly white context where, one can assume, they struggled daily for recognition. The Black national anthem's final line of the first stanza reads, "Let us march on, til victory is won" (Johnson, 1900, para. 1). Reflecting stasis, as purposeful defiance beneath the ordinary, readers should assume that Parker and Brown planned to be at the metaphorical forefront, motioning all those that would follow to "march on" toward a picture of victory made with and for Black people. Additionally, the context for this photo presses to the forefront. Whereas, for Black people, making a place for themselves in the collegiate context was rife with tension, Yale, like other Ivy League institutions, held deep ties to slavery.

The call for Black Power by Black beings, emblazoned with Yale across their chest, vibrates across the image and cultural context loudly, upsetting white normativity and contending with progressive logic that might deem two Black men at Yale as something worth celebrating. Self-fashioning occurs in the image that refuses to be drowned out or put on display to appease Western humanism. White peers and white alumni surround the two men, and in this way, Parker and Brown function as the proverbial canary in the coal mine, demanding that the white gaze image and imagine otherwise. In addition, the unspoken words between Parker and Brown resound across the photo. They are the only two in the line of cheerleaders who are standing side by side. Their raised arms, echoing Smith and Carlos achieve an arc of unity, as if to say to each other, you are not in this alone, challenging the individualist idyllic that high-performing collegiate cultures can embrace. I hear in their silence the tense grammar of fear, if not in their downward-gazing faces, then by the tremble in their lifted arms.

Neither Parker nor Brown's arms are fully extended, which doesn't defeat their instantiation but does capture, in some ways, the flesh's instinctual sense of constraint that seeks to insulate the body from danger, real or perceived. In this way, it cannot be understated that Parker and Brown were in danger. At a moment in history when Black people were victims of legal and extralegal violence, Black people had to negotiate their compulsion for dignity and meaning, without the reality of safety. The tilt and tension reflect agentic Black flesh actively pushing against repressive forces that taught Black people to stay in their place. As noted, Parker and Brown's performance is particularly heretic given that they are nestled squarely within a white cultural setting. The muscular refusal to straighten denotes Black being as a site of meaning that is never wholly liberatory, nor an instrument of abjection. Instead, Black ways of knowing and being are as complex as the ever-present threat of anti-Blackness, creating possibilities for what Campt (2017) called "reassemblage in dispossession" (p. 60). I take up this idea in the next photo.

158 | On Blackness, Liveliness, and What It Means to Be Human

Figure 6.2. Six women raise their fists in protest at a "Free Huey" rally (1968). *Source*: © The Regents of the University of California. Courtesy Special Collections, University Library, University of California, Santa Cruz. Ruth-Marion Baruch and Pirkle Jones Photographs.

Free Huey Newton Rally

Campt (2017) discussed reassemblage in dispossession as "everyday shifts in the social order of racialization that temporarily reconfigure the status of the dispossessed" (p. 60). Here racialized folks reimagined power relations in subtle "unintended ways, with unexpected consequences" (p. 60). It is the practice by which dispossessed people make effortful statements with depleted or minimal resources at their disposal. In this striking photo (figure 6.2), six Black women redeploy their bodies as agentic against masculinist politics within their communities and misogynoir in the larger public sphere. The photo was taken at a "Free Huey" Newton Rally in 1968, with five of the six women identifiable—Delores Henderson, Joyce Lee, Mary Ann Carlton, Joyce Means, and Paula Hill. Dixon (2019) stated that the photo "provides a testament to those who actualized the daily operations of the Black Panther Party" (para. 1). This sentiment echoes Farmer (2017), who wrote, "If a central goal of Black Power mobilization was to overturn editing structures and cultures and replace them with Black-centered ones, then redefining [Black] men's and women's roles was a seminal step in the 'revolution of the mind' required to engage in this political project" (p. 4). Black women were actively reconstructing the gender imaginary in society, making room for their ideas and movements in the freedom struggle.

These six women's image adds to theoretical arguments that sought to insert Black women into the largely masculine ideas of Black liberation. Unlike the first image at Yale University, when Parker and Brown knowingly situated their bodies as instruments of defiance, fully aware that they would be the center of attention, these Black women's demand that viewers look at them was achieved organically. In the case of a high-profile rally, it is not likely that they expected to be the center of attention, and yet, with nothing more than their bodies, they command the white ethnographic gaze to take notice of their will by seemingly calling it out. In the photo, the six women can be seen with their mouths agape, perhaps singing or following an organized chant. Whether singing or chanting, the sounds of their voices bellow and linger on the viewer's ears. It is clear that they do not intend to be silenced, pushing emphatically against tropes that Black women should be seen and not heard.

Their heads are slightly tilted back as if they were attempting to fill their lungs and project. Whatever the message is, it appears to be occurring in unison and at the same frequency. Though the sound-making looks to be forceful, the strain to project that sound does not overwhelm the women as they comport themselves with a seriousness that suits the occasion and the larger sociopolitical moment. An inference here should read that declarations to *"Free Huey"* went far beyond the immediate release of one Black man; they were proclamations for and on behalf of Black people broadly, and in this scene, Black women in particular. Even if freedom was not part of the chant, these women motion for nuanced attention to the idea, as one that recognizes imprisonment of minds and bodies, mentally and materially.

Moreover, readers should note that this image was taken in a public place, beyond any sense of safety that might accompany white institutions. Black people live with the threat of social death because of the ways their bodies have been mapped as dangerous and in need of control, especially in the public sphere. This truth makes their muscular tensions all the more noteworthy, as the women's bodies, straightened and deliberate, their raised arms, tightened and reaching, "shift the grammar of Black futurity to a temporality that both embraces and exceeds their present circumstances" (Campt, 2017, p. 59). Their bodies beckon for what's noted above, as a future they want to see in the now. Through the lens of stasis, viewers are witnessing, still, only what these women project for viewers; it should be assumed that there is muscular tension in this image that is unstated or held at bay and is mobilized outside of visual display.

A final observation must recognize the women's relation to one another. Indeed, a rally invokes a sense of solidarity among those who protest together. This image, however, signals a camaraderie that exceeds strangers meeting in a public place. One gets the sense that their political ambitions are aligned and that they share a common struggle. There is no image before or after this photo, so viewers do not know how the women came to be arranged in that specific moment, but readers should resolve that without each member, and the equally compelling expressive acts, the photo loses its provocative potential. Again, one must wonder how each member's presence contributed to the enfleshed praxis that each woman put forth.

Analysis of Hands Up, Don't Shoot

Images, as proposed above, emit sound. The first part of this analysis employed the notion of stasis as an analytic listening tool. In this section, I key into the quiet registers of futurity. I understand futurity, or the future, as "time that is to come hereafter; something that will exist or happen in a time to come; condition, especially of success or failure to come" (Campt, 2017, p. 15). In her analysis of quiet photos, Campt (2017) asked, what forms of futurity are made both visible and audible through quiet photos? I want to suggest that the quiet frequencies of Black image-making can make audible the dreams and imaginings of Black people. Futurity for Campt (2017) is tied to aspiration and desire. Poignantly, however, the future is in a "tense relationship to an idea of possibility that is neither innocent nor naive. Nor is it necessarily heroic or intentional. It is often humble and strategic, subtle, and discriminating; it is devious and exacting. It's not always loud and demanding" (p. 17). Hands up, don't shoot, is a quiet image. It is not as exacting or deliberately provocative, outside of a United States cultural context protesting police brutality, as the Black Power salute. Yet, on the bodies of Black people, the positioning represents Black futures and maroon imaginings.

Howard University Photo

I begin first with an analysis of an image of students at Howard University taken by a former student of the university, Megan Sims. In a *USA Today* interview titled, "Hands up: Howard U. Photo of Students in Solidarity Goes Viral" (Lee, 2014), Sims noted that approximately 100 students gathered to take the photo after an alumna, Mya White, was shot while protesting in Ferguson, Missouri, shortly after the murder of Michael Brown. At first glance, the number appears to exceed 100 students. A sea of Brown and Black people, with their arms lifted, confront the photographer, and subsequently, the viewers of the photo. Their faces rehearse a seriousness, stoicism, and purposefulness, with a message of solidarity that they hope travels from Washington, DC, to Ferguson, Missouri. The staging of the photo, at new student orientation no less, cannot be ignored. At a first order of listening, which is simply viewing the image, it raises questions about the authentic nature of a pose first erected by the thought that a Black person was killed with their hands up. Still, at the first order, it's possible to pull from the photo a sense of community and general collective regard for the well-being of Black people. On one register, viewers of the photo may wonder what relationship students at a prestigious institution like Howard University have with the masses of Black people outside of its gates, and people who do not attend institutions of higher education. Thus, listening in this first order can too quickly divorce students matriculating in and through the collegiate context with the larger sociopolitical context.

Attending, however, to the lower frequencies in this quiet image, I can push past the serial nature of the pose and the possibility of uncritical participation, to the humming recognition that it is routinely assumed Black people lack a capacity to feel and do not have or are not permitted to possess any human sense. Raised hands in this image point toward alternative diasporic survival strategies that have always included the prospect of Black disposability. Here, listeners are tuned into refusal, a maroon claim to futurity that remembers Michael Brown's stolen mobility. These were first-year students, many of them the same age as Brown and, following the pose's openness, by consequence of their existence in Black bodies and minds, are regularly prone to destruction.

Resisting the urge to create a fictive kinship among Black people that suggests these students could have been Brown, I am led to wonder what was lost, what did, or will, these students have to let go of in their encounters with society? When the staging is complete, what will they need to fill their hands with as they move throughout their worlds? In the quiet of this image, students give voice to a common theme—yearning. Every set of viewable eyes is fixed on the photographer. In this way, these Black students are refusing to disappear; instead, students locate their windows as it were, and lean into, up, between, or around potential blockages for the opportunity to be regarded—to matter—calling for a future that has to happen.

Ferguson Protest

Pain. Sorrow. Resolve. The scene of solidarity in Ferguson, Missouri, and the surrounding region, arrests vocal cords. The frequency apprehends several sensorial capacities—sight, sound, feeling. In an essay written by Jasmine Banks (2014) titled, "Black Kids Don't Have to Be College-Bound for Their Deaths to Be Tragic," there is an image of a Black woman, on her knees, seemingly weighed down by the heaviness of the moment or making a desperate plea. She is clear, her eyes lucid, open, and fixed. Her hands are not only up, but they are open, and her fingers are fully extended. Just below her, viewers can see the hints of the yellow divider, suggesting that this assembly is in the street. Metaphorically, one reading of this photo might be that a line has been crossed. The image was taken days after Michael Brown's murder, roughly fifteen minutes from the site. In these early moments, in the aftermath of murder, Black people redeployed a cultural pose from one that portrayed a casual presentation of innocence, worship, and celebration, to a political image invested in new forms of Black futurity. The hums beneath this image are "a quotidian practice of refusal that exceeds the sayability of words" (Campt, 2017, p. 43). Though the pose is often used in unison with the chant, "Hands up, don't shoot," the pose's quiet registers perform essential maroon work.

The inherent refusal instigated by this freedom motion "highlights the tense relations between acts of flight and escape, and creative practices of refusal—nimble and strategic practices that undermine the categories of the dominant" (Campt, 2017, p. 32). The pose, at face value, purports surrender, or to give oneself over to the dominant, and yet, represented on the bodies and lips of Black people, doubles as a transient space capable of giving voice to Black desires for a future in the now. Black people in this image express their dissatisfaction with norms in society (namely, society's violent regard to and for Black liveliness) and rupture the public domain with a pose that is typically used by those in power to constrain

Black movements. Police and state-sanctioned authorities apply this technique when they want to apprehend a situation or person. The familiar aphorism is often "Freeze," whereby suspects then gently lift their hands above their waist and shoulder to symbolize surrender—they submit to the context and deliver over their agency to the ranking authority. The pose, nondefensive in nature, suggests to an authority figure, that "I am not a threat." However, post-Ferguson, Black people, in recognition that no sense of safety follows, redistribute the logics of a pose that has functioned to curtail their bodies, into one of power and positional authority—it places demands on viewers.

Again, listeners are tuned into the simultaneity of vulnerability and liberation, and the incomplete nature of both. Toward the center of the photo, viewers bear witness to a Black man dressed in black, flanked by what appears to be two younger observers. Demonstrating the ways Blackened movements echo across time, the younger observer to the right has their hands lifted, as they look to the elder for evidence of rightness. The young observer's quiet reading is an education in Black futurity that reassembles anti-Blackness's crushing realism with a liberatory discourse that refuses to read Black beingness as inherently wrong. The familiar protest image and statement prop up this sentiment—I AM A MAN—held up by another young observer a couple of feet away. Notably, though rooted in the freedom struggle for Black lives of decades prior, and persisting as a critical race project in that moment, on its own, the signage is an incomplete aestheticization of the moment. However, juxtaposing the sign with the affective, enfleshed registers, taken up by others in the picture, soothes some of the rigidity that makes the future a space for some Black people, and not others.

Living Presence

Analysis of these images homed in on themes and strategies theorized through James's (1999) concept of limbos, which considers the various ways Black people negotiate contested spaces despite the structural patterns that function to stall their activity in the world. During my close read of each selected image, I used open coding writing notes/phrases in the margins that evidenced stasis. I followed that open coding with memo writing (Saldana, 2009) that responded directly to the research question. I listened to the images (Campt, 2017), asking what is each holistically expressing? In doing so, three critical findings surfaced concerning the work of presence in Black people's lives in and beyond educational contexts. First, the deployment of these images, and subsequently, presence, is an effort to claim and legitimate Black livings' intimate interiority. This finding is particularly invested in challenging the epistemological framings that have constructed the narratives of Black liveliness. Second, presence in and through images was invested in altering semantic fields of vision, that is, how Black being was read and interpreted. Finally, as acts of refusal, that are sensitive to the ontological grounds described above, these images annotate the practice and rehearsal of freedom for Black liveliness.

Legitimating Black Interiority

The Black Power salute and hands up, don't shoot pose highlight the fact that enfleshed interventions have an aesthetic and conceptual value. Together, they preach a belief in Black flesh as a site of value. The actions, first, are taken upon the flesh and carried out as extensions of its inherent worth. The actions, then and now, make clear that Black people possess an otherwise way of knowing and feeling in the world. Instead of making those claims verbally, however, they represent Black being as a form of lively discourse. In addition, though indignity and material death were the impetus behind these emergent gestures, the futurist and maroon refusal to invoke death as part of the claim should be read as an act of refusal and departure from the practices that have depended on the unspeakable Black flesh. While resourceful and revelatory, images in the social imaginary that call for Black humanity have tended to take up the beaten flesh or repeat and display the brutalized flesh (Hartman, 1997), recalling these scenes and the subsequent trauma they evoke. Listening to the images above, however, attends to the quiet intensity and subversiveness of these movements. For educators and researchers working with Black students and communities, it would behoove them to consider the potentialities of images, archival and contemporaneous, as opportunities to access a deeper, more complex, register of aspiration and desire. Educators might invoke imagery and invite embodied meditations—What does this image make me feel? What is the sound of the image? What feelings does this image provoke?—on Black aesthetics to remind students that there is a different way to engage ways of knowing.

Altering Semantic Fields of Vision

The visual field, as regarded by Fleetwood (2011), is a performative field. Butler (1993) adds to the notion, writing, "the visual field is not neutral to the question of race; it is itself a racial formation, an episteme, hegemonic and forceful" (p. xx). Black people then exist as racially marked beings who render hegemonic insights to those within their fields of vision. These renderings were constructed before them, and as anti-Blackness would have it, will survive after them. Presence, however, expressed in the poses analyzed, interrupted fields of vision and the associate meanings mapped onto Black people within some contexts. Presence renders or makes Black people over with multiple meanings, thereby rupturing, however temporarily, semantic fields of vision. Educators ought to consider how they might move away from the singularity of Black presence and visibility in society. For example, following Woodson (1933), and others, how might educators trouble semantic fields by meaningfully incorporating Black aesthetic productions into the classroom?

Rehearsals of Freedom

Presencing is ephemeral, deliberate, and rebellious in nature; these aspects of it combine to offer a rehearsal of freedom that can live on Black bodies and serve as the prompting for otherwise worlds they envision and want to experience. Moreover, presence is a form of preparation for the possibility of threats and violation, but also for taking up new modes of being. Presence assumes that freedom as an affective register must be felt before it can be lived in full. Presencing, in this way, can become new patterns of flight for and escape out of epistemological and ontological boundaries that restrict Black people's sense of self and being in the world. Additionally, presences function on the level of memory—the flesh remembers its movements for and toward freedom dreaming and building, carrying with it the possibility of metabolizing across communities and generations. For educators and researchers, this finding raises pedagogical and methodological questions. Pedagogically, how might educators create space for Black students to actualize freedom movements as part of their learning?

Educators can be intentional about naming and lifting the aesthetics of Black being as a site of meaning and healing (for example, unlearning practices of Western humanism in their comportments and visuality). Methodologically, how might researchers ensure that Black participants materially benefit from their support of a study in ways that enhance, or at very least allow them to imagine, how their lives, life chances, and communities could bring about new futures? Transactional research, where Black students, for example, are asked to share their stories and pain with no appropriate plan to help them resolve the potential re-injury, replicates exploitative and harmful practices. Can researchers provide on-site, free counseling? Can they train participants in somatic practices that will support them long past the research? Presence as a rehearsal of freedom ought to be more than a theory devoid of practice.

Black and Alive: A Conclusion

I am curious about what gets committed to social memory, as in what society remembers and how. I worry about the Trayvon Generation, what Alexander (2020) calls the young people coming of age in the past twenty-five years. My concern is what they will remember as they encounter the sight of Black death and dying, and perhaps, more, how academic knowledge production will contribute to that memory and the order of knowledge that it legitimates (Wynter, 1994, 2003). Black people, as demonstrated above, refuse death and dying, whereas refusal is practice honed by the socially dispossessed; it is more than mere rejection of a thing, but creating possibility amid constraint and negation. My interest in this chapter has been on how presence, as an aesthetic of Black liveliness, teeters between "clarity and opacity, and how this oscillation illuminates a politics of liberation" (McKittrick, 2017, p. 4). Where the circulation of images instructs people about their embodiment, possibilities, and vulnerabilities, this analysis was interested in how Black people see, understand, and create breathing space for the self against the terror of white, heteropatriarchal, normative boundaries. This work, however, is incomplete and ongoing. King (2016) reminds us that practices of getting free are always subject to shift amid anti-Black structures of capture and fungibility. As structural oppression is prone to change and adapt, freeing oneself will require a review of former and current practices, and dreaming and imagining others (Okello et al., 2021): "Modes of freedom existed in garret spaces, leaving the body, going insane, suicide, interracial sexual liaisons, same gender love, gender play, setting fire to the slave estate, murdering the Settler-Master, revolt, escape, or just surviving" (King, 2016, p. 1038). The Black Power fist and hands up, don't shoot images grapple with possibilities of how to be under the duress of enclosure, offering exemplars of image-making and imagination—presence—as praxis.

∼

> August,
>
> I love your discernment, your patient way of deciphering "how to be" and where that being might occur, with people and in the world. I know you to be caring, kind, and good-natured–you warm the air around you and light opens up at the acoustics of your smile. I have seen you move in between worlds–frozen, liquid, and vapor, you are agile. You are generous, but you do not smile on command, or turn yourself over to others without "sizing them up" first. You observe, and listen, and collect information. From the moment you opened your eyes to this world's fleeting, made-urgent desire to capture (read: photograph), you have questioned the lens. While [we] have tried to stage your being, you have been teaching me about the imperative of being. Love to you for leading me to others' intentions, their spirits, above and beyond how they show up on paper, or for what I can do for them. It is brave to seek purposeful connection. Not everyone has a right to your space, to see you in full, to know all of who you are–your joy and fullest expression, at all times, on demand. You are no one's entertainment, conjured, made to appear and disappear. You speak without words, your body a language of movements, unpredictable and unconfined. You are fierce, and present and expansive and rupture–evading capture, always in formation and taking shape. There will be attempts to name you, to piece you together into and under conventional definitions, and when it comes, feel free to move/question/elide, as you have always done.

7

"Make it intact"

Toward Ethical Regard in Higher Education

Figure 7.1. In Dogon cosmology, Ya Sa Dyongou is one of the eight divine human ancestors, four pairs of male-female twins from whom all of humanity descends that were molded in the womb of the androgynous Dogon Creator Amma. Having descended to Earth in a mystical ark from Amma with the sacred Nommo spirits, Ya Sa Dyongou is in charge of births, aids women in childbirth, and guides the fetus from the Blackness of the womb into terrestrial existence. *Source*: *Ya Sa Dyongou* by Mikael Owunna. Used with permission of the artist.

How *Ya Sa Dyongou* inspires this chapter

Liveliness requires accompaniment, and accompaniment is a matter of ethics. In *Ya Sa Dyongou*, I think about the feeling of care and being cared for as a presupposition for knowing and being in the world. I am curious about the existence of models of care that might be sturdy and as sure as the receiving hands of Ya Sa Dyongou. This photo works alongside this chapter's recitation to affirm Black liveliness as distinct from human ethics of regard and, as such, that which ought to be stewarded differently.

∼

In a January 2020 conversation with Ta-Nehisi Coates, Nikole Hannah-Jones, talking about the ways anti-Black institutions exact violence on the bodies, minds, and spirits of Black people, resolved, "if you make it, make it intact" (Coates & Hannah-Jones, 2020, 00:03:22). I understand Hannah-Jones as referencing the erosion of self that must occur to acquiesce in and to predominantly white educational spaces. It would seem "making it" is not the goal so much as humanely regarding the self amid the spoken and unspoken expectations that demand otherwise. The caution is all the more poignant because the professed expectations of many educational institutions is one of holistic regard, which is to say, institutions have espoused good intentions for Black people and expect those intentions to be socially accepted in good faith. The underlying assumption, here, is that educational institutions, higher education, in particular, can holistically regard Black people, and instances when they do not are unfortunate occurrences or hiccups in an otherwise holistically affirming experience. History vehemently argues against the capacity of educational institutions to holistically regard Blackness, which ought to raise questions about the nature of those good intentions. Without trying to gauge the goodness capabilities of institutions, one way to think about how institutions relate to or regard individuals is through the language of ethics.

Revision, as a process of habit formation—making of otherwise versions of human—is the catalyst of Black ontological possibilities for Black people as they compete with new stimuli and negotiate existing social, historical, and political demands. Conceptually, revision intervenes on the understudied question of ethical regard in student/early-adult development literature, and the overemphasis on the promotion of ethical regard espoused by educational institutions seeded in Western humanist valuation.

This positioning necessarily implicates educators and practitioners in higher education as those who reinforce the dilemma due to their commitments to the logics of Man as human. In other words, by taking up the central question of self-definition of "how to be," this chapter posits that Black being is an ethical dilemma for higher-education contexts. Beginning from the place of Blackness complicates this dilemma all the more as it conceptually holds the permanence of anti-Blackness and instantiations of Black liveliness and living, in tension.

Generally, society is guided by a set of standards that, whether spoken or unspoken, direct a community's deeply held beliefs and values. One way of understanding these standards is through the language of ethics, which helps to clarify how individuals within a community might behave, engage their social worlds, and inform how individuals relate to one another. In mapping these contours, issues that run counter to ethical systems are those that are contradictory or conflict with a standard solution. This sense of incompatibility might be understood as the ethical dilemma. In what follows, I outline ethical practice in higher education as a way to consider how institutions relate to Black people. Next, I detail the ways Blackness is a quintessential dilemma in what I explicate as a racialized ethical imaginary, as it is unmoored from the constancy of codes, statutes, and principles that might otherwise inform decision making and structure society.

ETHICAL PRINCIPLES

The ethical systems that have shaped Western beliefs and values reflect Aristotelian thinking (Fried, 2003). This connection emphasized community values and how ethical inquiry ought to prioritize benefits to the individual, namely, the community. Accordingly, one's private virtues are connected to public conduct and the *citizen* was expected to act in a manner that advanced the public welfare. Higher education is governed by standards developed by the Council for the Advancement of Standards in Higher Education (CAS) (see Council for the Advancement of Standards, 2006). CAS is an interassociation body made up of forty-one professional associations that have actively worked to develop and disseminate quality standards of good practice. Drawing on a review of ethical principles from across associations, CAS compiled principles that were consistently upheld as essential for good practice. Delineating ethical codes from ethical principles, Kitchener (1985) surmised that ethical codes have "omissions" and bump up against conflicting obligations. Ethical principles, on the other hand, offer a framework for decision making regardless of the obligation or dilemma. In this sense, ethical principles were "more general, abstract, and fundamental than ethical codes. As a result, they provide a more consistent vocabulary or framework within particular cases or issues can be considered" (p. 19). The CAS ethical principles borrow extensively from Kitchener's (1985) work, and, as such, I outline the ethical principles in their entirety to accentuate their fullest intended meaning as guideposts for practice, but more broadly and for the purposes of this book, as a general frame that structures how institutions relate to Black people and what it should mean for how Black people relate to white institutional frameworks. The principles, as a set of ideas concerned with achieving the highest sense of good, have guided what is perceived to be ethical decision-making in Western societies.

Higher-education institutions generally consider themselves to be communities, and as such, individuals within them are expected to put forth notions of care and concern that work toward the wellness of the entire community. These principles shape the ethical imaginary, or the rules and practices, spoken and unspoken, that inform how individuals relate to one another and are "premised on a world of selves and others. All selves are also others, and all others are also selves" (Gordon, 2017, p. 23). Their use presumes that they reflect universal values that will be/are consistent over time. Blackness unsettles, again and again, complicating the ethical imaginary as it creates a category of people, namely, Black folks, as neither possessing a self nor that which can lay claim to expressions of humanity (read: recognized as human).

Founding Order of Knowledge as the Racialized Ethical Imaginary

Hannah-Jones's commentary on making it "intact" implied tension, suggesting that making it, negotiating white institutions and logic, is an ill-structured problem, or a problem that is not easily resolved. Notions of making it with some sense of intactness is a meditation on anti-Black social imaginaries, and more specifically, the codes[1] by which they abide. Wilderson (2010) called these codes a form of solidarity, writing, "The structure of the entire world's semantic field . . . is sutured by anti-Black solidarity" (p. 58). Notions of solidarity symbolize continuity and an established set of agreements, often unwritten and assumed, that structure the sociopolitical imagination.

Anti-Black solidarity as a framing is instructive for understanding how racialized discourses, practices, and policies cohere on and around notions of the Black as nonhuman, and for all intents and purposes, other than human. Or, the durability of the world and the various hierarchical arrangements therein, are legislated by the antagonistic relationship that society has with the position of the Black. Solidarities reflect an alliance of thought, acceptance, and willingness to share in the fate and potentialities of a practice. What's more, anti-Black solidarity establishes boundaries within those spoken and unspoken relations, and with boundaries, the ability for some people and institutions to sanction behaviors, attitudes, and practices (Jenkins, 2021). Taken together, grammar might be thought of as a code of racialized ethics—a material and symbolic governing practice.

Ethics as Material Existence

Ethics as a structuring apparatus for society can be understood as ways of knowing, being, values, and beliefs that organize spaces and places. Ethics circulate in society as images, text, discourse, socially held stories, and actions that move beyond the individual. In many ways, ethics frame what we know about a space, and the people within it, how we know it, and how these guiding principles—primarily cognitive—are legitimate, material, and perceptual. To understand how Blackness functions as an ethical dilemma is to grapple with the coloniality of *Man*. The coloniality of Man, as discussed by Wynter (2003, 2006), proposes several ideas. First, the notions of ontological difference, inscribed by systems like anti-Black racism, anti-Indigenous racism, and the like, have been operationalized through the formations of Man, which organized living in the United States social imaginary since 1492. Columbus's expedition, alongside Copernicus's discovery that the earth moved on an axis and was not the center of the universe, launched the epoch of the Christian, where categories of humans were formed in a triadic model, as follows: Christian—those who heard and accepted the new word of Christ; infidels—those who rejected the word of Christ and were thereby enemies; and the last group, idolaters—"those pagan polytheistic peoples who had either ignored or had not yet been preached the word" (Wynter, 1995, p. 29). This point, for Wynter, was a fulcrum: "It was to be the figure of the Negro (that is, the category comprised by all peoples of Black African hereditary descent) that it was to place at the nadir of its Chain of Being; that is, on a rung of the ladder lower than that of all humans" (Wynter, 2003, p. 301).

Related to ethical formations, Wynter connects the emergence of Man to the "epistemological transformation of the Renaissance to the reconfiguring of civitas—a reconfiguring that was underwritten by consequence and the architectures and procedures of colonial power it engendered" (Da Silva, 2015, p. 93). Thus, the naturalization of Man elevated one mode of the human as the rational, right standing, and good as it disavows all others. A second epistemic shift, following the Reformation and Enlightenment, was the evolution paradigm, or what Wynter called *Man 2*, which, like Man, selectively advanced one version of human. This version, however, was determined by science and economics. The evolution paradigm extended Darwin's theory of natural selection and divided the world into the selected and deselected, coding the social imaginary as those who are subject to full citizenship, and diametrically, those who will experience social and symbolic death. These two periods bind secular/religious (Man 1); scientific, political, and economic (Man 2); and cultural ethics to Blackness, creating an asymmetrical relationship that would be *Man versus human others, meaning those who fall outside of the founding category of humanness*, are "not-quite-human" and "nonhuman." These colonial ruptures account for the ways humans were constructed through onto-epistemological racial codes. Furthermore, within these ruptures, one can find evidence of discourses that intended to organize society in a way that affirmed and protected white, Eurocentric, male, and propertied values—Western humanism.

As scholars of coloniality have noted, to establish a governing set of principles, "you need to destroy a person's history, knowledge systems, language, and religion, while simultaneously arguing that they have no value, are inferior, and are therefore incongruent/incompatible with a modern world" (Rose, 2019, p. 30). Colonialism's grammatical project is the unmaking of personhood and humanity, ensuring the Black and all human others are expelled from the ontological boundaries of Man-as-human: "Hence the way in which the positive/negative value connotations cum differential between 'whites' and 'non-whites,' and most totally, between 'whites' and 'blacks,' must be rigorously maintained in our present order of being and of things, as the condition of the instituting of our ethnoclass, or Western bourgeois conception of the human Man" (Wynter, 2006, p. 169). Dominant power requires mechanisms that facilitate rigorous, discursive legitimation that elevates notions of the Western Man to the singular and recursive way of being and worldview. Rigorous maintenance unfolds in what has been discussed as the afterlife of slavery, where histories of anti-Blackness and coloniality structure Black living, as Black people are routinely subjected to "skewed life chances, limited access to health and education, premature death, incarceration, and impoverishment" (Hartman, 1997, p. 6).

Closed Systems and Recursive Practices in Higher Education

Maldonado-Torres (2007) explained that coloniality is part and parcel of the air we breathe, kept alive in academic criteria, patterns of socialization and engagement, and objectives and outcomes. In higher-education contexts, uncritical deployments of curriculum can advance anti-Black structural conditions, behaviors, and attitudes. As an extension of this grammar, the "dominant curriculum is derived from, normalizes [sic], and preserves homo-economicus, an individualized, accumulation oriented Western genre of human based on free-market capitalism" (Desai & Sanya, 2016, p. 6). Where it relates to pedagogy, Black people's contributions to epistemology, ontology, science and technology, and memory writ largely are devalued, if not altogether abandoned in text and the arts—music, poetry, and dance. More broadly, Baszile (2019) called academic writing one of the fundamental tools in the making of the Western order of knowledge, as "the process itself epitomizes the European concept of 'legitimate' thinking; what is written has importance denied the spoken. It is one of the White world's ways of destroying the cultures of non-European peoples, the imposing of abstraction" (p. 12). She continued, writing, "[It] is a site wherein the power relations and understanding of the world established by/through European colonization and enslavement is maintained alive, as it works to reproduce the colonized consciousness" (p. 13). The academic publishing complex, in many ways, is an engine of reproduction that reinforces Western humanism as it works both to exclude and delegitimize endarkened onto-epistemologies. Conventions of this narrowing template are discernible in distinct separations that academic writing reifies such as subject-object, reason-emotion, and theory-experience, all of which can find a basis in the human/not-quite-human/nonhuman hierarchal order.

Legislative efforts like those of Executive Order (EO) 1395042 in September of 2020, which withheld funding from federal entities that promoted nine categories termed *divisive concepts*, and the dozens of bills put forth by states to ban CRT adjacent material, are examples of the ways writing and the convergence of the Western Man militate against diverse onto-epistemologies. Such a basis has been critiqued by scholars who have interrogated European critical theory and its general bend toward epistemic violence by denying the values of knowledges outside of the superior Western Man. Not to be missed in the *epistemic* violations are the ways writing produced ontological consequences. As a medium, writing was and continues to be a mechanism of the anti-Black social imaginary, wherein the regulation of enslavement and its afterlife can be traced to ledgers, storybooks, advertisements, disciplinary texts, and legislation.[2]

Legislation continues as a central site of legitimate truthmaking, and by extension functions to define the contours of ontological exclusion, not-quite-human/nonhuman. As an example, the crafting of laws and policies, enforced judicially and extrajudicially, as a practice of withholding, traces back to literacy laws (restricting who could read and write), what could be taught and to whom, and in the contemporary literacy norms that conspire to facilitate the achievement chasm.

On the question of ontology, and more aptly, bodily autonomy, Spillers (1987) noted how the theft of the body came to mark Black people as property, and thus, unprotected/able and without bodily autonomy. She noted that under the violent circumstances of enslavement, the captured body was separated from its autonomous will and desire. Those conditions ensured that, at minimum, gender differentiation was severed from the Black. A reminder is important here that as property, the Black body became a social, political, and economic territory to be bought, sold, and exchanged—fungible, with no respect to gender differences. Here, the captive body could be violated at will to fulfill the sensual pleasures, as it simultaneously and inextricably is a source of social, political, and economic thingness by the captor (see chapter 4). With no acknowledged subjectivities or personhood to speak of, as an object, Blackness inscribed nonhumanness, otherness, and, therefore, powerlessness. This racialized schema materialized during enslavement as Black women's sexual and reproductive servitude in conjunction with, alongside, and *as* forced labor, which together comprised the catalyzing force for the institution of slavery and profit making in the West. Stated differently, nonhumanness is the grounds for rejection of bodily autonomy, or the freedom from nonconsensual and violent acts—autonomy from the violent state and extrajudicial violence; autonomy over gender and sexual decisions and experiences; autonomy of relationality. During enslavement and in its afterlife, violence registers as a social norm, where Black women and men, trans folks, women, LGBTIAA, and others are subjected to the choices and decision-making bodies not made by them, inclusive of the State and family (see *Dobbs v. Jackson Women's Health Organizations*). This ethic, the lack of a recognized bodily autonomy, lingers in the contemporary, consistent with both the incompleteness of progressive liberal agendas that lack an intersectional purview that might interrogate the compounding nature of anti-Blackness, heteronormativity, and patriarchy, and more fully, as the "terrain which represents, and therefore dehumanizes, the subjects who are both liberating themselves and in need of liberation" (Rose, 2019, p. 30). Failure to address the terrains of the human does nothing to unsettle the nature of the Black as inherently, and more precisely, morally wrong in higher education.

Moral Wrongness and Privacy

Whereas Black people are not structurally regarded as human, but are considered to be deficient and unable to achieve the rightness of Man, they are, thus, wrong, problematic beings in the United States.[3] I have explained the ways that the Black has existed outside the realm of humanness and how socially relating to the Black is engendered by anti-Black solidarity coalesced, held in place, by a materially and symbolic governing practice—ethical imaginary. While there has been some critique of ethical standards in higher education, namely, the tendency to accept dominant worldviews at the expense of those nondominant belief systems, there has been much less discussion about the terrain that props up ethics. Fried (2010) ventured into this terrain, writing, rightly, that a positivist epistemology, with assumptions about truth, rationality, and objectivity, is foundational to the ethical discussion. Positivist epistemology acts as its own set of ethics, bounded by its emphasis on universality. The position of the Black in society as nonhuman, on account of the Man-as-human demands an onto-epistemological shift in ethical orientation. For the Black, as I have mentioned, it means understanding that the self, and one's relationship to space in the United States social imaginary, is to live in and be responsive to precarity. In what follows, I examine what is regarded as higher education's code of ethics, the ethical principles that direct how educators ought to engage students. In doing so, I consider the ways anti-Blackness troubles these ethics, and what such an analysis means for Black living.

A Grammar of the Outside

If the racialized ethical imaginary, in its current form, is constructed by and with positivist epistemologies and reliant on a set of universal values that, above all, are premised on notions of citizen and citizenship that are wholly unavailable to the Black, then to account for Blackness will mean exceeding, getting beyond, or unsettling boundaries of the current grammar. Borrowing a maroon ethos (Roberts, 2015; Trouillot, 2005), these maneuvers coalesce as a *grammar of the outside*—unfinished, liberatory activities, be they emotional, psychological, spiritual, or social. This grammar of the outside becomes necessary because of the captive nature, enclosure, and potential suffocation of being on the inside, though never absolute. A grammar of the outside reconstitutes the terms of Black livingness as conditioned by Black specificity and away from white logics, methods, and protocols that would seek to resuscitate and recycle old liberal humanist modes of being to create "post-structural and postmodern forms of violent humanisms" (King, 2019, p. 10). A grammar of the outside can add ontological language to Black being in the world as it rescripts standards toward Black specificity. Furthermore, devotion to the outside is to consider otherwise ecologies and socialites that transgress the regulations of property and self-possession, ownership, and citizenship in a Western sense. That said, a grammar of the outside does not amount to, nor does it intend to exaggerate complete sovereignty. On the contrary, given the ongoing force of the wake of anti-Blackness, it becomes difficult to separate the condition of the outside from the notion of flight—fleeing, escaping, or running away. When the movement of Black people is surveilled as part of the racialized ethical imaginary, the prospect of living fully is and must be measured by the thing that militates against it, the ongoing and always proximate threat of enclosure/captivity. In this view, it is important to read grammars of the outside as activities, unbounded and unfinished. To shift the grounds by which we might constitute Black living, I think with the *Black shoals and Black outdoors*.

Outdoors and Offshore: Black Terrains as a Theoretical Frame

A shoal is indeterminate—as part ocean and land, it is unstable and uneasily mappable and yet knowable. In this way, shoals slow the movements of vessels—they force the velocity and momentum to change direction, adjust, and at times come to a complete stop. King (2019) reads the shoal as an interstitial, analytic, and theoretical orientation, constituting moments of gathering and assembly. The *Black shoal*, otherwise stated, creates productive tensions. I take seriously that Blackness tends to precede the shore that we understand as common practice and ethical protocols, and thus, theorize Blackness as an occasion of stoppage—a site where our movements cannot proceed as usual. In relationship with the Black shoals, *the Black outdoors* theorizes being that exceeds the constraint of an inside. The concept illustrates how Blackness is cast as always outside white discourses of legitimacy—unsettled, unhoused, and unmoored from notions of self-possession, propertied personhood, and sovereignty. The Black outdoors gesture for an opening up, entering, and moving through the uncleared and overgrown. Summoning a maroon ethic, the Black outdoors is concerned with producing "thought of the outside while on the inside—the enclosure is brutal, but the practice is always about finding a way to produce an outside within that space" (Carter & Cervenak, 2016, para. 11). In these ways, a grammar of the outside might call forth a philosophical slowness over and against cultures of resolution and production. Slowness, or the willingness to tarry, relocates one's energy from product to presence, demanding that one take in or be taken by the scene—sonically, haptically, affectively—and notice with more intention.

Together the Black shoals and Black outdoors punctuate the ways that much of what passes for theorizing about Black liveliness and living emerges from, is located in, and is in tension with a racialized ethical imaginary confined to the shore, inside—within the constraints of white epistemologies, values, and belief systems. If we are to urgently attend to Hannah-Jones's *intactness*, what I read as the probability of adaptive ethics that responds to the racialized ethical imaginary, then theorizing must keep questions at its center that transgress the confinement of white protocols and what white civil society requires as the conditions for possibility. To be clear, I am not arguing for a singular category of rightness as it pertains to words such as *ethical*, and ideas such as *wellness* and the *highest form of good*. My point is not to resurrect unnecessary divisions; rather, I am suggesting that redefining the human, theorizing Black liveliness, is paradigm-shifting, not an adjustment of language or postures.

In this chapter, I commune with the Black shoals and the Black outdoors to bring about otherwise viewings by reconstituting Blackness as a site of disruption, a slowing of momentum, and a process of rearrangement. Here, Blackness is an otherwise space, always in formation (expanding or eroding) and not already overwritten or captured by the conceptual constraints of traditional ethical protocols. I am thinking of Blackness as another proceeding, a praxis of engagement, an ethic of care, and a way of noticing the otherwise possibilities amid the gratuitous violence and degradation that confronts minoritized folks. As an affective and relational meditation that might situate the self in relationship to the ethical imaginary, the Black shoals and Black outdoors push Blackness toward a posture of refusal that occasions several ways of thinking, being, and valuation. First, this framing of Blackness unsettles the orderliness of the liberal human subject. Alternatively, it searches for grammar, listens, and feels for utterances and moans beneath the surface and outside of white modes of speech and protocols for reflection; it occasions a metaphorical and embodied slowing down. This sense of looking, listening, and feeling for *what else is happening* militates against prescriptions of ethics discourse. Second, as the Black shoals and Black outdoors refuse constraint, Blackness makes room for productive friction, contact, and encounter that would ask how, and in what ways, does tension abound with an object of analysis and, as a result, what is created, or what condition is one's presence creating? This sense of refusal disputes objective claims that work to relocate people to spaces of innocence, consequently rendering them unaccountable to or free from the reach of power dynamics. Relatedly, this position refuses explanatory conclusions, normative thought patterns, and habits of Western empiricism as the parameters for truthmaking.

Moreover, as the tradition of the Black shoals and Black outdoors are experiments against the threat of enclosure, they motion for a labor of navigational temporality that would ask, *where am I now, and now, and now?* (Gumbs, 2020), refusing knowledge as something that happens, singularly, while still. If the assumption is that Black shoals and Black outdoors are embodied formulations while also unmoored and shifting, one's examination of Blackness cannot be static and stationary. The intimation here is that Blackness is not a closed system in and of itself, containing a singular story but a matrix of convergences. By noticing, assembling, and rubbing past and present recognitions against one another, unexpected perspectives emerge as disparate renderings are brought into relationship (King, 2019). Finally, deploying movement as an essential praxis of discernment, Blackness must be in dialectical exchange with the inside and outside, public and private. By this, I mean to disentangle the "will to know everything from an interconnected will to disclose everything" (Jackson, 2013, p. 158). Plainly, everything is not for everybody; refusal puts notions of disclosure in dialogue with opacity as a meditation on *who needs to know what* and, ultimately, what will remain private.

Black Terrains Critique of CAS Ethical Principles

Where the Black is located outside of the realm of citizen and human regard, ethical principles rooted in and reproduced by Western humanism ought to be critiqued for their capacity to account for Black livingness. As discussed above, the general set of ethical principles that has functioned as the standards for engagement in civil society follows a Eurocentric framing of the world that placed Man-as-human at the center of the world. This perspective on what it meant to be human effectively displaced God (or the notion of deity) as the center of a philosophical worldview and replaced it with the rational seeking, reasoned Man, from the fourteenth century through the Enlightenment periods of the seventeenth and eighteenth centuries. The rational Man has evolved into what the current social order embraces as the Western human, which privileges individuality, competition, and the larger capitalist system as its basis for civil society. Of import in this tracing of Western humanism, is what has carried over across time. The shift from a religious paradigm to one that placed the rational, reasoned Man at the center, brought with it elements of Christianity. In this way, the residue of Christian/religious ideologies and values that placed the good-right-standing individual over the ones who were categorically evil-wrong, linger and influence societal values and ethics across time and into the present. Thus, as Christianity was bounded to imperialism from the fifteenth century onward, "the ideal version of the human" (King, 2019, p. 16) was being written and legitimated by an insistence on keeping human others fixed in their place—outside—as lacking the reasoned capacity for ethical regard—autonomy/sovereignty, nonmalfeasance, beneficence, justice, fidelity (Kitchener, 1985). Juxtaposing these principles alongside the condition of the Black raises questions about their universality in society as a guiding metric for good practice in higher education.

Autonomy

For many, the notion of autonomy is so intrinsic to the contemporary understanding of freedom that it was an unenumerated right protected by the due process clause in the Fourteenth Amendment. The basic liberty, which falls under the substantive due-process interpretation of the amendment, states, broadly, that autonomy should never be taken away from the individual. Reading this ethical principle alongside figurations of the Black exposes the fragility of the idea as an unsubstantiated idea about those (Black people) who ought never to have been considered autonomous beings in the first place. Stated differently, the Black has existed outside of rights protections, and, more specifically, in an antagonistic relationship with rights and ordinances, to the degree that Black people, enslaved or free, held no rights by which constitutionality was bound to respect (see *Dred Scott v. Sandford*, 1857). Political legislation is but one scene of rights discourse that contends/contended with Black liberties; others are directly related to Black education. While there is general critique of legislation, the intent of those policies lingers as precedence. Thus, what CAS promulgates as an ethic of autonomy is seemingly overdetermined by Western humanist ideals. In this way, even as the boundaries have changed, the fundamental fact of the human remains, and so, too, racialized discourses that refuse the autonomous rights of Black people.

Do No Harm

Where Black people are concerned, the pledge to nonmalfeasance overstates its claim. Taking Hartman (2007) and her thesis on the afterlife of slavery at its word is to reckon with the continuous and discontinuous realities of slavery in which the Black inherits nonstatus, which is apparent in the violence exacted on Black people in and beyond the educational institution. One can see the intention and expressions of harm in the predictable forms of dehumanization that accompany existing while Black (Okello, 2022); the grounds of everyday existence are fleshed with mundane and invigorated possibilities for brutality in and on the Black body, mind, and spirit. The principle question that a Black terrains approach brings to nonmalfeasance is, who counts under the protections of do no harm? The category of student, colleague (faculty and administrator), and custodian, for example, carry implications of humanness that must be unsettled to challenge the epistemological and ontological assumptions of Man. As it is written, nonmalfeasance proposes a generality regarding the human that elides the tension of racialization and the making and unmaking of humans. The cruel irony of the do no harm principle, is that the invention of Blackness and Black (dark) lands as uninhabitable, were essential in defining the terms of imperialist expansion and conquest (King, 2019). The necessity of Black harm, again, extends as a requirement for Western humanism, a conclusion that Wilder (2013) clarified in explaining the rise of academic institutions, and the labor that facilitated that rise.

BENEFICENCE

An ethic of beneficence is described as a sense of altruism, or having or showing concern for the general welfare of others. This ethic, as approached through the viewing of Black terrains, unravels the ways society and institutions structure benefits and expressions of goodness. Organizations act in ways that might universally be perceive as good for individuals, and by extension, the field and organization. The commitment to goodness does not account for the ways white institutions, as racialized organizations, determine benefits based on who one is and where one is in an organization. By this, I mean that the ethical imaginary, in conversation with racialized organizations, names how the allotment of benefits, thus, flows through racialized channels. One's capacity to experience benefits is shaped by their position in the sociopolitical hierarchy and the agency attached to that positioning. Whereas Black people exist beyond organizational codes of ethics, the assurance is that they are not able to influence policies and procedures, and, in this case, the conditions for goodness, and promotion of one's health and welfare. A Black terrains viewing can see how Black people are not intended beneficiaries of racialized institutions; rather, white emotionality—sense of ease, safety, anxiety free, feelings of goodness—is the primary beneficiary of these standard ethical ideals. Pursuing altruism through the Black terrains trouble the terms of goodness and how that goodness would come to exist.

JUSTICE

A Black terrain reading of the ethical principle of justice reckons with the degree to which a racialized ethical imaginary can promote dignity, equality, and fairness. By degree, I mean that each of these qualities can and does exist in relationship to an onto-epistemological orientation. The tenets of justice as shared by CAS confirm this point, as the language of justice is interchangeable with ideals of equality. It would seem by these indicators that justice is operationalized as degrees of fairness, diversity, belongingness, and notions of multiculturalism, reflecting an attachment to the symptoms, or the map, instead of the terrain that allows for Black dehumanization. In fact, a view from the Black terrains grapples with the insufficiency of critical orientations, critical race theory, and the multiculturalism movement to address the problem of Man in descriptions of justice. What passes for critical takes on justice are proposed discourses that obscure the violence of anti-Blackness for an integrationist ethic that understands fairness and equality in the liberal humanist view. This approach readily elides racialization, as if Blackness (for example, social, political, economic relations) has been resolved. The goal of the neoliberal plane is to legitimize Western humanistic notions of fairness (for example, equality of opportunity) as the fundamental pursuit of dignified living, at the expense of liberatory agendas that would upset the current episteme. This sense of justice, untethered from liberatory logics, is operationalized as neutrality. In alignment with the racialized ethical imaginary, efforts to promote equality are often performative and ceremonial while doing nothing to change the condition of those on the bottom rungs, or left out of the origins of ethical regard.

Fidelity, Veracity, and Affiliation

The racialized ethical imaginary, founded on Western humanistic, universal norms, are expressions of bad faith. Where bad faith marks the attempt to hide the self from being responsible or held accountable, the racialized ethical imaginary, embraced by institutions of higher education, unsees its commitment to narrow versions of humanity constructed on the premise that not only are Black people inferior to all others, but that they are not fully human. These decisions to unsee are underwritten in refusals to confront the Western logics and methods that guide institutional ethics and values. Fidelity is both an agent of, and principle of the ethical imaginary, because it asks of all those who desire to take part in the institution to commit to its workings. For those on the outside, it requires that one take on the Western Man, if you are to be seen as human. In this way, fidelity can become a mode of denial, and for those attempting to *make it* in and against white institution, a form of self-denial. Thus, as the racialized ethical imaginary promulgates fidelity, it chooses not to take responsibility for the breath of Blackness, but asks that individuals trust these ethics and that the social world, guided by them, is arranged in the best interest of Black people. Fidelity, as viewed from the Black terrains, is a sphere of power that assists in the creation of proper human subjects, loyal to American grammar (Spillers, 1987) and the social goals reinforced in educational environments that align with that grammar. Notions of truth telling, and connectedness were added to core ethical principles proposed by Kitchener (1985). Like the foundational principles, veracity and affiliation centralize a commitment to racialized institutions that calls on agents of the university to speak and labor with integrity toward the general welfare of those who are part of the institution. As coinhabitants of a space, the reward for Black people would be that they are recognized and acknowledged as participants. A Black terrain reading of these principles discerns the politicized nature of these principles as one's that work to protect institutional interests by establishing a political correctness. If the racialized ethical imaginary is buttressed by Western humanistic codes of civility, then how are Black people to grapple with these realities, *how do they be*? Stated differently, people have ethical beliefs that result from what they have learned about "what they ought and ought not to do" (Kitchener, 1985, p. 44), so in the wake of an anti-Black public sphere as the ordinary grounds of existence, attention to Black livingness means revising one's relationship to the racialized ethical imaginary, and anchoring ethical dispositions and standards on a different set of assumptions altogether.

Toward a Praxis of Revision

Blackness, as a sociopolitical project, is not just an ethical dilemma; instead, Blackness, and more aptly, the refusal of Blackness is the point and pivot for ethical regard in the normative sense. Here, it is important to remember that ideas of ethics in the Western imaginary are inextricably tied to enlightenment logics that privilege individuality. For the one who is Black in an anti-Black world, conceptual individuality is not possible as the residue of slavery.[4] On this plane, thinking with regard to the Black terrains, I am less interested in theorizing ethics that would expand the current template to fit Black livingness. Again, attempts at inclusion do little to upset onto-epistemological logics. Instead, I am interested in ethical imaginaries that make Black being possible because they are invested in Black specificity. Through a praxis of revision, riffing on Moten's existential departure, Black people can refuse that which has been refused to them (Hartman & Moten, 2016) and subscribe to a different set of ethics altogether, what I propose as a *Black dispositional ethics*.

One should not read refusal in oversimplified terms such as opposition or resistance; rather, refusal is the renunciation of terms that have structured Black being (that is, racialized ethical imaginary) and the articulation of new terms that might direct current and future actions, and nonactions. This model of refusal and potential site of transcending racialized ethical imaginaries for Quashie (2021) turns on enunciations of Black ontological possibility, particularly constituted through Black female first-person expressiveness. Black female articulations are useful as a heuristic here because of the audacious manner by which they claim being over and against a world that denied them of it, and persists to do so. A praxis of revision as insurgent, contestation, and fracturing, might appeal to what Hartman (2019) called anarchy, longing to be free and refusing to be governed. Referencing the riotous behavior of colored girls at the turn of the twentieth century, she discussed their refusal as "treason *en masse*, tumult, gathering together, the mutual collaboration required to confront the prison authorities and the police, the willingness to lose oneself and become something greater—a chorus, swarm, ensemble, mutual aid society" (p. 205).

If readers attend differently—look, listen, and feel for—it is possible to notice the ways Black writers have rewritten ethical regard and offer insight on the shape of Black dispositional ethics. In the section that follows, I look, listen, and feel for ethical regard in "Poem About My Rights" by June Jordan (2005). The poem reads as follows:

> Even tonight and I need to take a walk and clear
> my head about this poem about why I can't
> go out without changing my clothes my shoes
> my body posture my gender identity my age
> my status as a woman alone in the evening/
> alone on the streets/alone not being the point/
> the point being that I can't do what I want
> to do with my own body because I am the wrong
> sex the wrong age the wrong skin and
> suppose it was not here in the city but down on the beach/
> or far into the woods and I wanted to go
> there by myself thinking about God/or thinking
> about children or thinking about the world/all of it
> disclosed by the stars and the silence:
> I could not go and I could not think and I could not

stay there
alone
as I need to be
alone because I can't do what I want to do with my own
body and
who in the hell set things up
like this
and in France they say if the guy penetrates
but does not ejaculate then he did not rape me
and if after stabbing him if after screams if
after begging the bastard and if even after smashing
a hammer to his head if even after that if he
and his buddies fuck me after that
then I consented and there was
no rape because finally you understand finally
they fucked me over because I was wrong I was
wrong again to be me being me where I was/wrong
to be who I am
which is exactly like South Africa
penetrating into Namibia penetrating into
Angola and does that mean I mean how do you know if
Pretoria ejaculates what will the evidence look like the
proof of the monster jackboot ejaculation on Blackland
and if
after Namibia and if after Angola and if after Zimbabwe
and if after all of my kinsmen and women resist even to
self-immolation of the villages and if after that
we lose nevertheless what will the big boys say will they
claim my consent:
Do You Follow Me: We are the wrong people of
the wrong skin on the wrong continent and what
in the hell is everybody being reasonable about
and according to the *Times* this week
back in 1966 the C.I.A. decided that they had this problem
and the problem was a man named Nkrumah so they
killed him and before that it was Patrice Lumumba
and before that it was my father on the campus
of my Ivy League school and my father afraid
to walk into the cafeteria because he said he

was wrong the wrong age the wrong skin the wrong
gender identity and he was paying my tuition and
before that
it was my father saying I was wrong saying that
I should have been a boy because he wanted one/a
boy and that I should have been lighter skinned and
that I should have had straighter hair and that
I should not be so boy crazy but instead I should
just be one/a boy and before that
it was my mother pleading plastic surgery for
my nose and braces for my teeth and telling me
to let the books loose to let them loose in other
words
I am very familiar with the problems of the C.I.A.
and the problems of South Africa and the problems
of Exxon Corporation and the problems of white
America in general and the problems of the teachers
and the preachers and the F.B.I. and the social
workers and my particular Mom and Dad/I am very
familiar with the problems because the problems
turn out to be
me
I am the history of rape
I am the history of the rejection of who I am
I am the history of the terrorized incarceration of
myself
I am the history of battery assault and limitless
armies against whatever I want to do with my mind
and my body and my soul and
whether it's about walking out at night
or whether it's about the love that I feel or
whether it's about the sanctity of my vagina or
the sanctity of my national boundaries
or the sanctity of my leaders or the sanctity
of each and every desire
that I know from my personal and idiosyncratic
and indisputably single and singular heart
I have been raped

be-
cause I have been wrong the wrong sex the wrong age
the wrong skin the wrong nose the wrong hair the
wrong need the wrong dream the wrong geographic
the wrong sartorial I
I have been the meaning of rape
I have been the problem everyone seeks to
eliminate by forced
penetration with or without the evidence of slime and/
but let this be unmistakable this poem
is not consent I do not consent
to my mother to my father to the teachers to
the F.B.I. to South Africa to Bedford-Stuy
to Park Avenue to American Airlines to the hardon
idlers on the corners to the sneaky creeps in
cars
I am not wrong: Wrong is not my name
My name is my own my own my own
and I can't tell you who the hell set things up like this
but I can tell you that from now on my resistance
my simple and daily and nightly self-determination
may very well cost you your life[5]

An Analysis

Jordan begins the poem with the immediacy of her exemption from the scene of mattering, as the reader encounters the terror of her beingness. On the violence of misogynoir that unfurls as epistemic, ontological, and spatial terror, Jordan details the precarity of Black femaleness (nonhuman/nonbeing) as she weighs decisions to engage with the public sphere. Brought to the fore in the opening lines is an embodied consciousness, something Jordan fundamentally understands about the ways her body moves through space and time. *She* is synonymous with Black women and thus disregarded; *she* is terror's embodiment, a site available to violence in all its forms. It would seem that the decisions Jordan, and more broadly, Black women must make must occur within a matrix that considers self-preservation, history, care, and the surveillance of anti-Blackness that monitors her coming and going. As if looking upon a completed poem to say, "and the work is still unfinished," she lamented that even if she can articulate what is happening to her, she is none the more capable of shifting the ethical imaginary to regard her as fully human and deserving of autonomy and the benefits of the citizen that fold into that racialized ethical imaginary. In fact, Jordan seems particularly clear that not only does she fall outside the categories of protection, but that there is a structural set of assumptions that ensure "she can't" belong, and that, to be regarded, in so far as she was not promiscuously courting danger, would mean acquiescence to the social sphere. Jordan's contestation with society's antagonism is responding to a broader set of conditions about gender identity and what it means to be woman. Her life experiences are doubling as a beholding that extends beyond the self and enunciates the worlds of those with whom she is in solidarity.

Jordan situates herself in relation to African-ascendant women, and the tensions that abound at the intersection of Blackness and woman, and temporality and the making of citizens. In needing to "take a walk and clear / my head," she bears the weight of being by which I mean "beholding oneself as the object of and for one's study" (Quashie, 2021, p. 36), or being the theorist of one's being and simultaneously theorizing one's becoming—the thing being made resultant of one's theorizing. Tabling for a moment the thing being made, Jordan is claiming a right to be of one's own knowing. She conceptualizes experience and expresses her feeling about that knowing as seen in the lines "because I can't do what I want to do with my own / body and / who in the hell set things up / like this." Hers is a claim of regard, as she moves from the first person to the interrogative pronoun "who," effectively laying bare the issue of wrongness that the racialized ethical imaginary has projected onto her and other African ascendant women.

Jordan moves in and out of particularity, both honoring her living experience and the terrors confronting diasporic women. Definitively, the poem is concerned about and intends to bring to the fore the violence of sexual assault, specifically rape. She is precise in her use of language to name the violence of the matter, such that there is no way to ease out of or away from the issue. Jordan refuses to sanitize the language, seemingly recognizing the ways purposeful misreading can occur that would interpret alternative meanings to avoid grappling with the urgency of the call. Enlarging the scope of the violence, she makes visible the ways the "monster" of settler colonialism and coloniality are exacting similar methods of domination, and how Blackness carries as the animating site of wrongness for that domination: "we are the wrong people of the wrong skin on the wrong continent." While these lines perform, perhaps, a clearer sense of relationality, they nonetheless flow from a Black woman claiming a sense of being in solidarity with others. The poem swells all the more from this point, gathering momentum from history and personal memory, governments, and parental anecdotes to detail how the logics of inherent wrongness materialized as decisions and behaviors that encase the lives of Black women. Jordan proclaims a certain indispensability to the racialized ethical imaginary that, echoing Spillers (1987) says, "Let's face it. I am a marked woman . . . my country needs me, and if I were not here, I would have to be invented" (p. 203). Jordan's rending is a cogent meditation on Black ethical regard, because of the conceptualization of herself as a site by which living can be understood: "I am the history of rape / I am the history of the rejection of who I am / I am the history of the terrorized incarceration of / myself / I am the history of battery assault and limitless / armies against whatever I want to do with my mind / and my body and my soul."

Returning to particularity, she proclaims, that "I have been the problem everyone seeks to eliminate." Holding both terror and opening (Hartman & Moten, 2016), Jordan confronts racialized ethical regard, too, with how *to be* in a racialized ethical imaginary that regards her being as nonhuman. Jordan announced, "let this be unmistakable this poem / is not consent I do not consent." Again, Jordan is not after a sense of particularity that is singular such that the "I" represents Jordan exclusively. She assists the reader in understanding the larger task at hand, by leading with "this poem." This forwarding puts Jordan in conversation with African-ascendant women broadly and therefore the demand of consent echoes from the multitude of voices, a consistent and unbending declaration about one's ethical regard. How do I (we) exist in the Black body is an ethical question of relation, and in these lines, Jordan authorized a right to full existence untainted by structural forces or familiar patterns, whereas no one—mothers, fathers, teachers, the FBI, idlers—has a right to infringe on the emotional, psychological, or sociality of Black (women) living.

It is tempting to read the poem as a deliberate affront to racialized patterns of thought and organization. Yes, Jordan reckons with what it means to exist in the anti-Black and antiwoman social structure, and yet, the ending confirms the poem's clear intention—the affirmation of Black living on its own terms. This intention is made clear as Jordan holds notions of wrongness up to the light in the final stanza. She stretches it out to make visible its inherent flaw when she declares "I am not wrong: Wrong is not my name." These lines are part of a larger praxis that, against projections of wrongness, dares to be, dares to imagine that Black folks have the capacity to make and remake worlds of their choosing, to create habitats of existence. The poem's final lines not only make claims about how to live, but it is also clear about how decisions to live more fully will upset the status quo, compel more humane ways of being.

Black Dispositional Ethics as Entry into Revision

Whereas educational institutions are microcosms of society, to be Black is to exist in the wake of anti-Blackness, to be on the receiving end of sanctioned and extralegal punishment, and structured in relation to a world that militates against Black living in all its forms. If institutions, as precedent, routinely relate to Black people through a racialized ethical imaginary, then the task of being for Black people is in doing so in terms other than those generalized for society and adopted by institutions. Sitting with ways Black people, broadly, and Black women, in particular, have come to regard the self in and against structures of Western humanism is to raise critical, existential questions that disprove the totality (completeness) of anti-Blackness, on the basis of revision. I understand revision as a process of habit formation that occurs as individuals encounter, relate to, and engage with various settings. Here, I explicate variability of that process as the *inclination, articulation, and activity* of becoming something that did not exist before. Drawing on Jordan's poem, particularly the last stanza, I theorize on how Black dispositional ethics might guide a praxis of revision.

Inclination

I have tried to be clear that the realities of coloniality, conquest, and enslavement have established unequal terms by which Black people are to negotiate living. The United States social imaginary, and for the purposes of this chapter, racialized ethical imaginary, governs and is beholden to logic that bends toward dehumanization. The inclination, will, and earnest desire for Black people is toward liveliness, which reflects both an articulation of what militates against them, spoken or unspoken, and a right, or activity, of existence on their own terms. In the poem Jordan carries this tension of awareness and rights, as the felt sense of how the world ought to be (future lived in the now) and reality of her "status," converging on the rhetorical question, for example, "who in the hell set things up like this." There is a future that is called forth, or more precisely, called back to the fore, by this inclination to liveliness and living that values presence as a holistic form of engagement. Western knowledge production depends on automation, unquestioned scripts that instruct the public on how to regard the self and others. Fueled by logics of production, the self is often valuable insofar as they are means of production. It may be difficult, if not impossible for such institutions driven by capitalist logic to be life-affirming.

Jordan redirects the reader—hers is an inclination to reflective presence, to celebration and the reminder of worth over and against those, and that which disregards. Discontent with survival, Jordan models how a practice of presence can facilitate clarification of living or the difference between how society views me, and what I imagine and create for myself. Western valuation does not often prioritize the time and space for presence, which offers some insight on why notions of survival are so prevalent and self-care is popularized as the language of conscientiousness. Survival is an achievement. That Black people survive is an achievement in racialized contexts, and as Jordan makes clear, those terms are unlikely to shift, so the work may be to take up presence as clarification, a deeply felt yearning and reminder to keep your name—your being. Presence enables one to return to a core sense of self that can be drowned by the noise of wrongness, "I am not wrong: Wrong is not my name." What may seem like an arrival at the end of the poem, is more readily the always already yearning to name—to live in the fullness of those who loved and named us, to self-definition. How does fullness look, feel, and sound?

Articulation

To be inclined to something is to look, listen, and feel toward. Responding to that pull, articulation as part of the praxis of revision is to materialize what is seen, heard, and felt. Here, articulation is not beholden to speech patterns, pronouncing syllables, or to be regarded as intelligible in grammatical terms. Articulation builds on the conviction of inclination as an embodied form of implementation. Jordan does more than affirm an ideal state (Roberts, 2015); her refusal is actually about desire that considers past, present, and future possibilities: "my name's my own, my own, my own." Here, repetition is a deliberate act on the time register and claim on existence as lived not just now, but into a future not yet known (Okello, 2018; Okello et al., 2021). Repetition as more than ideation is an invitation into a practice of encountering the self (and others), of rehearsing stabilizing postures in an ever-shifting wake. I take Jordan to mean, too, that repetition is a must because of the ceaseless antagonism of the wake. Articulation, thus, does not imply arrival, or that asserting oneself now or into the future will lessen how society relates to notions of Blackness. The imperative, however, shifts the direction of mattering from societal terms to how one regards the self, in turn, creating loopholes of retreat (Jacobs, 1987; Okello, 2024) that do not conspire with Man's narrative constructions. Articulation, on demonic grounds (McKittrick, 2006), in the flesh, reworks notions of the human toward more-than-human, as flexible for Black living on its own terms, over and against the structural, abstracted, and dematerialized constraints that fix Black ways of knowing and being into a place.

Activity

The realm of the Western Man demands framings of Blackness as nonbeing, as a necessity for its continuance. Revision, as adherence to deeply felt beliefs about one's fuller existence, materialize, or come into view through articulation. Therefore, one should understand activity as the multidimensional, embodied formation of another way of being. The defining principle of activity, as echoed by Jordan, is its constancy. Jordan's endurance, metabolized as "simple and daily and nightly self-determination," reckons with the realities of existence in an anti-Black world, while simultaneously refusing its totality and remaining committed to more-than-human living. The case of the interstitial, or in-betweenness of revision, is poignantly made here, as Jordan does not expect a utopian frontier where Black people will live uninterrupted lives. She is not after notions of "non-interference" that, as Roberts (2015) noted, aspire to lives free of threat or coercion. The racialized ethical imaginary writ large does not lend to absolute security. Rather than focusing on the imposition of racialized ethics per se, activity resolves to make living out of the everyday, in the interstitial. By interstitial, I am referring to an in-betweenness that troubles the boundaries of private and public spheres, where a certain amount of freedoms exist for agents. Interstitial spaces are critical because they enable individuals within to challenge the boundaries of social, intellectual, and political practice. The interstitial spaces are punctuated by flexibility and degrees of power that may enlarge understandings of how to be. Activity is to conjure vocabularies, legislation, and institutions, broadly understood, that champion more-than-humane living in the interstitial.

Make It Intact: A Conclusion

Making it intact, as Toni Cade Bambara understood it, is "no trifling matter," in part because the racialized ethical imaginary is constructed on Black separation from the realm of being. Reading Jordan as fleshing Black dispositional ethics is to engage a collective rendering, accentuating revision as the inclination, articulation, and activity of becoming something not yet, but necessary. Woven into her expectation is revision as a work of mutuality that asks, how do we push deeper in our relationships beyond obligation and imagined commitments? Making it intact, for Hannah-Jones, and Black folks, is to reckon with Black separation as not only disconnection from an ethical regard of self, but also, the communal imperative to care for and love flesh (Morrison, 1987). Making it intact on these terms is to take seriously the immediacy, and constancy of revision as a praxis of liveliness and living.

∼

> August,
>
> Every morning, while we are preparing for the day, I ask you two questions, the first, what did you dream about? I assume that you dream–of galaxies and worlds, of smiles and laughter, of melodies and spirituals and sing-alongs. I want to affirm that dreaming is something you do, that we do, and that we must remember, ours and those of others. Dream, August. I follow with a question of intentions; I ask about your desires–what do you desire for today? Right now, it's beautiful utterances of outside and puppies and bicycles, and jumping. Tomorrow is another day that may demand another way of being, other desires and things that you want to hold. Desire belongs to you, is you. I want you to know that you can hold things, big and small, material, but also spiritual, and kinetic and felt. You can hold joy and love and presence and inheritance. In your hands and within. Set your intentions, August. Practice and protect your blessings, August.

Part III
Carcerality and the Radical Imagination of Self-Definition

8

On the Possibility of Black Thought to Guide Educational Policy and Practice

Figure 8.1. Opening Their eyes, Amma, the Dogon creator god, emerges from Their womb and creates the *po* seed first among Their creations. In the primordial blackness of space, Amma molds the *po pilu* in Their hands and places within it all of the signs of creation from Their infinite womb. The po is the image of the creator, and it remains invisible and inaudible as it spins between Amma's hands, scattering particles of matter and the essence of creation. *Source*: *Amma Creates the World, Molding the Po* by Mikael Owunna. Used with permission of the artist.

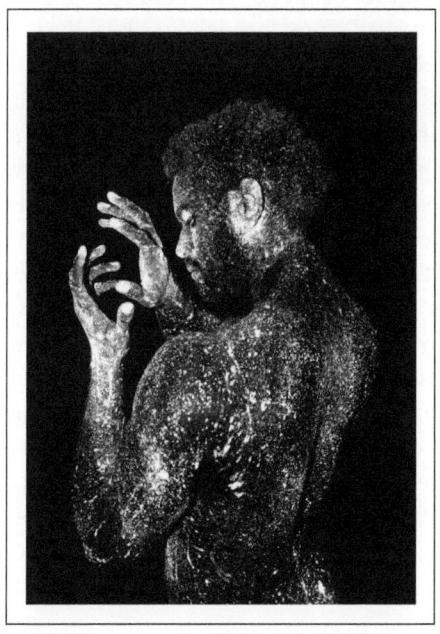

How *Amma Creates the World, Molding the Po* Inspires This Chapter

Black people create from dust, parables, and indigo. The language of worlds seems appropriate here but also feels small once it settles, as perhaps too restrictive. All the more, I am struck by the deliberative opacity, as Amma works against dominant desires to know, see, surveil, and document Black activities in the world. To understand what is being created, then, requires a different labor. *Amma Creates the World, Molding the Po*, I think, is urging viewers into a viewing practice that refuses the dominant, white gaze and its attendant sensibilities, as it too demands a laboring with Black ways of knowing. The photo is instructive, thus, as this chapter attempts to reorient educators and researchers to an otherwise policy praxis.

∾

The idea of schooling in the United States and the construction of Blackness are inextricably tied. Educational policy related to Black people cannot be discussed without its relationship to slavery, and plantation politics. This premise presumes that the plantation and the politics therein (McKittrick, 2013; Williams et al., 2021) track across time and have taken up residence in contemporary educational policy and practice, specifically in the ways "it folds over to repeat itself anew throughout black lives" (McKittrick, 2013, p. 4). As exploited labor, the establishment of institutions of education, namely, higher education, was dependent on Black nonhumanness. Black people's labor built and serviced institutions, particularly in the colonial college era, which mirrored the anti-Black logic that governed the order of society and knowledge. Or, as West (2000) put forth, anti-Blackness functioned to reinforce that Black bodies are "ugly, their intellect is inherently underdeveloped, their culture is less civilized, and their future warrants less concern than that of other peoples" (p. 85). The brutal exercise of power deployed by white institutional logics, however, was never absolute. Though formally forbidden from participating in education during this period, Black people consistently challenged the discrepancy of written virtues by those beholden to the slave economy.

Scholars have routinely noted the site of education as central to emancipatory aims, as Black people in and against the force of anti-Blackness, imagined a social, political, and spiritual sense of place. Even under the surveillance of the plantation, and the plantation politics that dictate/d higher education policy and practice, sites of anti-Black oppression can also locate plantation futures (McKittrick, 2013). An orientation to plantation futures revisits and remaps geographies of slavery, postslavery, and Black dispossession providing opportunities "to notice that the right to be human carries in it a history of racial encounters and innovative black diaspora practices that, in fact, spatialize acts of survival" (McKittrick, 2013, p. 2).

Following this claim, Black freedom-making has demonstrated a will to live over and against stated sanctioned calls for sociopolitical death, or Black freedom dreaming is a site of imagination. I note this with caution—I want to resist the temptation to read Black living as locked in a space of ongoing survival, or the common images of Blackness as suffering and violated, or ushered along a linear trajectory that is no longer subjected to racialized violence and terror. Instead, I am after a mode of Black being uninterrupted by Western humanism, which is produced and sustained through inequities. Stated differently, my interest is in calling forth a theoretical scaffolding that, in shifting our relationship to knowledge production and what it means to be human, might account for the complexity of Black liveliness and living. Evidence of that beingness can be located in historical attempts at Black specificity, such as the official calls for Black institutions, which demonstrated the actionable promise of education to disrupt current orders of knowledge, creating an alternative forum made for Black ontological possibility.

The draw to Wynter (1994, 2003), and, specifically, her comportment toward the Black Arts/Studies/Aesthetics movements has as much to do with what is affirmed during the era as it does with what is refused. Schooling processes, insofar as they have been imagined and implemented in the United States, have functioned as an instrument of socialization; young people are initiated into the traditions and, as such, particular ideals of and for society, in and through academic processes. Western humanism, as discussed, has been at the center of those logics, working behind and underneath pedagogy, policy, and practice to align and reproduce the social order. The battle, as it were, is not a cognitive struggle, one to be resolved with rational claims and solutions; the confrontation is an onto-epistemological warring against anti-Black logics that structure liveliness and living in society. By interrogating the order of knowledge, one might understand curriculum, in a social and academic sense, as a regime that structures consciousness and keeps the United States social imaginary in its place. Where it relates to education, "the function of the curriculum is to structure what we call consciousness, and therefore certain behaviors and attitudes" (Wynter, 2006, p. 10). In this way, systems of knowledge become inseparable from the empirical arrangements in society—otherwise stated, the policies and practices that govern institutions.

With respect to direct policies affecting the education of Black people in a US context, the Freedmen's Bureau, during the reconstruction era, was charged with integrating freed Black persons into the social fabric. I introduce this periodization and institution for two reasons. First, I am interested in how Black people construct Black worlds, and this era is a critical juncture at which notions of self-definition were brought to the fore for public debate, translated as the Negro Question. The Freedmen's Bureau, as I will show, reflects an institution by which the (white) architects (Watkins, 2001), were interested in a broad equality/antiracist agenda, continuant white, Western humanist logic as it relates to who and what Black people could be/become in society. A closer look at Black education policy and practice during this era complicates narratives of schooling as a means of Black self-actualization, determination, or self-governance.

Generally, outside of Black people amassing community resources and curating their own sites of education, educational policy and practice for Black people were reluctantly instituted to the appeasement of Western logic. By conducting this closer reading, I am interested in juxtaposing the legacy of the Reconstruction policies with the emergence of Freedom Schools in the 1960s, as sites through which tenets might be explicated for a policy and praxis intervention that moves beyond the breadth of nondiscrimination and, antiracism broadly, to consider Black specificity. The Freedom School movement is an extension of the multifaceted efforts that Black people have wielded in the United States toward self-definition. Most importantly, there is a sharp distinction in how Blackness is accounted for as a lens for guiding educational policy, praxis, and pedagogy. Juxtaposing the Freedmen's Bureau's approach to Black education and Freedom Schools, I think with Wynter's map and territory analytic as a decolonial (Fanon, 1952) way of addressing race, space, and social/spiritual death in a manner that is predicated on Black living. Thinking about the racialized logics of educational institutions (McKittrick, 2013; Williams et al., 2021) "sheds light on the ways . . . racial histories hold in them the possibility to organize our collective futures" (McKittrick, 2013, p. 3).

Freedmen's Bureau

No sooner had the Civil War ended than what shall be done with the formerly enslaved? had become the preeminent question. The question itself was the thrust behind the Civil War and found no resolution in its afterlife. As noted, enslavement was and is part of the architecture of the US sociopolitical, economic imaginary, an imaginary that fixed Blackness into nonhumanness. Still, the Freedmen's Bureau represented an interesting attempt by which the US attended to the social condition of Black people. Freedom from chattel slavery did not transform Black people in the minds of slaveholders, who were beneficiaries of the slave economy. Ending enslavement, in many ways intensified anti-Black antagonism, and the work of federal programs like the Freedmen's Bureaus' efforts to resource Black people were met with hostility. Beyond the south, northerners, too, grappled with an embedded sense of racialized hierarchy, racial animus, and anti-Black logics and methods that structured enslavement. As such, the dominant ideological discourses that penned Black people as less intelligent, able, and deserving of the benefits of Western humanism became the epistemic grid for theorizing Black policy and placemaking in society.

White architects, a sect of abolitionists, Northern white philanthropists, and educational administrators, were epistemically committed to a social order that would never unseat their perceived status, and rather, reified anti-Black logic and methods that justified enlightenment rationality to delimit who was considered human. Decisions made at the dawn of emancipation, thus, substantiated routinized and quotidian schooling practices that privileged mechanisms for controlling Black aspirants on the belief that the combination of freedom and education would make freed people less willing to acquiesce to subservient roles. What's more, there was an overwhelming fear that Black people might consider themselves on an equal plane with the former slave owner; therefore, policies were designed to reengineer the social order. On the matter, Watkins (2001) wrote: "The practical decision to not interfere in long-standing racial relations served the North well. The conquering of the South could be mollified with the continuation of racial and social privilege. Accommodationism best described post–Civil War race relations in the South. Blacks must learn their 'place' in the new industrial order" (p. 23). Educational policy, fueled by eugenic-inspired, enlightenment rationality, intended to reify an existing social order by creating an infrastructure theorized from these origins. These theorizations would legitimate the racialized organization, top-down reforms, and social control. Major foundations and philanthropists, in the years following the Freedmen's Bureau, worked to construct Black education in ways that would maintain the social hierarchy. More broadly, the idea of the social sciences and "department structure," were both products of foundation finance. Individuals like Samuel Armstrong, founder of the Hampton Institute (now known as Hampton University), principally, sought to maintain this order, and "mastered the art of crafting social change without changing society . . . of promoting social reform without disturbing existing economic and racial arrangements" (Watkins, 2001, p. 45). While contested, the advent of mass public education at the public expense, in the southern United States, was accommodated by the bureau, if not unsupported. Black people purported the idea, even as they pursued education on their own terms beyond the scope of those accommodations (for example, conducted learning on plantations, in churches, secret societies, etc.). The residue of Western humanism directing educational policy-making and practice may best be exemplified by Brown I and II, which argued that Black students needed integrated spaces, both symbolically and epistemically (Ladson-Billings, 2004). In this instance, the focus shifted from the pathology of white supremacy to the inherent deficiency of Black people (Ladson-Billings, 2004; Siddle-Walker, 2013), in effect, dismissing the long-standing arguments of Black institutions.

Education as Praxis

Notwithstanding the deliberate antagonisms for equity in education, Black educational desire did not wither. If one is to account for Black liveliness and living, one must take seriously "what the Negro [wants/ed]" (Logan, 1969). Black sociopolitical thought during the 1960s was organized around the confluence of legal battles and emergent social organizations such as the Southern Christian Leadership Conference and the Congress on Racial Equality. As it was decades earlier, discussions about Black being and becoming, loosely, if at all, were predicated on Black self-definition, which in turn, did little to achieve racial equity or justice, or deinstitutionalize racialization. To examine the potentialities of Black specificity, one might look at the organization of Freedom Schools, which emerged as an alternative network of schooling that would also become a central arm in advancing Black self-definition. The network of schools engaged learning as an intellectual, social, and political formation that began from the place of Black consciousness. Borne of the Student Nonviolent Coordinating Committee in 1960, Black college students were active participants in the movements for racial equity, while learning, in praxis, how to link their convictions to actionable policy and practice demands. The demands included no less than the eradication of the discriminatory social and educational laws and the radical transformation of values and racialized schema—rules and routine to resources. Guided by a pedagogical vision of grassroots, group-centered leadership (Ransby, 2003), Freedom Schools epistemically eschewed the Western humanist order of knowledge that was dependent on top-down, charismatic leadership as it believed in the beingness and power of Black communities to organize their futures, a frame that was a direct breach of existing existential arrangements. The pedagogical function of this learning prompted southern Black students to imagine futures with a different reverence for anti-Black oppression, namely, one that refused to concede to its myriad encroachments. A 1963 report that helped to shape Freedom Schools made the explicit connection to education as the praxis of freedom: "education—facts to use and freedom to use them—is the basis of democracy" (Perlstein, 1990, p. 302). Bob Moses reflected on this design when constructing a literacy project, noting: "I had gotten hold of a text and was using it with some adults . . . and noticed that they couldn't handle it because the pictures weren't suited to what they knew. . . . That got me into thinking about developing something closer to what people were doing" (Perlstein, 1990, p. 303). Similarly, Charlie Cobb, an architect of the Freedom school, would write that schooling in its current design was a "complete absence of academic freedom . . . geared to squash intellectual curiosity," and maintain "social paralysis" for all students. Cobb concluded that reshaping policy and practice meant building "our own institutions to replace the old, unjust, decadent ones which make up the existing power structure" (Perlstein, 1990, p. 303). Notions of "unjust, decadent" institutions confirm what Wynter discussed as the order of knowledge that would frame Black people as unrealized versions of human-Man, and where No humans are involved, Black people are affixed to Western humanist sensibilities. The Freedom School movement, however, offered a break from the breathtaking paralysis of policy and practice that legitimated Black nonbeing, pushing for more than inclusion, more than the (Western) human, but as Baszile (2019), reading Wynter, noted, the movement, in concert with the Black Arts/Aesthetics/Studies/Power movements, produced discourse and practices "that sought to claim a vision of humanity that was less a request for inclusion and more a willful articulation of humanity in our own likeness and on our own terms" (p. 16). Wynter (2006) emphasized this effort

> as the first stage, however then incomplete, of our coming to grips with the real issue . . . The issue of being now compelled—as "black" and "native" intellectuals who have hitherto only been permitted to use the Word of Man, thereby willy nilly, serving to willingly further Man's Project, overrepresented as if it were the Human—to create now our own Word, by separating discursively as well as institutionally the notion of the human from the notion of Man. (p. 161)

Thinking alongside and with the rhetorical and material procedures of the Freedom School movement in the 1960s–1970s, several themes emerge as a critical intervention on policy and practice if educational leaders are to insist on the fullness of Black liveliness and living. Otherwise modes of being hinge on an explicit focus of the interlocking workings of society and Blackness, a critique of historical processes that culminate in long-standing, uneven racial policies, while also centralizing that the idea of possibility, or what Wynter (1971) might call the plot and plantation—a social order built within the context of a structurally oppressive system. Mustaffa (2017), thinking with McKittrick (2011), suggested that anti-Black contexts did not disabuse Black people of agency. Black people "always engaged in life-making through forming literal, political, and imaginative Black senses of place" (p. 714). As such, McKittrick (2013) regarded plantation futures as sites during enslavement that embodied the coordinates for both anti-Black oppression and Black possibility.

Reading Possibility in the Freedom School Movement

Locating both the interworking mechanics of racialized policy and practice, as well as possibility, demands a deciphering practice (Wynter 1992) that might, first, identify the normalizing mechanics of a system, wherein Black subjugation is a necessary component of a racialized system; second, policy and practice as exemplified by the Freedom School movement requisites habits of noticing one's participation in and commitment to the reproduction of a system as natural and ordinary; and third, lessons from the Freedom School movement instructs practice that imagines how Black specificity puts forth a knowledge that is produced outside of the status quo, thereby, rejecting Western humanist logics, and, in turn, envisioning otherwise futures and genres of the human.

Naming Normalizing Mechanics

Taking the first principle, Freedom Schools deliberately named the antagonisms of anti-Black logic in the schooling practices that governed the social and education curriculum for Black students. The recognition here was important in that it compelled those who professed a commitment to Black living to interrogate structures (for example, curriculum, pedagogy) and schema (for example, ideologies, epistemologies) and how the latter reproduces and reinforces the former. Structures are upheld by ideologies that manifest in disparate and inequitable opportunities and resources. Whereas reconstruction, and post-Reconstruction policy and practice related to Black education, structured life, formally and informally, Freedom Schools named anti-Black schemas and how they got expressed in educational institutions (for example, segregation academies, tracking programs, etc.).

Clarifying Participation

Concerning the second principle, Western logics and methods in education are normative, and in so far as society is concerned, they are ordinary and neutral. The United States has never organized institutions on an equitable basis. The disparate experiences of nonwhite folks is a condition of deeply held beliefs (for example, Black intellectual inferiority) about who is deserving of education. White property interests remain implicit and legitimate the uneven distribution of resources. Some institutions, though developed in response to white institutions and anti-Black exclusive logics, can reinforce racial hierarchies, while former policies and programs such as affirmative action or diversity programs are disruptions to the normal state of things. The neutrality of anti-Black logics, importantly, extends beyond intentional expressions of discrimination. Under investigation here is the racialized deference, rituals, and otherwise normal practices and behaviors of an organization, or the guiding epistemologies.

Imagining Black Specificity

Freedom Schools were formed to love Black flesh, a poetic treatise for what it means to imagine Blackness as a fulcrum and beginning for political mobility. The model for Freedom Schools materialized out of the nexus of inspiration, legislation, and liberation, in that before formal access to schooling made any inroads (and thereafter) in the United States, Black people were creating and producing. Freedom Schools rejected the Western humanist institutional logics of higher education that enforced respectability politics, normalized Black exclusion from faculty and student bodies, lifted up objective notions of worthiness and qualifications, and promoted ladder altruism (Kendi, 2012). Rather, foregrounding education as deliberately political, the curricular design intended to support Black students in clarifying their felt desires, demands, and questions for and of the social order. Following Kelley (2002), the model assumed Black aesthetic practice, asking what are Black students dreaming about? For "we know what they are fighting against, but what are they fighting for?" (p. 8). I believe that revolutionary dreams emerge from the deep study of Blackness, Black Study, which can engender new questions, new policies, and otherwise modes of being and relating to one another.

Freedom Schools were a site of political engagement, grappling with the specificity of Blackness as political, which supported students, teachers, and communities in naming their realities, and empowered them toward living they could experience on their own terms. Among the ideas challenged were notions of citizenship, which could otherwise be understood as the profile of and for what it means to be human. Freedom Schools critiqued dominant narrations of the human as flawed and uninhabitable, thereby inviting students to imagine otherwise modes of being. The coordinates called forth by Black specificity direct a Black policy praxis, as discussed in the following section.

Toward a Black Policy Praxis

Thus far, this text has deployed tools of Black Study to inform theorizing on the premise that if educators and researchers think differently about how Blackness circulates on and around the lives of Black people in and beyond education, then they will pursue the work of education with a more complex treatment. By posing the question, how might Blackness differently orient us to policy and practice? this next section, informed by the theorizing across this book, introduces a Black policy praxis to inform higher-education policy and practice.

Theoretical Perspectives

The carceral imagination is consistent with what Zuberi and Bonilla-Silva (2008) describe as a pragmatic, problem orientation to direct research activities, evaluation, and policy analysis. On this premise, a positivist paradigm rooted in rational norms and traditions is actualized by linear, recursive models and practices that institutionalize how we know and what can be known. Moreover, the carceral imagination is positioned to favorably address social problems that meet the conditions of Western humanism. Thus, policy evaluation and analysis directed by the carceral imagination cannot ethically consider Black liveliness and living, even when Black people are the proposed subject of investigation. Drawing on Mills (1997), in order to liberate researchers from the carceral logics of policy making, we must learn to "oppose the epistemic hegemony of conceptual frameworks designed in part to thwart and suppress the exploration of such matters" (p. 119). To accomplish this, I offer a Black policy praxis (BPP) as an otherwise approach to unsettle the Western humanism of policy making and practice processes in higher education.

I model a BPP as an interdisciplinary practice, constructed at the nexus of theoretical tools from Black Studies (Dei, 2017; Wynter, 2003) and critical policy studies (Young & Diem, 2018), to reorient policy makers toward liveliness and living in policy making and practice. Blackness challenges the category of the human, on the premise that the social sciences naturalize who is human in the modern world and on what grounds, thereby clarifying who is not considered to be human (Henson, 2021). I put this framing of Blackness, and the critique of racialization therein, in conversation with calls by critical policy studies to attend to ahistoricity and the neutrality of processes that reinforce anti-Black regard. Here, I follow Du Bois (1898), who refused conventions that problematized Black people by reducing them to charity at best, and a problem to be solved at worst. He surmised, "Facts . . . are elusive things" (p. 23), and, therefore, employed creative, aesthetic modalities to curate a more expansive portrait of Black living. This line of thinking assumes that categories of analyses should be critiqued and data needs to be informed by experiential knowledge, which, in the form of a question might ask, what does a problem *look* and *feel* like (Womack, 2021)? What kind of aesthetic innovation would engender a more dynamic series of interventions? In doing so, I aim to challenge the perceived neutrality of policy and praxis development, and the universal foundations of knowledge that inform who and what counts in agenda setting and implementation. More to the point, taking up Black aesthetic practice is to refuse a mapping toward inclusion, for a territorial frame aimed at shifting the epistemological point of reference. Against the expectation of finitude, I use the term *praxis* to articulate a methodological process, not an empirical outcome. In praxis, I convene multiple disciplines (Black Studies and education) and methodology (critical policy studies) to intervene on policy processes.

Blackness

Following hooks (1992), "Unless we transform images of [B]lackness, of Black people, our ways of looking and our ways of being seen, we cannot make radical interventions that will fundamentally alter our situation" (p. 7). hooks's note about "our" functions to illuminate the condition of Black, and minoritized people broadly, as they are understood in the United States social imaginary. Policies and practices in education are set in place by Western logic and methods (Zuberi & Bonilla-Silva, 2008) to perform anti-Black disregard materially and ideologically. In order to understand how anti-Black policies and practices have gained supremacy, educators, leaders, and policy makers must interrogate constructions of society, in particular, the making and unmaking of the human.

Repetition and replication, the process of autopoiesis, describes the process of writing the self into being. This project of self-making (Wynter, 1994), which has a long, protracted global history, represented attempts by European coloniality to write the white subject as the rational, thinking subject who would, and should, rule over lesser humans. These conditions set in place rigid ways of knowing and being, and clarified those who could participate in this conditional citizenship. In essence, the naturalization and acceptance—reasonable or otherwise—of universal ways of thinking and being in the world, are part of an order of knowledge that was recursively written into place and thereby normalized. In this order of knowledge, those closest to the Western Man, through various deployments of power, constituted themselves on the basis of an objective truth. Beings come to life, or they become understood as living entities with stable, socially recognizable characteristics and life trajectories that can be plotted, as determined by laws of truth that were/are drafted in the interests of the Western Man, thereby positioning Black people as out of place—nonhuman. This basis disavows positions that "all lives" matter, as it were, or all categories of people are purposefully and equitably situated in the world. They are not. Moreover, the making of human beings in this way outlined a process for classificatory logic to take hold, manifesting in spatial and temporal forms.

In this way, I intend to think of educators, leaders, and policy makers as engaged in autopoiesis toward the construction of policies and practices that affirm Western humanism. King (2019) termed this type of mapping, *conquistador humanism*, and more specifically, "the crafting and sustaining of European human life and self-actualization through Black and Indigenous death" (p. 84), or concepts of Western humanism, and the figure of the Western Man, come into being insofar as genocide, Black enslavement, and settlement are enacted en masse (see preliminary vocabulary). The arc of this work demonstrated that the notion of the human has various meanings across time, purposefully pulling together, superseding, and reinterpreting policies and practices into the amalgamation that is Western thought and reason.

The sense of imperialism that underlies conquistador humanism is expressed by and through a myriad of material modalities that include but are not limited to the social politics, economics, and modes of force like police and military regimes. In like manner, conquistador humanism revealed itself in discursive forms such as aesthetics and literature (King, 2019). Historically, colonizers have written themselves into authority (read: policies and literature) and cartographically situated themselves on landscapes (read: organizational precedence, hierarchical practices) through overt and sophisticated forms of spatial fixity, effectually keeping Black people in their place. One should read the intention of spatially fixing Black people in place as part and parcel of a larger agenda. The university is always about expansion and growth in ways that expand the institution's reach, without having to change its core sense of ethics. Amplifying this point, Wynter (2006) wrote: "The central task of all human social orders is that of their production and stable reproduction. Nevertheless, our oversight of the imperative centrality of this process is itself due to the fact that as Godelier points out, while it is we ourselves who are the individuals and collective agents and authors of all such societies, from our origin as human beings, we have consistently and systemically made this fact opaque to ourselves by means of a central mechanism" (p. 134). Taken together, the emergence of the Western Man-as-human must be the starting place for understanding policy construction. This conception of Man, held in place over time, is fixed by an organizing framework on two mutually constitutive ideas, conceptual whiteness (constructed on the basis of the Western Man) and its progenitor, conceptual Blackness, which symbiotically inform one another. On this point, Makalani (2017) posited, "to insist on a world where Black lives do matter brings into view those mechanisms by which Blackness continues to provide a baseline for a racialized US democracy, where Blackness remains visible as the point to which whites must never fall" (p. 534). Thus, to engage Blackness is to reckon with its formation as a political, cultural, social, and economic rule of life, and not the exception.[1] The force of this claim makes clear that Black people should not be assumed rights bearers in constructions of humanity. Doing so assumes that racialization is a cultural phenomenon and not a political orchestration that forcefully articulates what is nonhuman- and not-quite-human.

The naturalization ensured that polices would appear as the norm, unquestioned, and opaque to those situated within a particular context while still imposing.[2] Wynter's tracing of the emergence of Man brought necessary attention to discourse that has functioned to deny a sense of Black livingness, on the mandate that they could not be human. Where it relates to education policy and praxis, this discourse "reifies its own civilizational racism through the systemic productions of discourses" (Rose, 2019, p. 33), like the "achievement gap" and the "prison industrial complex." For Fanon (1965), however, this state of being, what he would term *damnation*, can also be a beginning of possibility for a new conception of the human. He wrote, "Let us decide not to imitate Europe and let us tense our muscles and our brains in a new direction. Let us endeavor to invent a man in full, something which Europe has been incapable of achieving" (p. 236). The human remained important because it is central to securing "the well-being, and therefore the full cognitive and behavioral autonomy of the human species itself/ourselves" (Wynter, 2003, p. 260). As policy makers fail to interrogate the human and its relationship to and against Black people, they are complicit in maintaining anti-Black racism, coloniality, and principles that are forged in support of Western humanism. An approach to policy and practice construction that thinks with Blackness in the spirit of liveliness and living, can think with the map and territory (see chapter 1). This approach means that the foundational onto-epistemological structuring of society is addressed with specificity.

Beginning with Blackness might ask "what is denied for Black students as they represent the most extreme form of human otherness (non-being)?" (Rose, 2019, p. 40). A further question for consideration might be in what ways are we participating in projects of containment, for fear of what Black specificity could mean? Also, how does a focus on eliminating racism (read: the racial incident) draw us away from the ongoing and quotidian manifestations of anti-Black disregard?

Critical Policy Studies

Policy makers are responsible, largely, for contributing to conditions that advance the general business of educational institutions, which can be understood as helping students meet prescribed outcomes and organizational growth. Consistent with the neoliberal university, policy makers are exhorted by society and boards to create organizational cultures that are quality driven, customer conscious, and invested in distinguishing itself in a competitive market. As higher education has adopted corporate aims and modalities, there is a mounting political and public expectation that institutions, and the leaders therein, demonstrate their usefulness, prove their worth. To move toward these external goals, policy makers are at the forefront of creating conditions that will help students meet particular outcomes. A secondary goal of policymakers has been to consider inequality in education and address these inequalities in varied ways. I begin in this way to make plain that the idea of postsecondary education has never squarely considered Blackness, notwithstanding the establishment of historically Black colleges and universities. Quite the opposite, "The white elite were explicitly identified as the benefactors and beneficiaries. Higher education was designed as a place for the burgeoning wealthy class to send their young men to establish social connections and secure their places as power brokers (e.g., judges, governors)" (Rodriguez et al., 2022) or "an academic archetype indelibly linked with a real and imagined colonial past" that is "influential and vivid in the American imagination" (Thelin, 2004, p. 1). Recognizing this, in 1968, Black educators, students, artists, and activists convened at a conference at Howard University named, "Toward a Black University." As publicized,

> The function of education in any society is to acculturate the younger members of the society: it instills in them a certain idea of the life they should live. The concept of a Black university is revolutionary. It merges out of the frustrations of Black students, educators, activists, and community leaders who recognize that present institutions of higher learning has no relevance to the total Black community and who realize the contradiction of allowing themselves to be acculturated into a society that debilitates Black people. (McQuirter, 2018, para. 1)

Clear in their goals, they continued by writing, "the Black University must help to build a new social structure by providing its students with a viable alternative to the status quo and the freedom to create values, lifestyles and norms" (McQuirter, 2018). The proposal emphasizes the ways white institutions, policies, and practices, that feign interest in Black people (read: race and racism), do so insofar as those interests converge with the status quo (Bell, 1980). Milner (2008) is instructive on this point, issuing the reminder that race and racism are deeply embedded in the foundation of education, whereas interest convergence stressed that racial equality could be pursued and advanced as they align with progressive liberalism. When methods, particularly those of opposition, contend with power in (il)logical ways, racialized policies and practices are slower to find support. It should be noted here that racial equality, as performatives of diversity and inclusion, often define what passes as critical policy and practice. On the premise, educational policies, curriculum, and practices (for example, pedagogy) have the interests of the Western Man at the core (Milner, 2008; Wheatle & Commodore, 2019), leaving unaddressed the workings of anti-Blackness. As a result, "policymaking is the result of racialized political power, whereby policy elites act as gatekeepers in an effort to maintain their hierarchical position as the sole arbiters of defining policy problems and their solutions" (Rodriguez et al., 2022, p. 521).

Blackness as point of departure for policy making reveals the ways policy and practice may be understood as a verb (Gildersleeve, 2013). Policy and practice act "as both intervention and the intervening, as both movement and the moving" (p. 2). This viewing regards the ways norms move about an institution, in and through policy, thus, securing dominant ideological discourses and material objectives. To consider Blackness might begin with the "violence of abstraction" (Saunders, 2008), whereas the preconditions of anti-Blackness and coloniality converged at enslavement and the theft of land that gave way to the rise of higher education (Wilder, 2013). By explicitly naming these histories as well as the breadth and depth of their implications, policy can be wielded differently. In this line of sight, Blackness (indigeneity) would become pillars of policy, as exploitation and subjugation of Black and Indigenous people were a necessity for the establishment, and maintenance of exclusivity. *Policy* as a verb is anchored to a place that says an individual's beliefs are always and already racialized. This position disavows neutrality as a position-taking project, understanding that "policymaking cannot . . . ignore history and racialized political power . . . in doing so, [it] contributes to the maintenance and reification of the [Western Man]. Put differently, one cannot divorce the racist history of governance and racial hierarchy from beliefs about concepts such as fairness, equality, and the role of government" (Rodriguez et al., 2022, p. 556). In conjunction with an interrogation of beliefs, a critical policy studies approach would consider notions of deservingness. Here, leaders must recognize the sorting function of education to (hold in) place according to social positions based on narratives of deservingness and merit. Critiquing deservingness, in this way, would be a central core value in policy building (Rodriguez et al., 2022). Next, it is worth considering how problems are defined, as problems are socially constructed and tied to "who we are and what our social goals are" (Baachi, 1999, p. 53). How problems are framed carries assumptions as "language works to structure the possibilities of policy proposals" (p. 40). Otherwise genres of being, again, require a historical lens that would grapple with Blackness as abstraction, and the historical conditions necessary for the problem to exist. Relatedly, as problems are constituted by regularities, liveliness and living as an approach ought to question the function of a process. Finally, in critical policy studies, sacrifice is necessary for equitable change, and for the purposes of this discussion, Black self-definition. Sacrifice, however, requires those in power to give up things of interest and start anew; it requires imagination.

Speculative Methods

Western humanization cannot be equated with Black living, attempts at universal definition enable innovations in policy preoccupied with righting the errantry of Blackness (Jackson, 2020). Returning to Black aesthetic practice, in order to get beyond the critical race impulse, however important, to make known and compel policy to potentiate Black living (which I understand as categorically different from responding to or attempting to refashion toward inclusion), we must begin from an elsewhere, not the hold; it is to critique the *carceral imagination*.

Carcerality indexes the ways society reproduces social hierarchies through anti-Black forms of social control. This lens reflects how the racial calculus of society moves beyond the most obvious patterns of subhuman regard, to clarify how the carceral imaginary is embedded in social life. Otherwise stated, the carceral imagination has created the conditions for corralling, coercing, and designing solutions to the problem of Blackness (Benjamin, 2019; Jackson, 2020). These foci become all the more critical because it is always already backed by a carceral continuum that enacts direct and epistemic violence (Jackson, 2020). Here, I am interested in carceral dimensions and how Black futures occur over and against these antagonisms (that is, Freedom Schools). The current order of knowledge, which extends to and through educational policy and practice, is a defensive claim about who or what can be regarded as human. *Defensive*, as I use the word here, is indicative of how carceral logics outline the parameters of citizenship and, ultimately, being. As a social technology that is reinforced by the allure of objectivity, policies, like technoscience, materialize as anti-Black responses to educational problems, the content of which tends to reflect the motivations of its creators, funders, and agencies. Policies erected through the carceral imagination presume that Black people can mature toward or into the figure of the Western Man. Black people are and do otherwise. As a portal to elsewhere, I situate BPP in speculative methods.

Speculative Methods as Imagining Poetically

Interrupting carceral-imbued processes such that educational leaders might create pathways to differently engage Black living will mean engaging the imagination. Poetic knowledge, as a Black aesthetic practice "is born in the great silence of scientific knowledge," as the experiential takes precedence over the question of sharp analysis (Kelley, 2002, p. 9). For Kelley, thinking with Aimé Césaire, the poetic knowledge is not just an outcome, but the "emancipation of language and old ways of thinking" (p. 9). It might be said, then, that policy makers have a problem of imagination, as they are often working in response to conditions of life in unimaginative ways. Imagination here is not additive; it must be at the crux of both radical assessment and creation, for if we are to "see things as they really are, [we] must imagine them for what they might be," and then consider otherwise (Bell, 1995, p. 893). Furthermore, "without new visions we don't know what to build, only what to knock down. We not only end up confused, rudderless, and cynical but we forget that making [policy] is not a series of clever maneuvers and tactics" (Kelley, 2002, p. xii), it is a poetic process. Appadurai (1996) issued a similar claim, noting that the imagination is "no longer mere fantasy (opium for the masses whose real work is elsewhere), no longer simple escape (from a world defined principally by more concrete purposes and structures . . . [it] is central to all forms of agency" (p. 31). Where policy, like technology, occasions coded inequities that appear desirable, impartial, and claim to be predictive in ways that point to social progress, what's necessary is an abolitionist ethic that is able to both bring about an end to harmful policies and envision alternatives.

An abolitionist ethic is committed to the divestment of resources from harmful structures and entities (Benjamin, 2019). I also understand this ethic as an epistemological divestment from the carceral imagination in ways that make room to create. Abolition, as a speculative method for processes might begin not with the question, "what do we have now, and how can we make it better?" Instead, it asks, "what can we imagine for ourselves in the world?" (Kaba, 2021, p. 3). An insistence on speculation, on what isn't, but perhaps must be brought into the present (Campt, 2017), begins with the self. Imagination is not about changing policies so much as it is changing the self, loosening the self from the encroachment of the carceral imaginary. Speculative practice, thus, is fiction as refashioning (Benjamin, 2016), as experimental practice that plays with "different scenarios, trajectories, and reversals" (p. 2); it is ongoing study without the convenience of resolution, or solving the issue. By experimentation, we must orient ourselves away from the goal of "gentler" harm (Kaba, 2021, p. 5), which is tethered to Western humanism, and toward a belief that everything can change. What might it mean, for example, to think with Ella Baker toward a radical form of democratic leadership, or the Dream Defenders when considering the various investment projects attached to a university or organization? The demand, here, is for a different set of questions—questions willing to abandon our fidelity to logics of "applicability" and "practicality" in policy making. Interrupting these logics is discursive, and raises questions about our reception, desire for, and love for Blackness.

Praxis

Revisiting Fanon's (1952) endless creating is to actualize praxis. This claim to one's potential inventiveness pushes against Western humanistic logic that might otherwise regard life in an anti-Black world as existing in a hopeless overdetermined state. Inventiveness edges closely with calls to locate Black aliveness (Quashie, 2021), otherwise ways of knowing and being, and methodologies of care and livingness (McKittrick, 2014, 2016; Sharpe, 2016) that would assist researchers, but also educators, policy makers, and pedagogues with looking, listening, and feeling for Black desire (liveliness and living) against a tendency to focus on Black people as damaged. Blackness is not simply consigned to death, despite the structural antagonism that raptures its existence. Blackness is and can be a condition of possibility insofar as it is engaged in a site of possibility, or what Wynter might call, being human as praxis. This notion of being human as praxis both acknowledges the press of historical facticity, and also commits to making and remaking the self against historicized rules and rituals. It might be said in this way, that the orientation to praxis is to appeal to ceremony (Wynter, 1984), ushered in by Wynter as a ritualized critique of the governing systems of knowledge that order society.

Wynter mobilized the idea of ceremony as a praxis space where the order of knowledge could be disassembled, appealing to a transformative paradigm, specifically, the Black Arts/Studies/Aesthetics movements as cosmological discourses, that could provoke an epistemic shift. Otherwise stated, ceremonies for Wynter could be transformative. As projects of liberal humanism, namely, that Man 1 and Man 2 (Wynter, 2003, 2006) have taken hold as the overrepresentation of the human ideal, Wynter's work teaches that breaks from the normative logic are possible, and that the familiar ways of organizing society, which depend on Western humanism, are alterable. Being human, or a version of humanity untethered from traditional framings, is a doing—praxis—because of the heretic-like maneuvers imperative to disruption of the normative systems of knowledge. In this way, being human, or to service, advocate for, and advance a humanity that might account for Black living is to look without turning away at structural formations that create barriers to access, mobility, survival, and need; it is a form of engagement that is malleable and open to change, or living invention into existence (Fanon, 1952).

As a process that is ongoing, Black policy praxis is anchored in the collective—the collision of thoughts, feelings, and vibrations of sociality—at once grappling with the ways the past is written onto the future, and imagining what will need to have happened if a livable future is to take form. Importantly, thus, praxis is a messy and imprecise process that is formative in nature, and treads beyond notions of binary thinking/theorizing and resolution/completeness. Finally, praxis as life-affirming work is to also submit to improvisation, or the process by which the creation of new ways of doing policy and practice "emerge within the context of an already existing way of approaching or doing something" (Brown, 2013, p. 331). Improvisation, generally, describes an in-the-moment act or response that is unplanned. Here, the notion of praxis is adaptable and able to move as the situation may demand. Improvisation as praxis is not an anything-goes approach; it is deft, applicable, relevant, and contingent to context. Making room for improvisation allows policy makers, and those with whom they are in the community, the space to collectively make sense of information and processes in context without being tied to a specific set of methods or strategies.

Thinking with Diem et al., (2014), praxis as a component of policy making involves the interrogation of processes, symbols, and rhetorical devices, as well as the delineation between rhetoric and reality. Interrogation should be understood here as a practice of deep questioning to identify complexities and contextual nuances within an organization or policy. As mentioned, a praxis approach empowers leaders to comb through multiple viewpoints to decipher how ideas become/became reality and normalized by asking questions such as, "how categories work, and how do they become fixed, and how do we need to constantly challenge the categories?" (Diem et al., 2014, p. 1076). Principally, this questioning is not just at the level of the policy, but also at the level of epistemology, on the premise that the epistemic informs what one affirms as real, true, and legitimate.

Relatedly, a praxis, directed by Blackness and critical policy studies, would ask, "how policies emerge, what problems they are intended to solve, and how they reinforce dominant culture" (Diem et al., 2014, p. 1083). Praxis is attuned to the distribution of power (and voice), resources, and legitimacy, as in who is deemed a knowledge holder and potential contributor. Considering power, one might ask, "what is the role of power in making knowledge . . . which is always shaped by power relationships" (Diem et al., 2014, p. 1077). Last, as a habit of mind, praxis is a dedication to agency and advocacy. Along these lines, I read the Black in Black policy praxis as a provocation; a call to meaningfully center subjectivities, voices, desires, and concerns that are structurally unthought, or considered insofar as they fit within an antiracist agenda.

From "Theory to Practice" to "Theoretical Practice": On Accessibility and the Work of Precision

Rodgers and Widdick (1980) proposed a formal model for theory to practice along several phases: (1) the selection of a problem faced by a specific population in a specific context; (2) the selection of appropriate and useful scholarly theories; (3) the translation of those theories into the context of practice; (4) the formulation of goals for the intervention and/or program; (5) the design of the intervention and/or program; (6) application of the intervention and/or program; and (7) evaluation of the intervention and/or program. The proposed process presumes that problems can be identified, and as those problems are identified, they can find proper resolution by the application of theory or a concept. This procedure, too, assumes that individuals have correctly addressed an issue, have a firm grounding in theory, and are prepared to address said issue using theory. Fundamentally, this process sidesteps what I want to suggest as a quintessential component of a would-be practice of liveliness and living, and how theory happens on and through the individual. Of interest here is not one's capacity to assign theory to a problem but the pursuit of a *theoretical practice*.

While there have been critiques of theory to practice models, there is less discussion on the workings of a theoretical practice. Interrogating theory to practice models, Reason and Kimball (2012) presented a model for integrating scholarship, context, and reflection. Their models lifted the importance of formal theory, institutional context, informal theory, feedback loops, and practice. Regarding formal theory, Reason and Kimball (2012) noted that educators and practitioners "must have a broad-based, advanced education in [formal] theories that allows for an informed, eclectic approach to theory selection at all administrative levels" (p. 368). Institutional context calls attention to the ways "environment informs institutionally supported student development goals and provides guidance to student affairs professionals about how these goals are best achieved" (p. 368). Building on Parker (1977), which proposed informal theories as bodies of knowledge that allows practitioners to make implicit connections, informal theory "implies a desirable level of critical consciousness and reflection that implicit theory does not" (p. 360). And, relevant to this discussion, practice is the application of informal theory, informed by institutional context and formal theory. The model prioritizes the reflective practitioner, who is able to describe the formal theories, institutional context, and some understanding of the theory in context alongside the goals of an intervention.

Moreover, the reflective practitioner is directed by two important questions, first, "how is my perception of practice outcomes incorporated into the informal theories that I employ? The second asks: how does practice inform the way in which I understand institutional context relative to formal theories and localized understandings of student development?" (p. 372). Broadly, the approach is an important step in the realm of translating ideas for pragmatic purposes. More specifically, the model is explicit about the important role of theory in practice and asks practitioners to be cognizant of their positionality and beliefs and how those positions shape their practice. Both questions, and the tenets writ large, however, understate the totalizing effects of Wynter's conception of Man, and how institutions are not only a reflection of that logic, but how that conception defines policy making.

Theory to practice models, thus, tend to refuse ambiguity in favor of technical knowledge, linear thinking, and a legitimization of theory as useful for institutional good. Whereas theory to practice often means "coming to terms with (which usually means move past)" (Sharpe, 2016, p. 20), Black being, instead, demands an epistemic departure from these logics toward configurations of policy making that would stay in the wake, and in doing so, inhabit a "blackened consciousness that would rupture the structural silences produced and facilitated by, and that produce and facilitate" (p. 22) Black social, psychological, and spiritual death. Reconfiguring theory to practice toward a mode of attending to Black living is necessary because the stakes of not doing so unrecognize the endemic nature of anti-Blackness.

If educators, researchers, and policy makers are to take seriously what it means to pursue new genres of humanity that seek to affirm the life and dignity of Black living, it will mean a confrontation with established priorities, namely, the rush and resolve to incorporate ideas into practice/policy solutions, often in the absence of theoretical grounding. Yes, education is an applied field, and reflexivity is important, and, if educators are not careful, this common referendum can become the basis by which theory or ideas that are not neatly presented and easily digestible, are written off, or deemed to have no practical relevance. This general tendency, in some ways, reflects a version of professional training and socialization, wherein theory, while introduced, is not required for practice, even if that work claims an equity or justice orientation. What passes for equity and justice policy-making, more or less, tends to be based on progressive liberalism that educators believe can be repurposed to level the playing field; the language of equity is used, but diversity and inclusion remain the implicit solutions, not unlike the Freedmen's Bureau, except for the explicit labor to reify racialized hierarchies. In this way, critical approaches too often signal a progressive, antiracist agenda as opposed to meaningfully grappling with the epistemological, ontological, or values systems that prop up structures of inequity. Theory, particularly as is discussed in relation to Black scholars, is dismissed for its informality; it is chided for being impractical, dense, unclear (Christian, 1987). These infractions reify scripts of Blackness as incapable of being a legitimate site of knowledge, and, further, renders Black theorists and theory making as illegible, disassociating them from true science. Thus, discussions about theory to practice should grapple with the racialized core principles that undergird the logic of theory to practice, those being accessibility and translation.

Accessibility

Curating policies that affirm Black living will not grow out of scholarly discipline to methods; instead, rhetorical disruption that can intervene on normative approaches is needed (Benjamin, 2019). This disruption assumes "a kind of blurring of speech/writing to mark a different mode within the same mode" (Moten, 2017, p. 6). Precisely, the issue at heart, the overrepresentation of Man-as-human, should not be framed as a neat, discrete, and focused problem of practice that is unresolved only because of failures to rigorously execute theory to practice. The construction of the human is rhizomatic and ever shifting; as it cuts across disciplines, contending with it depends on creative theorizing that is radically interdisciplinary in nature. Interdisciplinarity as frame for thinking about practice and policy is to break from normative conventions of policy praxis (Rodriguez et al., 2022), which, above all, demand ideas that fit within the logics of practice (read: can be readily taken up and used widely). Plainly stated, Black aesthetics (and so too thought and praxis) does not, and should not be understood as easily intelligible. This is not to suggest the writing and discourse should be purposefully imperceptible; rather, expansive versions of the human cannot be written into being without disrupting the template of thinking and practice, and also what is read as accessible (and therefore useful). Here, there are no clean- or clear-cut departures, just "new things, new spaces, new times [which] demand innovation and intervention, formal maneuverings that often serve to bring to the theoretical and practical table whatever meaning can't" (Moten, 2017, p. 17). Wynter (2006) gestures toward this point, writing,

> I WOULD LIKE TO FEEL THAT EVERYTHING I SAID HAD A LIBERATING AND EMANCIPATORY DIMENSION. That's what she [Aretha Franklin] has. Black singing, at its best, it has this—like Gospel. That I wanted. But also, I was always aware that it wasn't that I was thinking anything linearly. It never came linearly. It tends to come the way a flower blooms. It comes unexpectedly; and it has nothing to do with "genius." It has to do with this beginning to question your own "consciousness." It's the idea of poesis, again; there is also a poesis of thought; a new poesis of being human. These concepts don't come in a linear fashion. They build up. They build up, you know? (p. 34)

Wynter's disruption of linearity is an important reminder about the sovereignty of Black aesthetics and praxis as wayward meshing, movement, frictions, and marronage (Hartman, 2019). Black liveliness and living are of complexity, produced as shifting bodies, ideas, ways of being and knowing. In like manner, Wynter stitches together language and concepts in a form of radical interdisciplinarity that calls forth multiple and varied ways of seeing/feeling/knowing/being. What might be read as incomprehensible is not an attempt at intellectual density; it is engendering a new mode of study that perhaps might destabilize the routinization of educational policy and practice. Here, policy makers ought to be willing to study and sit with theory, and not just components of a concept that they deem accessible or useful for real-world implications.

If policy makers are to support self-defining praxis, the central positional commitment is to, first, be the living site of intervention, "constitute[ed] by systemic theoretical practice and this is her 'instrument,' forever and anon" (Spillers, 2003, p. 456). Said, differently, the instrument, as it were, for the policy makers is the willingness to take seriously what it means to read deeply, deeply study, and to question. Taking up this process, policy makers will be able to put forth a set of demands that gets at the epistemological crisis that defines and stabilizes the field of higher education and educational policy-work. This positionality is concerned with the ways theory passes through the *I*, as the central object of analysis, before any discussion of application. Moreover, the approach tempers ideals that favor empiricism and application on the recognition that the rush to practice and solutions are fueled by anti-Black, colonial logics. That said, theoretical practice requires precision.

Precision

The urgency to change higher education as espoused by policy makers is not new. Advocates for change, however, are committed to behaviors and performances that fail to address the logics of Western humanism that instruct institutional formations, practice, and policy. Ergo, as we misrecognize onto-epistemological dimensions as the object of analysis, replacing it with recognition and symbolic gains, we mistake the map for the territory. To counter this logic, educators, practitioners, and policy makers must commit to precision. By precision, I am following Spillers (2003), Moten (2018), and the host of scholars, creatives, and grassroots activists who uncompromisingly believe that sustained engagement—reading deeply, deep study, thinking in community—are the instruments that will facilitate more humane environments. Moten compared the conviction to sustained engagement as the activity of rehearsal: "The notion of a rehearsal—being in a kind of workshop, playing in a band, in a jam session, or old men sitting on a porch, or people working together in a factory—there are these various modes of activity. The point of calling it "study" is to mark that the incessant and irreversible intellectuality of these activities is already present" (Wallace, 2018, para. 9). The call to rehearsal should be read as the exercise of giving explicit attention to onto-epistemological foundations that structural inequity as the essence of system-changing response. Addressing these conditions of being and knowing not only says that they have largely been absent in systems thinking processes, but that systems work is the translation of individual theoretical practice. Perhaps then the only question is, "To what extent do the 'conditions of theoretical practice' pass through" (Spillers, 2003, p. 456) us as the site of intervention? Plainly, translatable research, or theory to practice cannot occur devoid of theoretical practice.

Being Involved: A Conclusion

Discriminatory policies are an algorithmic code, supported and reproduced by Western humanism. Confronting these codes necessitates not just a process of unlearning, but commitment to a departure, an ethic bent on imagination; an aboveground praxis that would allow theory to first occur on and in an individual, before they are able to do the work of actualizing the practice; and being human as praxis (McKittrick, 2015) as an entry into practice. The ideal of being human as praxis begs, what does it mean for one to *be* a theoretical approach, and then to be *involved* in a work of practice. These ideas, as part of the neoliberal enterprise, are incompatible and, on the surface, pull away from one another. Theory, which can be read as tools and logics that are rooted in rigorous methodological study, is restricted largely to the cognitive domain, which, as has been discussed, removes the body as a site of knowledge, but also as a site of sensemaking. With regard to the latter, the implications for exclusively thinking with theory do not allow for one *to be* involved in how theory is deployed. Stated differently, one regards theory as much as they are able to think with it toward a specified outcome. Living as the site of intervention can stage both disruption—avoid rescripting Western humanism—and potentialities that carve out new directions for Black living plumbed from the depths of our imagination in curricular and institutional practice.

∽

> August,
>
> We met with your teachers today. These meetings always make me anxious–I haven't figured out how to reconcile my distrust for white institutions and their inability to see you fully, to love you at all, and our desire for you to engage with others, make friends, and play with others. During this particular meeting, early in your time at the center, the teachers told us of your beautiful and kind spirit. I know these things to be true. You are wonder and care, bound in curiosity. The teacher talked about the various markers they have identified with regard to development–even at this age . . . especially at this age, there is language, and metrics, and milestones, and markers of normal or typical, how many words you should have, what you

should be doing, all held together by the loose decree that all children are different. Sigh. I am uneasy with the descriptions and markers because of how Blackness, how your Black being, is always figured outside of childhood, that is, the simplicity and innocence attached to childhood is racialized as white and, more precisely, not you. This is how I show up to parent-teacher conferences, now and into the future.

Toward the end of our meeting, the teacher shared some information that affirmed my hesitations. She told us that [white] children were pulling your hair. For context, you are a Black child. This is the language I used in our initial meetings with the center, and I will continue to do so. There are few Black children in the center, and I want to make clear that caring for you, fully, is not attending to you without recognition of the ways Blackness moves in the world. You are not just different, though I am clear, however unconvinced I may be, as to why early childhood centers will use that term, you are Black. So, as the only Black child in your class of mostly white, and other non-Black children, there are already ways that "pulling hair" will be/is to be addressed as "normal" childhood behavior, innocence. It is not. The teacher said that children have done this more than once, that they had been pulling at your hair for weeks. To be clear, not one of these three regular teachers in the room saw it as appropriate to share this information with us, your parents. Furthermore, by way of intervention, they told the children that they can't pull your hair, but they can pet, as in stroke your hair to satisfy their curiosity. The teacher told us that the children's actions made you upset, that you screamed when it happened. Even in this moment . . . I am having to pause . . . to collect myself . . . to breathe. I started to cry in that moment, but there was no time for tears. . . . The teacher was ready to move on . . . to end the meeting, content with the admonishment she gave to you to say "no." I refused her desire to move on, her expertise, her training, and her innocence.

"It is not okay that we are just learning about this behavior," I quipped, as I simmered just short of rebuke. I needed her to know that she, no teacher, has a right to make decisions about you without the permission and involvement of those who love you. I told her, again, that you were a Black child, refusing her appeal to racial innocence, and inability to name the racialized dynamics in the classroom. It is of "no benefit" for you to ignore this fact, I told her. She was embarrassed and quiet, and attempting to explain the situation as difference. I declared firmly, unmoved by her pleas and unaccountability, "Our son is not a petting zoo for other children's curiosities."

August, I knew the day was coming ... when I would have to explain the unexplainable. I have been preparing for it. The most important part of my day is the time I spend with you in the morning. I tell you that "your curls and locs are beautiful," that "no one has a right to your body," while you flip through pages of Black joy, affirmation, and regard. We look in the mirror together and smile and greet the morning. I want to you to remember how to access joy and regard, all the days of your life.

We reset the terms of engagement in that meeting, reminding her, and I am sure the entire building, that we are watching, and present, and will be involved. I cannot promise that white institutions will love you, August, I do not believe that to be sure. But in that absence, I will continue to push, to show up, to imagine the possible, for you and others like you.

9

"I can't be a pessimist"

Carcerality, Black Study, and Staging Black Futures

Figure 9.1. Throughout the United States, and especially along the coasts of Georgia and South Carolina, stories persist to this day of enslaved Africans who escaped bondage by taking flight and returning to their African homelands. Hypotheses persist as to the origin of this myth, but many point to the 1803 slave rebellion known as Igbo Landing on St. Simons Island in Georgia, where a group of enslaved Igbo people walked into a creek, drowning themselves rather than being reenslaved. As they entered the water, they chanted, "The Water Spirit brought us, the Water Spirit will take us home," and were thus transported to the primordial Blackness from which everything emerged. *Source*: *The Flying African* by Mikael Owunna. Used with permission of the artist.

> Having had to accept Amen: and learned to sing Hallelujah: some of us know that love is the key to life and that life is stronger than death. We know that because we have had to teach our children that.
>
> —James Baldwin, *The Hallelujah Chorus*

> I can't be a pessimist because I am alive. To be a pessimist means that you have agreed that human life is an academic matter. So, I am forced to be an optimist. I am forced to believe that we can survive, whatever we must survive.
>
> —James Baldwin, *A Conversation with James Baldwin*

How *The Flying African* Inspires This Chapter

The image has melodic resonance, composed in blues and jazz, and birthed elsewhere. To fly, one has to learn how to breathe differently, in low, in no air. Flying in space is to do so without air, the element most central to respiration. *The Flying African* compels me because of how it has made use, made living of rebellion as activity—not a rebellious act. The activity of rebellion is the animating rhythm that creates the frequencies that course through *The Flying African*. This final chapter opens with *The Flying African* as one meditation on staging, making room for Black futures.

∼

I am watching Kenneth Clark's interview with James Baldwin, and I am struck by his line of questioning: "what do you see as the future of the Negro and the future our nation?" Of the many questions that could be asked, "that's what [you] came up with?" I lamented. Reading the question, even now, I am led to wonder, "how do it [that question] free us?" to echo poet Sonia Sanchez. And, while I am not interested in a universal, essential us/we, Black specificity cannot be a false choice that leaves space but for one answer. The moment, the question was a strawman, all the more arresting because of what I knew the response *had* to be, as it has been proved time and again. The future of Black people, in a Western epistemological order, and US context, in particular, is foreseeable so long as those futures are in relationship to Western humanism. Those futures, as Baldwin would note, are "insoluble." He makes this assertion against the natural flow of the conversation. The interviewer was piecing together a question about the future of Black people and offering their analysis of the, perhaps, linked trajectory of the two distinguishable worlds. Hearing the question took Baldwin to another place, beyond the interview, not fully present alongside the interviewer, as the antagonism on Black liveliness that constructed Black sociality came rushing into his purview. With clarity and a sense of deep sorrow that folded his lips and tucked his eyes away, he shook his head and resolved, "they're insoluble" (00:23:02).

Like someone forced into a decision, Baldwin's utterance seems bitter, as if it didn't taste right as it rolled out of his mouth. One gets the sense that there was something else bubbling beneath his spoken response. The embodied, unarticulated response, however, was itself a curricular text, that gestures to what is often incalculable, when interpreted through the lens of Eurocentric discourse. In the esoteric nuance of movements, shifts in tone, pauses, and breaks, Baldwin orients readers/viewers to broad conceptual ideas and, simultaneously, the particularities of Black beingness. In looking and listening for what else is there, I make a categorical distinction between what the interviewer proposed as the future of Black people and the makings of Black futures as a type of futuring, undisciplined from the carceral imagination, which must understand the future of Black people as tethered to, and thus, contained by Western humanism. In line with Clark's question, the quintessential query that emerges with regard to Black people and higher education, is "what are the (higher) educational futures of Black people?" Here, educators and researchers are lodged in carceral logics, manifesting as the carceral imagination, which is a constituting technology that determines the futures and life chances of Black people.

Thus far I have theorized "how to be" over against the mundane terrors visiting Black liveliness and living. My concern has been with how Black people have and might regard the self, even as they "inhabit, are inhabited by, and refuse" those terrors (Sharpe, 2016, p. 116). Self-defining praxis engenders practices for loving Black flesh against the shifting terrains of anti-Black regard. This concluding chapter, in the tense of Black futures, imagines the potentialities of Blackness with and beyond the tools provided. To engage in this type of labor is, as I have written elsewhere, to trouble the notion of Black educational futures as, first, relevant to Black people, and, second, achievable in the Western order of knowledge, which raises the central question of this chapter. Following Zakiyyah Iman Jackson, who thinks with Aimé Césaire, in *Discourse on Colonialism*, I move to consider, broadly, "how might we resignify and revalue humanity such that it breaks with the imperialist ontology and metaphysical essentialism of Enlightenment man?" (p. 670). My claim here is that within Western order, there is no conceptual frame for imagining, affirming, or attaining the ontological substance of Black futures. Such a reckoning fundamentally shifts the question from "what are the (higher) educational futures of Black people?" to one of praxis that asks, "what is the sound, look, feeling, and work of Black Study?"

I have tried to be clear that I am not interested in rescuing Black people to or for the category of the Western human; rather, I want to sketch the possibilities of a soluble, stand on and in its own, Black future. To accomplish this, I conduct a close visual reading of Baldwin's interview with Kenneth Clark, particularly the sequence of thoughts outlined in the epigraph. Upfront, the challenge of attempting to articulate Black futures mimics a familiar critique of student/early-adult development in that it is not site or outcome specific. Black futures are not subject(ed) to enclosed spaces that can be found in any classroom, institution, or outcome. One will not find Black futures in a curricular text or a set of readings. I use the epistemological field as a way to direct readers away from colonial attempts at capture and procedure, models of being that might attempt to cohere Blackness (or complicate Blackness) by naming the varied identity expressions therein. In this way, I am signaling for Black futures as elusive, fluctuating, undisciplined, and unable to be retained by the logics of anti-Blackness. Consistent with self-defining praxis, conceptually, Black futures is not after resolution so much as it is after a way of being in the world. Different from self-defining praxis, it is not a result of, or response to, the problem of anti-Black regard per se. I understand Black futures as an existential orientation that can be materialized, experienced—in texts, classrooms, and interactions—in ways that inspire otherwise liveliness and living.

I begin with an interview analysis, particularly, on the ways anti-Blackness troubles and necessitates social structure (see chapter 2) readings of Black expression. Put another way, any recognizable citizenship for the one who is Black is ascertained through the language of unity. In that analysis I am interested in what the United States social imaginary needs from Black people, and in that need, rids Black people of liveliness on their own terms. From there, I move toward a governance reading of the same interview, guided by the already Black futures question, who are Black people to each other? in order to discuss the conditions for Black futures making.

Reconciling Undeveloped Citizenship

Meditations, and in an educative sense, research and praxis that attempts to trace the experiences of Black people, have their use. One can also say that Black folks are studied often enough, an outcome of the social science research program that emerged postemancipation. In no uncertain terms, the entire premise of research investigations on the Negro question was that the Black was unfit for citizenship (read: underdeveloped). It's a premise that has reinvented itself over time. Some of those strategies are noted in previous chapters—Freedmen's Bureau, the Negro question, integration policies, the Western Man as the comparison group in research studies, the achievement gap, and so on. Resolving racism has long been considered a problem of proximity, a solution mitigated by interracial interactions and policies like *Brown v. Board of Education*, and the wave of progressive liberalism that would follow the ruling. The interviewer, Dr. Kenneth Clark, most widely known for "the doll test," the 1947 study that examined the racial preferences of Black children in an interracial setting, was an integrationist. The doll test, which would serve as evidence in the 1954 *Brown v. Board of Education* proceedings, concluded that Black children preferred white dolls over Black dolls. While an analysis of that study is beyond the scope of this project, I begin there as a way to interpret Clark's line of questioning as invested in an integrationist referendum. The title of the series under which the interview took place was called, "The Negro and the American Promise." This framing argues for a political orientation that centers Blackness in a United States context as a problem to be resolved, namely, by closing the distance between Blackness (and Black people) and the American ideal. The series would include preeminent Black speakers, all interviewed by Clark on the premise that they would contribute to larger discourse on the Negro question. The interview, recorded on May 24, 1963, is televised publicly. One lens for interpreting the interview and its public display is through the social structure.

The social structure, as discussed in chapter 2, engages the Negro question insofar as that thought aligns with or contributes to public discourse. Fittingly, this conversation on race relations organizes a narrative about Black humanity that fits with what's possible in the social structures—the Negro future insoluble to, and with, the future of the United States. Thinking about the interview as a curriculum, Wynter noted, the "system-conserving mainstream perspectives of each order (or well-established scholarship) therefore clash with the challenges made from the perspectives of alterity. . . . For, it is the task of established scholarship to rigorously maintain those prescriptions, which are critical to the order's existence" (Wynter 1992, p. 27). Dr. Clark's question to Baldwin, thus, is not particularly original, as Dr. Clark is simply conveying what the social structure has engineered as the most sensible path to progress. He leads Baldwin toward the response that the United States social imaginary has set in place: "I think the future of the Negro and the future of the nation are linked" (00:22:37). As such, to listen to his question, on the other end of Baldwin's commentary about the Negro and the nations insolubility, seems logical. Clark asked, "Are you essentially optimistic or pessimistic?" (00:22:48). The question is weighty, and while seemingly open for reflexive insight, it evinces the ethic of the social structure, which seemingly compiles Black thoughts without ever having to grapple with Black desire. Clark is not asking how Baldwin feels, or what he feels or where he feels it in his body—to make room for Black desire, catharsis, under the close watch of a national audience and production company that are holding on to every word during an increasingly explosive sociopolitical moment would be inconsistent social structure protocol. No, the safer and more predictable route is to explicate what the Negro thinks, and on these terms, what the Negro *must* think about their condition.

A social structure reading of the interview suggests that Clark understands the predicament, the conditions he has created, and the stage he has set for Baldwin. Clark knew Baldwin, if not personally well, he named how versed he was with Baldwin's writings. Baldwin in many ways is the archetypical bridge builder for the United States social structure as he incisively critiques Western humanism, and he simultaneously invokes love, imploring Black people to love that which will not love them. Baldwin, more than many others, reckons with intersubjective relationality, the question of citizenship, by calling society to a higher version of itself. Baldwin was inclined, in general, to reckon with the terror of Black being through the language of community and belonging (see Baldwin, 1963) that exceeded the mythical dimensions of the Western Man and invented distinctions of race. In this interview, then, the predictable response is offered, ushered in by the claim: "I can't be a pessimist, because I'm alive. To be a pessimist means that you have agreed that human life is an academic matter." This characterization objects to pessimism on the matter of Black being, perceiving such a position as an illogical conclusion on the premise of pulse and breath. Being (alive), here, is apprehended simply on biological terms, making it accessible for viewing audiences.

What's more, in the social structure, there is one humanity that is incorrigibly affirmed, and one version of human aspiration that is reified over and over again. For the social structure to survive, alternative versions of the human cannot be entertained; instead, the developmental aspiration is reflected in reconciling Black people into the "American dream." Put another way, "the problem is Blackness is and as underdevelopment" (Sharpe, 2016, p. 34). Baldwin functions as an intermediary of sorts on this latter point. His distinction qualifies him, with or against his will, as one who might advocate for Black possibility. His body, draped in love and "amens" is opportune. He is seemingly called on to confirm the promise of the United States and the value of a national identity as an American. What follows his claim is an interpellation to an unearned belief in what can be. Railing against the "tendency to see the worst aspect of things or believe that the worst will happen, a lack of hope or confidence in the future[1]," Baldwin commits himself to optimism, an orientation toward the future that is steeped in hope and confidence. The ideals of hope and confidence, again, are tied to the futures of Black people in the United States, a message to viewers who might, more broadly, implore, and maintain *hope in the American ideal*. Given the reckoning unfolding, then and now, Baldwin surmised that the collective we could survive, thereby casting pessimism and optimism as separate and incompatible orientations, and, establishing those who are for progress and those who are against it. Furthermore, the particular directive, as carried out by the social structure, takes the future of Black people away from them, and, in a sense, places ideations of the future in the lap of white folks. Baldwin (as cited in Standley & Pratt, 1989) continued, "But . . . the Negro in this country . . . the future of the Negro in this country is precisely as bright or as dark as the future of the country. It is entirely up to the American people and our representatives. . . . It is entirely up to the American people, whether or not they're going to face and deal with and embrace this stranger whom they maligned so long" (p. 49). While the bounded nature of Clark's quandary is clear, I want to move away from the more subtle seduction—the trap of singularly, and uncritically regarding Blackness. Clark's questioning stages one form of this uncritical praxis in that, first, the question is not about Black people, so much as it is about a white polity, and negotiations about who they will or will not allow. The question presumes that the nation-state is grounded in anti-Blackness, but in doing so, it appeals to Western humanism—an uncritical form of relationality—as the antidote for resolving the racialized pressure valve. Concomitantly, the carceral logic is reinforced in the invitation for Baldwin to choose one epistemological grounding for his catharsis, optimism, or pessimism. The underlying sentiment of choice reveals a general tendency to monitor the language and embodied vibrations of Blackness, which furthered the need for Clark's emphasis on optimism—an optimism that conflates citizenship, development, with the Western Man-as-human. Blackness, as on onto-epistemological field is capacious—a rendering that does not neatly fold into one particular orientation. Glissant called this conceptual break "rooted errantry," a poetics of relation (1990).

What I am trying to do is to suspend the appropriation of Blackness for scientific use, the study of it as an object of analysis (read: examinations of anti-Blackness), instead of presence, a field, mode of being, of relational capacities, flight. It is as important to understand what *Blackness motions against* as what it *is for*, something the social structure and its configurations are not constructed to hold. Whereas the social structure, which prioritizes the Western Man, demands enclosure, the governance structure proposes a heterogenous, choreo-sonic, abolitionist ethic that motions for Black specificity, unmoored from its conditional existence to Western humanism. For Baldwin, while he did maintain a devotion to the language of national reckoning, to understand him singularly on these "optimistic terms" would be to circumvent the ways he was attuned and in attendance with the specificity of Black being.

Reading Governance

Keying into the governance formation, as it was with the social structure, is to draw on the work of Carr (2020). The governance structure, again, is a rigorous attempt to tune into Black specificity (Wynter, 1989), to listen, as it were, for the *what else*, otherwise, what I want to elaborate on as *poesis*. To explain the inhabitance of governance, one can consider the choreo-sonic realm and the ranges of sounds that define, in general, the United States soundscape, and the idea that not all sounds belong. Noise, or the production of noise, lacks cooperation with the harmony of a soundscape. Noisy is disruption, antagonistic, a rupture to tranquility and conformity. Noise, as the enunciation of excess, a rupture in what could otherwise be understood as the solace of time and space, denotes that which is out of place. One might read noise as something that needs to be lessened, quieted, in order to establish, or reestablish, the central, socially agreed about arrangement of sounds. Noise is the excess, and, insofar as the Western Man is concerned, that which exceeds is a disruption to the coherence of society. Blackness, in this way, is quintessentially noisy; it refuses consensus in a Western order of knowledge. Blackness as noise, as excess, is an assault on the desire for harmony as linked to normative ideals, and by way of being ungoverned, is a fearful proposition that must be contained by Western humanistic logics (read: the carceral imagination). Blackness, or the sounds of Blackness[2] that reference the "deregulated, unregulated, reckless, unending, always anticipatory expansiveness, an excessive hum or buzz that resists repression," disrupt the harmony of quietude, the rest, and peacefulness of social order (Crawley, 2017, p. 244). There are, however, soundscape traditions that depend on what would be conceived as excess, or noise. Black people lived into this excess through "calls, cries, and hollers; call and response devices; addictive rhythms and polyrhythms; heterophony, pendular thirds, blue notes, bent notes and elisions; hums, moans, grunts, vocables, and other rhythmic-oral declamations, interjections, and punctuations; off-beat melodic phrasing and parallel intervals and chords; constant repetition of rhythmic and melodic figures and phrases" (Floyd, 1996, p. 6). I am less interested in the delineation that is the social imaginary that requires coherent sound and the "noise"-making traditions of Black being. I illustrate the distinction to say that beyond its break with Western thought traditions, excess, noise, Blackness is a definitive soundscape that stands on its own. Black music, as one example, is not for Western consumption, seeking to be read or interpreted, or legible by Western humanistic logics and methods (McKittrick, 2016, 2020; Wynter, n.d.). Governance, thus, sets the conditions of possibility for attendance—being present, in full participation, care. In this realm, the question of humanity is not argued for, or a problem of thought as aptly noted by Chandler (2013). Black being is assumed, and bringing Black liveliness and living into sharp relief is the matter of concern. What is needed then is a method for doing governance, institutional logics notwithstanding. I am motioning for retinal attachments (Okello & Duran, 2021) that take up Blackness as an optic that directs how one sees, understands, and accounts for oneself in the world (Sharpe, 2016).

Blackness as an optic that brings Black liveliness and living into view, causing it to be visible, noticeable, is the type of worldmaking capacity central to Black cultural production and Black theories of being like that which Sharpe (2016) puts forth as Black annotations and redactions. Notably, the potential of otherwise modes of being does not betray a commitment to reality. Instead, the modes of being are brought to bear "from the problems or plane of thinking in which we find ourselves . . . [and] . . . also reconfigure or reorient the plane precisely by being prompted by a problem" (Colebrook, 2017, p. 654). If only briefly, Blackness, as attendance, as care, confronts the failure of the carceral imagination to behold the fullness of Black being, and here, Black futures, with a sharper line of questioning. One way of shifting the gaze (Callier & Hill, 2019), where the gaze considers how bodies are in relation to one another and spaces, is through the performance of Black Study, which asks what *else* are Black people saying? Poesis, in this way, is the methodological activity of bringing something into view that was not there before.

Black Study

Working toward a *what else* line of questioning is to begin with the notion of Black Study. Black Study indexes a critical practice of sociality that is operationalized as an epistemological emphasis on Blackness. Fundamentally, the practice does not claim neutrality, or objectivity; it is not beholden to dispassionate pedagogies, nor does it maintain deference to impartiality. To allow for impartiality is to foster the partiality of the Western Man. Returning to sound and the vibrational excess that is Blackness in the social imaginary, where silence is regulatory and privileges limit in terms of thought and being, Black Study is attuned to, expects, and listens for the noise. The acclimatization is an embodied work, a leaning in, a shifting of one's gaze motivated by love like that of June Jordan, who inclined readers to look again. Callier and Hill (2019), as beneficiaries of Jordan's unrequited love, call attention to Jordan's directive: "I am black alive and looking back at you" (Jordan, 1969, p. 31), noting that "to be Black, alive, and looking back is to be known to yourself and to others" (Callier & Hill, 2019, p. 96). This reflection on Jordan is in reference to her book-length poem, *Who Look at Me*, a text grounded in the imperative of the Black Arts movement that was invested in art that articulated the depth, density, and texture of Black liveliness and living. Jordan outlined the shape of a Black world, demonstrating its possibilities to hold the complexity of Blackness and Black folks. Where it relates to Black Study, one should understand it as an epistemic and methodological innovation, again, part of a larger movement discourse that was engaged in unorthodox and aesthetically diverse modes of craft and representation, that took as its foundation and lens, Blackness as knowing, being, and doing. Care, as modeled by Jordan's decision to see otherwise, is to understand Black Study as an embodied and performative orientation that allows for the excess range of Black being.

Black Study as performance is a dynamic, marooning disposition toward the necessity of alternative ways of being in the world, and the higher-education context, in particular. Regarding the latter, the formal education context is sutured indelibly, to a set of ethics that prioritizes the neoliberal normative university/education context, and, as such, is not structured to critically regard Blackness beyond that of object (see chapter 7). The university, in this regard, is cramped space, the hold, the garret (Okello, 2024) an expression of carceral logics, the afterlife of slavery that attempts to constrain Black being. I use the language of "attempt" purposefully to indicate the ways Black folks, under surveillance, confined materially, have, and continue to devise Black worlds, still (Coles, 2024). As I have written elsewhere (see Okello, 2024), Harriet Jacobs's Black presence in the anti-Black social sphere marked her as a perpetual object available to violence. Her suspension to the garret space, however, simultaneously occasioned joy. Such a conceptualization is hard to fathom as understood through the frames of Western humanism. Confinement, be it externally imposed or internal resignation, figures as a state of punishment, an imprisonment that should object to joy. When read through a governance register, which necessitates multiple and layered renderings of Black living, Black joy emerges. Jacobs produced and aestheticized Black joy while in the crawlspace. There, I proposed that Black joy, thus, compels a set of questions attuned to the senses as it is unbounded by linear reasoning. Black Study, as a set of questions that enlivens the enunciations of poesis concerning Jacobs, might ask, what is the sound, look, and feel of Black liveliness and living? What is the body doing? What does it want to do? And, after those renderings are distilled, Black Study returns again, to generate and produce other possibilities, to conjure other worlds, to affirm the *what else*—poesis.

Baldwin's Both, And

If we work with the tools of Black annotation and redactions, we might put Baldwin's (1989) interview response in sharp relief. Through the aforementioned Black performative reading practice concerned with poesis,

240 | On Blackness, Liveliness, and What It Means to Be Human

one is able to locate Baldwin's interior excess, away from the representational logics that initiated his response. One might find, in the excess of the consigned choice, pessimism or optimism, another arrangement that complicates and reimagines both as useful in the service of honoring the density, depth, and texture of Black living. A governance reading troubles the frame of university impulses to collect Black responses (read: data points), to want to know the experiences of Black folks; it might evacuate Baldwin, as a stand-in for the study of Black things, from the realm of the object. Reading this interview aloud, listening, and watching the interview meets the social structures' epistemological failure and inability to accede to Black living with an inclination for listening, seeing, feeling, and beholding.

> I'm alive.
> human life is
>
> Negro
> bright dark future
>
> I'm
> here
> future
> of

If we look, listen, and feel for it, one might recognize how so much of Black living is redacted, made to disappear. The carceral imagination disciplines Black thought to meet the demands of the social structure. A preference for governance, rescues, however temporary, expression from the limited range of anti-Black options extended to Black living. Where the dysgraphia of the wake, to borrow Sharpe's (2016) language, is disorienting, governance is an invitation toward honoring the texture, sensibilities, and desires of Black flesh.

Redactions, as exercised above, allows desire to emerge in all of its complexity. Notice first how Black redaction militates against the ethnographic will to know, effectively deploying opacity as a way to say that "reader, you do not need to know everything, nor do I believe you to have the capacity to understand everything that I write or say" (see Introduction). Redactions are a way to keep some matters, articulations, and longings. It is the performance of refusal—being purposefully unresponsive to calls for clarity and explanation. Redactions hold intimate knowledge as uneasily translatable, and names, without saying as much, the ease with which expressions can be appropriated. When instituted for and about Black liveliness and living, Blackness becomes the grounds by which critical formations might surface. Moreover, Blackness is not the backdrop; instead, it is the prism that shifts our attention, increasing the ability to read for specificity, a practice of taking what is necessary. The first words readers are met with in this new order, this focus on Blackness, is a claim to life. Encased in Black (redaction), it is possible to live. If we take redaction as both the absence and presence of language, we might reread the opening as "Black alive," followed by a sense to the capaciousness of Blackness that reads "Black human life is." I read "is" as a state of being that is open and enduring. This sense of possibility counters the thrust of choice and ultimatum that frames discussions filtered through the carceral imagination.

In the governance formation, one is predisposed to trained vocabularies in the service of Black living. Whereas, for example, Negro is conceptualized as absence, vacuous, and pathological, beholding the term through the governance formation displaces the fictional accounts with terminology historically intended for whiteness—*bright*. Blackness as bright, again, is not an argument against the force of Western humanism, per se. In the governance formation, a Black world, Blackness is. Black, then, is already luminous, or that which brilliantly reflects light; it is vivid, dazzling, intensely radiant, and fleshly fluorescent (see Michael Owunna, *Infinite Essence*). I understand the vibrance of Blackness here, as too, auspicious, astute, and intuitive, perceptive, and proficient, gifted, and full of genius—bright. See also how dark precedes, opens into the "future," where, following Wynter (1970), "history has been rigorously concerned with maintaining futures predicated on the European, Western Man," through the performance of Black Study "we see, in glimpses, evidence of a powerful and pervasive cultural process which has largely determined the unconscious springs of our being" (Wynter 1970, p. 35). Blackness can be the terms by which we construct futures, a place of alterity that "offers us the possibility of thinking differently about what is at stake in refashioning what it means to be human" (Walcott, 2009, p. 57). Blackness, thus, is a futuring discourse that can envisage being human as praxis (McKittrick, 2015).

Shifting from an analysis of the transcript to the video Baldwin's response, Black Study as a governance formation, disrupts the legibility of foregone conclusions that are articulated in the discourse of question-and-answer exchange. Poesis, or listening, seeing what else enables one to engage Baldwin's embodied response. There, in that alternative register, one can see that Baldwin is grieved by the question. His eyebrows scrunch, he pauses, while peering into an abyss, as if hoping for a different reality to stare back at him. He is unsettled by the question, and, resisting the confrontation that awaits him, and Black people more broadly, he refuses the interviewer's gaze. The moment of noticeable despair should be seen as a sharp criticism of Western humanism, and more specifically, how that configuration of Man maintains its shape and organizes society. The body is communicative, and, as Wynter (1992) noted, "any attempt to dismantle those social hierarchies, must dismantle the acts of communication that motivate and demotivate specific behaviors" (p. 22). Listening for the Black livingness of Baldwin, I am focused on what his body wants to do as I notice the muscular tension that tightens his shoulders, raises his jaw, and lowers his head. Baldwin is reticent as he releases words that address Clark's question. Reticence, in a Black Study register, is part of a larger history of strategies for being, deployed by Black people, as they negotiate various terrains.

Herein, Baldwin is demonstrating one of the myriad ways of subverting the carceral imagination's regulation of Black futures. Reticence is not silence, or unfettered optimism, it is a complex rendering of Black affective capacities, that allows one to devise when and how to move toward the future. When attending to the affective frequencies, the facial reactions, the body's shifts and movements, viewers witness a sense of unboundedness occurring, the refusal to stay in one's proper place; refusal: "a rejection of the status quo as livable and the creation of possibility in the face of negation, that is, a refusal to recognize a system that renders you fundamentally illegible and unintelligible" (Campt, 2019, para. 17). Baldwin rejects the terms of enclosure that are admonished, called into place by the line of questioning. Whereas Clark's question prompts a denial of Black subjecthood and an appeal to normative conduct, Baldwin's emotionality negates the bounded aspiration of the social structure logic by enlivening the body as "a generative and creative source of disorderly power to embrace the possibility of living otherwise" (Campt, 2019, para. 17). I am drawn to the unruliness of Baldwin's body, which complicates the verbalized utterances that would have him to intellectualize, and in many ways, stalls the range of Black subjectivities that should accompany questions of being.

Looking beyond what we hear from Baldwin and attuning to what we might see on an affective register is to consider the subtle and imperceptible as enactments of Black livingness. There is, of course, a delineation made that chooses "optimism," but one observes a rush of emotion in what follows that represents, brings into felt reach, the desire for an elsewhere. If breathing, the double gesture of inhalation and exhale, is best understood as evidence of biological existence, then there is nothing to be made of Baldwin's deep inhale and exhale between the ending of his comment on survival (00:26:39) and before his next statement (00:26:42). But the performance of breathing, the show of Baldwin's breath here—audible and explicit—is a creative production of refusal; it is insurrection while inhabited by surroundings, and willingness to be unmoored from the decency of protocols.

There is general agreement that physiology and emotionality are in direct relationship, such that "what the flesh does and motive disposition are not easily disentangled" (Crawley, 2017, p. 47), or they are irreducible and productively fused. Black breathing, or breathing for Black folks, thus, is itself intellectual practice that refuses separation of the mind, body, emotion split that Western humanism prefers. And Black Study is a resource from which to resist the force of enclosure. It is in the pause, the break, that witnesses might bear the possibility of living. Black Study is concerned with openness, and Baldwin, through what I read as the intentional interruption of speech and "eruption of air, of breath and breathing" (Crawley, 2017, p. 43), creates such an opening, that allows for something else to gather, to collect, that might fill the space. Baldwin is animating a desire for breath, breathing deeply and more fully, in excess of the anxieties of the Western Man that desire silence and enclosure. Conceptually, Black

Study allows us to consider the fugitive nature of breath as producing a critical distance between what is espoused and what is felt, and, as such, to appreciate the range of subversive tactics that maintain Black livingness.

Taken together Baldwin's performance of breathing is an enactment toward Black futures that forcefully interrupts the anti-Black foundations of Western humanism. Black Study as a mode of attending to poesis, a practice of refusal, is attuning to otherwise being that refuses the need to affix Black people to futures within the frame of Western humanism. In what follows, I consider how self-defining praxis can be generative for attuning to, materializing, and sustaining Black Study. Taking up praxis as a possibility will demand a different set of ethics (see chapter 7). Crawley (2020) is an instructive on this point: "When we want to imagine otherwise possibilities—otherwise worlds—we must abolish the very conceptual frame that produces categorical distinction and makes them desirable" (pp. 28–29).

Staging Black Futures through Self-Defining Praxis

The carceral imagination plays out in myriad ways in higher-education contexts, the notion of human development is but one conceptual site for this logic. Wynter (1992) made clear how the Western Man-as-human structures curriculum, and, as noted in chapter 2, the notion of Man is foundational to student/early-adult development theorizing. The challenge for educators, thus, is a confrontation with canonicity, and the inability to release the self from Western orders of knowledge that structure life and living, an inability to imagine otherwise. Imagination involves habits and practices that require one "to pause, to doubt, to question, to wonder out loud about the assumptions, the conditions, the terms, the conventions, the values in relation to which, at any given moment, we pursue the projects we pursue" (Scott, 2002, p. 74). It is there, in the interstices of pause and doubt and question, that one is able to access the imagination in its more sovereign sense. Importantly, "the sovereignty of the imagination has neither to do with the sequestering of creativity from, nor its absorption by the world of affairs . . . by, the world of affairs. . . . [It] has to do with the active will to refuse submission" (pp. 74–75). One should read "submission" as the surrender, indoctrination, consent to the principles that require fidelity to anti-Black logics of being. Under and in this unimaginative space, one is guided into unloving practices that unsee the self beyond the templates for hope and aspiration that direct citizenship and community. This adoption of limitations goes by different names (for example, miseducation), but, at heart, conspire on and around coloniality (Okello, 2020). Whereas, decolonizing the mind (Wa Thiong'o, 1986) is well documented as fundamental to revolutionary projects (see Kelley, 2002; Trouillot, 1995), I understand the work of decolonizing as an embodied project that must attend to the ontological—visualizing, hearing, feeling, sensing. This is to say, beyond the practice of stripping down and through the layers of meaning that have been attached to Black existence, self-defining praxis emerges toward the what else.

Therefore, returning to the central question for this chapter—what are the tools for bringing *Black futures* into view?—I propose self-defining praxis as practices of pause, intimacy, pursuit, and commitment, as a set of tools invested in Black futures. Self-defining praxis is a claim to life's documentation, depth, density, and refusal, that are concerned with ethical and aesthetic formations of Black liveliness and living. Here, self-defining praxis, as "breathing, in everyday Black life, is a spectacular event" (Cox & Jean-François, 2022, p. 99), that allows educators and researchers serious about the matter of Black living to account for the porousness of Blackness and encourages futurity wherein new, revised, and multiple genres of human (distinct from the singularity of the Western Man-as-human) can surface. Herein, self-defining praxis—invention/inventiveness, intimating, presence, and revision—open, as both a being practice, "how to be," and coordinates for listening, relating to, discerning, and calling forth.

In what follows, I turn back to Owunna's art, in particular, *The Flying African* (image that opens this chapter), as an optic for staging Black futures. If curriculum in higher-education contexts is meticulously beholden to assumptions of the Western human, and expectations about how citizens are to pursue a certain type of future, then Wynter's onto-epistemological push is to shift and break open the rubric for study, or that which can constitute learning. On these terms, I make the case for beginning in, and with Blackness, as the site of Black Study, and portal to rewriting/recurricularizing (Baszile, 2019). The question that animates the next section thus becomes: How does self-defining praxis attend to Black Study?

INVENTION/INVENTIVENESS

Blackness fills the space between, as that which was and will continue. Flight is activity, as it simultaneously remarks on carceral dimensions. Activity should not be confused with aimless floating. When viewing *The Flying African*, one gets the sense that they are on their way somewhere, away from something and toward. Blackness, for *The Flying African*, is mutable and motile, a way of seeing into the past and the myriad ways the Black was a distinguishing signifier. Blackness, in the image, is compositional, constructed with various grammars that allude to the circulation that is expansion and contraction, moments of breath and attempts at the theft and regulation of breath. Blackness is of hieroglyphics. Reading hieroglyphics is one method for mapping anti-Blackness overtime, and the force by which it repeats. Black flesh is a charting of histories, and every motion is a refusal, something that was not intended to be. There is Black liveliness in the work of invention/inventiveness, though the labor of remembering and looking again is often tethered to uncritical repetitions of anti-Black violence, whereas the scenes of subjection become the sum total of Black living. This logic can be framed by the image, whereas Blackness could be seen as absence, or even the thing that haunts life. Black surrounds and is all encompassing. In the carceral imaginary, it is anti-Black logic that leads and overwhelms. The potential of invention/inventiveness as an analytic of disentanglement intervenes on those logics toward a rethinking of the scenes that exceeds linearity and ideologies of containment. Invention/inventiveness, in this frame, should be understood as an optic that brings life into view. It is the search for traces, however imperceptible or molecular. At the edges of the image, there is a smattering that is taking place, a gathering. I suspect that there might be a tendency to glaze over the infinitesimal, in its ephemerality, as insignificant.

The beauty and breadth of Black living, here, is all the more apparent by situating it in the governance of Blackness. Or, where carceral dimensions attempt to produce static, inflexible depictions of Black living as biocentric, "hidden beneath the surface of that violence, though very much present in the world, are orchestrations for breath that allow us to endure" (Cox & Jean-François, 2022, p. 102). The smattering could otherwise be the musicality of aspiration working its way into ensemble. Droplets, seemingly falling away, receding from the recognizable, are transformed into claims of existence that dispel fullness as completion. As a method of listening, invention/inventiveness interprets the smattering as essential moments of vibration, of echolocation, of pulsating rhythms that allow one to identify where they are, now, and now, and now (Gumbs, 2020). It is the refusal to move too quickly, believing that there is something here. Invention/inventiveness is not separated from its histories as that of an ethnographic observer; it is an active dwelling, gathering, and communion of tones, sighs, whispers, and that which is unspoken. It is placing our ears close to the rising and falling chest, believing that life, respiration, is present and must be accounted for.

Intimate and Intimating

Blackness, in a Western sense, is impure, and, as such, purity—of thought and being—is established in relation to its distance and detachment from Blackness. Black people, as the material embodiment of Blackness in the carceral imagination, are things to be avoided, objects of aversion. Aversion is a turning away, withdrawal, and decision to estrange oneself, a matter of distinction by distance. Where aversion is enacted, "such objects that produce aversion cannot produce the sensation of beauty" (Crawley, 2017, p. 112). We might conclude that beauty, then, is the territory of proximity, of closeness, of choosing to see and be with. The image, seemingly, takes the notion of aversion to task. While the gaze of *The Flying African* is affixed elsewhere, there is simultaneous intention on transparency, allowing the self to be seen in ways that expand notions of sociality. Affixed is not the same as avert, and *The Flying Africans*' looking away is not a refusal to see, feel, or experience. Instead, I read looking elsewhere as an indictment of voyeurism, and the conditions of capture attached, that make objects of study of Black "life." Blackness here is opaque, content to live, and refusing to submit oneself to that which will not handle it with care. Looking elsewhere is contemplative and social, as it refuses to be closed off under the guises of being seen, looking directly. In its sociality, there is gentleness to the image, like that of care—full holding, an embrace that says, "Let go, I've got you." Blackness feels like the tenderness of being, and being afforded the space to be. The image feels like unregulated play and refusal to comport oneself to be legible for particular audiences. This is what trust feels like, to be held, cared for, and not just an object, an artifact. In this Black world, I hear the artist saying, "I see you, Black and whole and deep." Africans in flight, in the space of governance, are not heresy, or even profound. Africans in flight as intimation are not interested in the limitations of form, or custom, or curriculum, whereas the latter is already organized by enclosure.

Intimating gestures toward Black Study, where the body is presented as instrument and instrumentation, as that which is shaped by and also gives meaning to the conditions of being. Holding in the carceral imaginary, operates as a mode of detainment and capture. Black intimating, here, should be read as a method of escape, unshackling the self from the grip of developmental discourse. Intimating is a form of inhabitance, the score that assumes and makes room for desire, "for meaning, for togetherness, for being a constantly reproduced entanglement" (Cox & Jean-François, 2022, p. 105), a foray into wayward, experimental forms of being. The figure is an intimate portrayal, illustrating the musicality of percussive desire, fugitive motions cascading and colliding. Black folks have desires if we would notice them. Black Study is borne of desire and, as the image reflects, is the clearing for desire's unmappable expression. Owunna's work is a call to mutuality and relationality, where one is uncovered and willing to lay the self bare, commingled with the expectation of being graciously held. Openness and holding are invitations, the work of specificity, and the bridge to loving practices.

Presence

The Flying African alters; aesthetically it produces a formation for being that unseats the Western Man as the symbolic aspiration. The piece performs this alteration by imbuing the frame with Black matters. There is the matter of materials (for example, colors, paint, canvas, lighting), and there is the matter of living, or Black matter (for example, sights, sounds, feelings, smells, sensations). Black aesthetic and cultural production intervenes on the carceral dimensions' failure of imagination by striving to produce differential, otherwise ways of being by manipulating not just the essence of matter itself; it proposes an alternative way for something/someone to matter. It shifts what matters. Matter in the compositional[3] hands and mind of Owunna, is a way of presenting Black liveness in excess of what it is "supposed to do." Insofar as materials are taken up and used in ways that disrupt the normative intent, they might become tools for presence. The image of *The Flying African* is an affirmation of the expanse of Blackness, but, more importantly, it reflects how Black matters, or how one imagines Blackness and to whom. In the hands of white institutions, social scientists, reformers, and data regimes, Black matter, the affective and somatic dimensions that define personhood, are reformulated as data, and thereby evidenced and isolated as novel data sources. Not unlike the "data revolution" that took place at the turn of the twentieth century, Black living is converted into "statistical integers, mere data," in the name of addressing Western humanism's fundamental assumption of the Negro (as) Problem (Womack, 2021, p. 2). Viewing *The Flying African* is to read against the grain of anti-Black regard and need, albeit important, to locate Black suffering exclusively. The image is an endeavor that refuses the ordinances of light, color, and flash that have been harnessed as technologies for the surveillance and study Black people. These materials, in the hands of Owunna, destabilize ordering tactics that would call for a specific use of materials. Black *matters*, is of consequence in a manner undisciplined from the representational imperatives of social science research. Accounting for the still elusive nature of Black living, Owunna is astutely undescriptive in the translation of Black living. *The Flying African*, as a project of presence, emerges as aesthetically dissonant and uncooperative against disciplining logic, systematic collection, and scientific categorization—it might be said that *The Flying African* is "unfit" to be enclosed to the strain and empiricism of data source. Black mattering, as a doing, as presence reconstitutes the conditions of possibility such that the materiality of Blackness reconfigures the conventional logic of Black presentation. The imaging trains us toward the vitality of Blackness, as capacious, fleshed with depth and exuberance. *The Flying African* allows us to locate these possibilities for Black Study as experiments in "how to be," in instantiations of Blackness that might loosen "the clasp that insists on reducing blackness to an object of knowledge, to data, to a racial calculus that always confirms black life's disposability" (Womack, 2021, p. 7). In doing so, presence affirms embodied variations within and beyond existing geographic formations as effected by necropolitical forces (for example, racialized surveillance) and imaginative capacities toward livable futures.

Revision

If breath had a shape, color, and sentience it would appear as *The Flying African*. A meditation on process and internal faculties and how they manifest, take shape, in the production of liveliness, the piece is an elaboration on creating and moving toward futures. It is customary to locate futuring (or one's investment in future achievements) as an external exercise, as in, a certain type of movement and thinking will generate a specific type of response that moves one closer to a desired future. Owunna's Flying African graciously affords access to the often-unspeakable components of Black folks' futures. While the logic of reasoning has a particular use, viewers bear witness to utterances layered beneath the surface, the internal strivings, spiritual longings, a world of activities and movement that circulate in the place of the bones, and muscles, and marrow. Liveliness, how to be, here, is interior. The sight of respiration, of air flowing across the body, is more than evidence of life against an anti-Black claim of non-human, no human involved. In this view, living isn't proven; Black flesh is the performative act of breathing that is enlivened by the repetitive force of inhaling galaxies and exhaling genealogies. For Owunna, the skeletal structure, the organizing frame that shapes the body—Blackness—is cosmic, and irreducibly vast, seamlessly meshing with and giving definition to the world outside of itself. Framings of Black being, or negations of it, tend to rely on renderings of Blackness as the inability to assimilate into social form, framings of citizens, justifying Black folks' nonfuture designations. Owunna blurs the lines between internal and external, where the flesh starts and where it supposedly ends, such that what emerges is sociality, breath entering and worlds forming in exhale. Revision, thus, as a method of Black Study, is occasioned by the repetition of being and becoming.

Thinking with Owunna, revision as a method for Black Study is a call to immersion and learning anew. Where Blackness colors in governance formations, anti-Black disregard is the imposition, rule, authorized curriculum. In this way, revision must be the labor of conceptually liberating the self from defined end points. Revision, like breathing, is in motion and at work in the production of living, in and beyond governance spaces. *The Flying African*, as a heuristic of Black Study, should be understood as an intergenerational practice of inheritance and becoming. In other words, *The Flying African*, in all the ways it speculates on otherwise possibilities and offers another grammar for being, did not evolve from nothing. The thought that such an idea was probable accounts for the range of Black histories, to affirm Blackness as ontological presence (intimating), and imagine and live into experiments of otherwise living. Revision is built with the longer genealogy of Black making and doing, of breathing Black liveliness of every day, of recognizing "lived subjection" and not only living in "subjection and as the subjected" (Sharpe, 2016, p. 4). Revision as Black Study cuts in where the music, so to speak, stops, and says, let us continue, there is more here. It is the refusal of the end of things—normative temporalities (that is, who counts as a normal, developed, human), constraining curriculum, linear progression in growth and development. Revision is the practice of annotating and augmenting, constituting study as an always unfinished praxis that enables us to cut across time and space.

Black Epistemological Territories: A Coda

The right to look is contested terrain (Mirzoeff, 2011). It is an authority, for Mirzoeff, that defines the "right to existence" (p. 477). Owunna's *Infinite Essence* series challenges the authority of visualizers, and their right to look upon Blackness in a way that confirms Campt's addendum to Mirzoeff's "right to look," with the *"the right to look away"* (Campt, 2018, para. 5). Against mundane acts of violence, and the proliferation of that violence, Owunna conditions possibility by refusing the very "authority of visuality that functions to refuse blackness itself" (para. 8). In doing so, Owunna asserts an awareness of, and refusal to be incorporated into authoritative registers of Western humanism that claim at once a right to unsee Blackness as legible to humanity, as well as the right to look away from Black suffering. *The Flying African* as a spatiotemporal optic is instructive in that it refuses to recognize the gaze of the current order of knowledge as deserving "or eligible" of the right to see, and thus know Black living. Here, I am interested in the ways *The Flying African* is leading us away from the entities that cannot love or affirm Black livable futures in educational spaces. Such leading away might direct us away from, "what are the futures of the Negro in America(n) educational institutions," and toward what ross discussed, as Black space in education. ross queried: "If we conceptualize the Black educational experience as existing within the afterlife of school segregation, where antiblackness precludes Black humanity and inherently positions Black children as uneducable. . . . If we acknowledge the egregiousness of anti-blackness, and the permanence of race demands a permanent move underground, underwater, (outer) space what then might Black space in education look like?" (Nxumalo & ross, 2019, p. 508). Black space, here, is conceptualized as a mode for attending to Black educational futures as those situated in and responding to the terror of anti-Blackness while also imagining futures (Nxumalo & ross, 2019). The articulation, here, is anchored in Afro-pessimism, which, for good purpose, is primarily accounting for the still-moving project of anti-Blackness. It rightly restates, and regards, the ever-present reminder that Blackness is unwelcome under the terms of Western humanism, and cannot *be* fully, or humanly, in the world. The Afro-pessimist project, as a whole, is consistent with what I proposed as two essential ways (see chapter 2) that Blackness can advance higher education in that, as a wider project, it is an urgency to document, analyze, and make known the centrality of anti-Blackness. Or, anti-Blackness is a problem of history. It demands an ethical practice that wants to be "free of air, while admitting to knowing no other source of breath" (Wilderson, 2010, p. 338); it is staying in the hold despite fantasies of flight. The necessity of this analysis will always be of import, and organizing spaces situated in, and extending, this specificity exact a political morality.

If we can agree that anti-Blackness, in all of its permanence, cannot support Black humanity, conceptualizing Black space in educational contexts must attend to the second advancement, onto-epistemology. Anti-Blackness as a problem of history is indicative of an ethical grounding that directs how one is oriented to Black ontological possibility. With unflinching regard for logics of containment, it understands that Blackness remains outside of the terms of normal/acceptable, even as it is brought into formal places, and even when it is invited into educational discourse. My detour, slight as it may be, concerns the epistemological affections conveyed by, and in the framing of Black educational spaces and Black proper subjects. In order to intervene on anti-Blackness, inevitably, one must remain in the hold such that a deeper reading of the Western Man-as-human might become more visible. Training and pedagogy that occur in this epistemological register, however informed by Black learning principles (Woodson, 1933) these practices may involve, are already occurring in the Western order of knowledge, and, thus, toward expedient versions of humanity. As a problem of epistemology, I am interested in the ways pedagogy occurs, and the corollary objectives of those occurrences. Crawley (2017) writes instructively on this point: "There is an important difference between learning spirituals on plantations during working hours or while stealing away in brush harbors and praise houses, on the one hand, and learning them in private classrooms with the goal of perfecting through rehearsal, away from the social world" (p. 206). Self-defining praxis is an epistemological enunciation that orients us to a different brand of study, away from policies that might infringe on Black curriculum and the placeness of Black bodies and minds, away from possibilities in response to anti-Blackness. Taking *The Flying African* as inspiration is to take up the speculative and affective (see chapter 8). On the value of the speculative, Benjamin (2016) is adamant that in a sociopolitical moment that questions assertions of liveliness, "facts, alone, will not save us" (p. 2). Where there is no safety to be found in classroom spaces (McKittrick, 2014), nor in discourses of diversity, equity, inclusion, and belonging, Black Study as a self-defining praxis is already running, in flight, and marooning. In a world that cannot see Black capaciousness, Blackness as otherwise, like Owunna, we must imagine, which is to make otherwise. To conduct and participate in this onto-epistemological worldmaking is to argue for the breadth and depth of Blackness in ways that gesture toward aesthetics of being, unmoored from the finitude of location and locution, or that which historically gives it meaning. Imagining that exceeds the space, time, and contexts that organize and depend on conceptions of what it means to be the Western Man-as-human, however deviant those conceptions may be, is to invite renderings of Black ontological possibility. Particularly, where the nonevent of emancipation (Hartman, 1997) extends to educational sites, self-defining praxis as an exemplar of Black Study is an otherwise ecological possibility, at the nexus of refusal and relationality, for staging Black futures.

I submit that, more than incorporating, for example, Black literary and cultural productions into the educational curriculum, educators must be oriented to Black futures, a premise engendered by specificity. Black specificity is an act of love that sets the conditions for Black futures. This statement does not advocate for an optimistic outlook, as optimism implies an expectation of improvement or inevitability. Instead, it embraces Black specificity as an appeal that enables a commitment to the concept of viable present and future experiences for Black people. I understand specificity as epistemic, affective, ontological, and axiological attunements that can exist as resonance and felt sense; it is valuation and expression of desire; Black specificity as an aspiration for Black futures conjures, and is speculative and given to fiction and invocations of what is not, but must be. Black specificity is not a place, or even a moment; rather, it is animated by an ethics of poesis that registers at and beyond the flesh—annotated comportment, tone of voice, breath, and utterances; it is fleshed as impulse, incitement, and tenderness and care. Black specificity is an act of witnessing, privately and publicly; it is an affective sensibility, unbounded, and always in the business of livable Black futures. Asé.

August,

For my birthday this year, your mother got me a telescope. She knows that I have always been taken by, drawn to things above and beyond me. If I weren't teaching and writing, I think I would have wanted to chart the stars, to travel in space. Bebe and Babu knew this, and thought it appropriate that I own a telescope as a child. The telescope wasn't particularly strong in terms of its lens, but it was their loving way of getting me off the ground and into the sky, to have a closer look. It was a wonderful gift. All these years later, I still value the idea of the telescope and was grateful that your mother remembered this. To my delight, she bought you a mini-telescope as well! How amazing it is, and will be, I thought, for us to peel back the layers and debris of this world. I love telescopes for what they enable us to see, to bring into view. More than that, however, I am thankful for the reminder they provide that there is more. There is elsewhere, August, and you have access to it. You are more. You are infinite essence. Asé.

Gratitude

I am because we are and because we are, therefore, I am. This book began with a question: how do I feel about being Black in this (the United States) country? So many people and communities have, in one way or another, given me space to pursue this question with all of its entanglements, intensities, contradictions, pivots, and turns. I learned how to ask better questions of myself and what I was reading during my summer in Massachusetts. The learning community at the Institute for the Recruitment of Teachers pushed me into knowing my capacities. I am grateful. It was early in my doctoral program at Miami University when I encountered the question mentioned above, and my doctoral cohort—Aeriel Ashlee, Kyle Ashlee, Mark Pontius, Shamika Karikari, Adam Duran-Leftin—proved to be an endless circle of support and encouragement for talking out my initial thoughts—thank you. I am a better thinker because of the master teachers I learned alongside in Oxford, Ohio, including Mahauganee Shaw Bonds, Peter Magolda, Kathy Goodman, Kathleen Knight-Abowitz, and Brittany Aronson. This project has been emerging for some time. Although different from my dissertation, my committee, consisting of my adviser and chair Stephen Quaye, Elisa Abes, Durell Callier, David Pérez, and Tammy Brown, is worthy of regard. Each of them has affirmed how I have chosen to do my work while being an engaged reader and thought partner. Thank you endlessly for your investment in me. Dominique Hill, my teacher, and big sister, thank you for still calling me higher and higher. I learned what deep study was while under your care. It was under your tutelage that I stretched and moved, where I learned how to stand in my voice, to take authorial risks, to let my body go. Thank you for being a brilliant interlocutor and teaching me how to trust my lungs and decisions, to chart a relationship to my reading and learning that honors genealogies. Denise Taliaferro Baszile is and has always been, a possibility model. In your class, I began honing my identity as an artist-scholar, one who was deeply engaged in Black Study and creativity. I learned that one could be a serious artist-performer and scholar. You are an exemplar as an interdisciplinary scholar in ways that I hope to honor with this writing and the creative activities that spring from it. To my mentors—Vicka Bell-Robinson, Jerome Conley, Rodney Coates, D-L Stewart, Annemarie Vaccaro, and Christa Porter—and those who inspire me from afar—Tina Campt, Greg Carr, Cynthia Dillard, Saidiya Hartman, Katherine McKittrick, Christina Sharpe, Hortense Spillers, and Sylvia Wynter—thank you for pushing my thinking. The rethinking that would become this book occurred while sitting on the shoreline in Wilmington, North Carolina. While there, as the world was waking up to multiple pandemics, a group of people held me. Thank you Candace Thompson, Donyell Roseboro, Laura Szech, Karla Zaccor, Andy Ryder, Kevin McClure, Symphony Oxendine, Denise Henning, Dar Mayweather, Shawn Savage, and the UNC Watson College of Education students and staff, for the opportunity to write, think, dream, and build out this project. To my village in Rhode Island, a state that became my home; my wonderful colleagues at Penn State and my circle in State College, PA; Youngstown, Ohio, continues to be a site of possibility—thank you for teaching and growing me. Friends are life-sustaining, and mine have been just that. I am grateful for all of my friends and life partners, namely: Clarence Howell, Michael Gibson, Carrington Moore, Lamar Sykes, Thomas Toney, Christopher Travers, Tiffany Steele, Natasha McClendon, Tricia Shalka, DeMarcus Jenkins, Kamaria Porter, Lydia Ocasio-Stoutenburg, FOCC #19 cohort, Candace and Dorian Hall, Jeremy Snipes, Derrick Tillman-Kelly, Edwin Lee, Kyle Brooks, Christina Morton, LaMesha Brown, Terah J. Stewart, Laura Hamilton, Kayla Griffin, Alvin and Stephanie Currette, ReSean Yancy, Bobby Oliveira, John Cruz, Rui Montilla, Andy and Jonai Cooks, Micah and Kristin Anderson, Darryl and Keya Anderson, Guy and Val Burney; my Ox Fam—Morrel Wax, Brian Streng, David Davis Modinat Sanni, Ken Bennett—I appreciate each of you. I apologize to those I missed, please know that you are appreciated. Keon McGuire, thank you for your generosity and time. You've been a consistent source of wisdom, affirmation, an interlocutor, and friend. Tiffany Nyachae, I appreciate your insightful and incisive reading of this manuscript. This book project was made better because of your sharp critique and abundant care. Sabrina Cherry, you reminded me to pause and breathe—the work could not be completed without you. Thank you.

Z Nicolazzo, thank you for all the ways you nudge me forward. Melody Moezzi, Caitlin Ryan, and Antonio Duran-Leftin read an early prospectus for this book—thank you for your careful readings, good questions, and friendship. To my brother and sister, Richard and Candace Okello, thank you for loving me still. At every turn, you both have been consistent, compassionate, and insistent in supporting me. I have all I have ever needed because I have the two of you. I am grateful to my God, and to a mother who dreams and prays, and a father who models how to keep moving forward. Janice and Serafhin Okello, I love you endlessly. I owe this project to your stewardship, tender love, and thoughtful discipline, which calls me to principled living, publicly and privately. To my Isenhour family, of which I am held, covered, and overflowing with love, you are my core and blessing; and to my late grandmother, who embodied radical care, I feel your presence, always. To the Wagner family who has embraced me as their own, I am grateful for you. To my partner and wife, Morgan Helene, who reminds me to be consistent, I am better because of you. I wrote this book in the middle of three moves, parenting, partnering, and doing life with you, and in these ways, none of this is possible without your grace and encouragement. I love and appreciate you. My godchildren, nieces, and nephews in love—Justice, Christian, Karter, Cara, Noémi, Cadence, Geno, Eden, Amani, Alex and Chance, Langston, Paisley, and Nassir—I think of you often and am dreaming of not-yet worlds for you.

I have shared portions of this work before caring and enthusiastic audiences at the Association for the Study of Higher Education, the American Educational Research Association, and the Academy for Anti-Racist Leadership at the Center for the Study of Higher Education (Penn State). Concerning the latter, I received indispensable support from my colleagues in the Center, particularly Alicia Dowd and LaWanda Ward. Earlier versions of chapters 3 and 4 appeared in the *International Journal of Qualitative Studies in Education*, and an earlier version of chapter 5 appeared in *Conceptualizing Blackness in Educational Research*, Routledge. Tamira Butler-Likely also conducted a close read of this manuscript, for which I am grateful. Thank you to the writers, essayists, poets, and thinkers, whose names I call in this text, especially June Jordan: "Poem About My Rights" from *Directed by Desire: The Collected Poems of June Jordan*, Copper Canyon Press, © Christopher D. Meyer, 2007; reprinted by permission of the Frances Goldin Literary Agency. I am honored to be part of the SUNY Press series, Critical Race Studies in Education. The anonymous readers of this manuscript offered critical and thoughtful feedback, as well as reader reports that supported and pushed this project along. The editorial team at SUNY read this project honestly and as I had hoped. Many thanks to the SUNY production team for their efforts. I sincerely appreciate Rebecca Colesworthy responding to my inquiry about a book idea and never wavering in her enthusiasm. Thank you for your important questions, helping framings, and belief in the project's potential. Thank you to Derrick Brooms for leading a courageous series, for the hallway conference talks at ASHE, and for seeing vision for this project. Deep bows of gratitude to Mikael Owunna for sharing your capacious vision of Black livingness and for trusting me with your work. Your art, which resonates with me still, is the aesthetic representation of everything I hope this book project conveys. I earnestly pray that this book's contents complement your emancipatory vision of possibility. Finally, this book is dedicated to August Asé Okello. Thank you for reminding me about the breath of Black being—the sound of it in your guttural and long laugh, the feel of it in your fearless curiosity, and the look of it in your unrestrained rhythm.

And, for the ancestors and elders whose names I will not know and for whose labor this is possible, I hope to be part of the chorus that says your work has not been in vain. Asé.

Notes

Introduction

1. The references informing this entry are Paul Gilroy, *The Black Atlantic: Modernity and Double Consciousness*; Katherine McKittrick, *Dear Science and Other Stories*; Fred Moten, *In the Break*; and M. NourbeSe Philip, *Zong!*

2. Throughout this book, where "Man" appears in upper- and lowercase, it refers to Wynter's usage.

3. Sharpe's (2016) notion of Blackness as an agrammatical is instructive in considering the ways Blackness animates, reorders, and distorts language, thought, and meaning.

4. I am thinking with Josh Myers's reading of W. E. B. Du Bois as hesitant, and the importance of *Sociology Hesitant*.

Chapter 1

1. I am thinking here with Denise Ferreira da Silva's (2019) reconceptualization of "how." She notes that "Because *how* refers to what has and has not already been done, to what takes place at this exact moment and in that other unimagined place, because *how* recalls infinity, all I do here is share with you another possible how, another black feminist doing, inspired by the kind of sensibility announced when one attends to doings that are always and simultaneously feats, deeds, burdens, artifacts" (para. 3).

2. Throughout the book, I use "the Western Man," "Western humanism," and 'Man-as-human," interchangeably. Conceptually, they are all rooted in the same thesis.

3. Patterson (1982) noted that "[Black people] differed from other human beings in that they were not allowed to freely integrate the experience of their ancestors into their lives, to inform understanding of social reality with the inherited meanings" (p. 5).

4. For Orlando Patterson (1982), discussions of slavery and slavery's formations deserve close attention. Outlining several conditions, or what he called dialectics of slavery, Patterson, noted first, that slavery is a relationship of domination. The first condition in this relationship of domination is "powerlessness in relation to another person" (Patterson, 1979, p. 33), originating, mediated, and maintained through force. Under these relations, enslaved persons are under the sentence of death, where a master is imbued with the power of life and death over those enslaved. Where the enslaved have no existence outside of those dictated by a master, the enslaved lose social connection and relevance, or they become socially isolated, interrupting their right to community. This second conditional element, natal alienation, denotes the enslaved as someone who "has been forcefully cut off from the protection and demands of [their] natal group" (p. 34). Moreover, it is the "forceful and enforceable alienation of slaves from all natal ties of 'blood' and sentiment and from any conception of having by right of birth any attachment to groups or localities" (p. 34). A third constitutive element of the enslaved condition is the notion of dishonor, which suggests that the enslaved can have no honor-dignity, membership within one's community, sources of protection, or independent authority. Honor as a constitutive element should be read as a sentiment that manifests in conduct and reputation. It is expected that the enslaved be regarded as an entity undeserving of dignity (Patterson, 1979, 1982). The components facilitate a strategic hold (Butler, 2017) on the enslaved, but they gain their strength from the sociopolitical context. Social unfreedoms, for that matter, are the result of a unilateral power relationship that transforms the aforementioned conditions into rights relationships. Further, according to Patterson (1985), the making, or ritual of enslavement incorporated four elements: "first, the symbolic rejection by the slave of [their] past and [their] former kinsmen; second, a change of name; third, the imposition of some visible mark of servitude; and last, the assumption of a new status in the household or economic organization of the master" (p. 52). Slavery as filtered through transatlantic slavery, and into a United States context, ushers entry into a living social death as articulated by Patterson.

5. The emphasis here on enslavement and its signification of social death is not to suggest that imagining otherwise should begin with enslavement, or that theorizing enslavement is the only way toward Black possibility. As my central critique is of the question of the human as constructed by Western coloniality, and how this rubric gets deployed in human development and knowledge production, I think with the idiom of enslavement to illustrate the will of liveliness.

6. Ungendering here follows Spillers (1987) as the dissociation of Blackness as attached to Black bodies as that which can be fully human, and, thus, a holder of the vitality markers of the human.

7. I am thinking here with Katherine McKittrick (2016), Rebellion/Invention/Groove and her meditation on Wynter's Black Metamorphosis.

Chapter 3

1. By countergravity, I am thinking with Tina Campt's (2021) conceptualization as a gravity that refuses the physics of anti-Blackness that exacts violence on Black living.

Chapter 4

1. While imperfect, the emergence of NIL (name, image, and likeness) and a May 2024 settlement agreement, part of a class-action lawsuit known as *House v. NCAA*, which allows athletes to receive pay directly from colleges and universities, is shifting the economic terms of the matter for some.

Chapter 5

1. I am thinking here of the slave ship, its constraint and enclosure.
2. For enslaved captives, dwelling in the cargo hold was a breathless, asphyxiating existence. On the similarities between the barracoon, prison, and the hold, Childs (2015) noted that the breathing air was miniscule and the moving cage immobilized the enslaved to the extent that it was impossible for them to straighten themselves. Lest the enslaved be considered, or consider themselves as passengers, they were packaged to "half the room afforded soldiers, emigrants or convicts on ships of the same period" (Browne, 2015, p. 48), with the expectation that should they disembark alive (in whatever ways we might conceptualize alive to be), they would do so marked as slave and not free. The hold, in this way, was generative and exacting on those perceived as nonhuman, ensuring that if, and in whatever state the enslaved emerge from the hold, they wouldn't do so wholly (Okello et al., 2021). One must wonder what happens/ed to their bodies in the hold, when held. The bound and stowed body marked the space/place "of no rights and no citizenship . . . And since, it [was] a rite of passage—indicative of no rights, no citizenship à la Dred Scott decision—[we] must ask what marks passage from, through, and to" (Sharpe, 2016, pp. 85–86). The transatlantic moment ensured that movements, as attached to Black bodies, minds, and spirits, be treated with hostility in an anti-Black social sphere. Plainly, the Black body/mind/spirit was to be understood as out of place. Octavia Butler (1979) offered a poignant imaging of the harsh, embodied effects of the transatlantic slavery on the Black folks when talking about Dana. It is because of slavery's hold that "[she] couldn't let her come back whole. . . . Antebellum slavery didn't leave people quite whole" (p. 498). For Butler, this meant that Dana would be stamped by the atrocity, as the always already pull of enslavement that held her (pieces of her) even as she lived into her present and future. Time and location change, the hieroglyphic resonance did not. Whereas the

vestiges of slavery repeat and take on new life, I am led to wonder how educational policy and practice functions as a carrying vessel.

Chapter 6

1. As discussed in chapter 1, outlining American grammar's regulatory epistemological boundaries, Hortense Spillers (1987) concentrated on the captive body that would become the Black flesh wrapped in socially fixed realities and inundated with inferior messages. She argued that this body/flesh is legible in the "the ruling episteme" (p. 68) as still captive, arrested in perpetuity to the "originating metaphors of captivity and mutilation" (p. 68) so that it is as if this captive body survives only as an object to be murdered (Johnson & Bryan, 2016; Spillers, 1987) by anti-Black policies and practices. These estranged conditions subject Black folks to social, cultural, and political impositions of dominant communities, a narrative firmly tied to its "seared, divided, ripped-apartness" in Western social, psychological, and political formations.

2. The need for presence is predicated on the existence of what Christina Sharpe (2016) called "the wake." To exist in the wake, for Black bodies and minds, is to live the historical-made-present remnants and reverberation of slavery as the grounds of everyday life. The elements of repression and capture persist as overdetermining properties (Spillers, 1987) that are "so loaded with mythical prepossession that there is no easy way for agents buried beneath them to come clean" (p. 65). In other words, slavery is encoded in culture and attached to Black people in ways that follow and raise normative standards of the Western Man around them. Anti-Blackness directs Western forms of schooling practices, and conceptually, it has been a functional analytic to discuss the ways Black students are positioned as inherently inferior (Dumas, 2014, 2018). Whereas anti-Blackness outlines an irreconcilable relationship between Blackness and what it means to be human, the same logic extends to theories of education that presume to understand Black people—how they think, move, and behave—through white, enlightenment constructs that privilege linearity and normativity (Okello & Turnquest, 2020). Furthermore, scholars note the ways Black students are trained toward self-hatred as the norm (hooks, 1989; Okello, 2020), expected to inflict spiritual violence within (Johnson, Stovall, & Baszile, 2017), and must contend with the imprecise and uncritical interrogations of their lives as uniquely susceptible to anti-Black violence and the traumatic responses that they conjure (Menakem, 2017). Therefore, loving flesh, or engaging in a practice of self-love, in the afterlife of slavery (Hartman, 1997), given the psychic trauma (Collins, 1990; Maldonado-Torres, 2007; Oliver, 2004; Woodson, 1933) "that lingers on the spirits of Black people" (Okello, 2020), is often understated and misunderstood as a purely cognitive endeavor.

Chapter 7

1. By codes, I am referring again to what Spillers (1987) would discuss as American grammar, or a set of rules and regulations that organizes the United States social imaginary as distinctly anti-Black. Whereas grammar refers to systems of language that include syntax, inflections, semantics, and the making of discourse, American grammar accentuated how the institution of slavery informed discourse regarding Black people. The logic was a holding, a binding, that fixed Black people—in a Spillersian case, the Black woman—to a particular realm of society and social order, namely, nonhuman, kinless, and noncitizen.

2. Castro-Gomez (2002) noted that "the written word constructed laws and national identities, designed modernizing programs, and organized the understanding of the world in terms of inclusion and exclusion. For this reason, nations' foundational projects were carried out by creating institutions legitimized by writing (schools, hospices, workshops, prisons) and hegemonic discourses (maps, grammars, constitutions, manuals, treatises on hygiene) that regulated public conduct. These institutions and texts established boundaries between people and assured them that they existed either inside or outside the limits defined by written legality" (p. 272).

3. To be clear, this is not to suggest that Black people are themselves a problem à la Du Bois's double consciousness. Some interpretations of Du Bois's question tend to construct the Black as the problem. Constructed as problematic beings, they are phobogenic objects, which is to say a stimulus to anxiety. As a phobogenic object, the Black came to symbolize all that white Europeans did not want to be, and therefore a biological danger in need of being controlled. Fanon (1967) noted that the Black has but one function and that is "symbolizing the lower emotions, the baser inclinations, the dark side of the soul" (p. 190). Furthermore, the Black formalized the underside of binaries, the evil beneath good, ugliness beneath the beauty, all which rationalized writing the Black out of humanity as a moral necessity to preserve the sanctity of the Western Man. For Fanon, white logic justified this repression: "In the remotest depth of the European consciousness, an inordinately black hollow has been made in which the most immoral impulses, the most shameful desires lie dormant and as every man climbs up toward whiteness and light, the European has tried to repudiate this uncivilized self, which has attempted to defend itself. When the European civilization came into contact with the black world, with the savages, everyone agreed: Those Negroes were the principle of evil" (p. 190). These discourses of wrongness would provide the conditions for the systems of labor extraction and the basis for continued expulsion from the realm of humanity, or what Gordon (1995) has explained as bad faith. The notion of bad faith speaks to evasive behaviors where individuals lie to themselves, lie to others, and lie about others in order

to provide a dominant group with a level of determinacy, over and against the possibility of irrelevance. In order for the Western Man to claim legitimacy, and secure their position in society, there is a need to problematize the other, in this case, Black people. To confront the condition of Blackness would mean to upset the ethics that structure Western humanism, and, indeed, it is Western humanism (expressed as anti-Blackness) that is the fulcrum by which society hinges. Ellison (1964) posited that anti-Blackness (as social, political, and economic assemblage) primarily emerges from a "need to believe," hence, the Black becomes the stand-in for white folks seeking "to resolve the dilemma arising between their democratic beliefs and certain anti-democratic practices, between their acceptance of the sacred democratic belief that all men are created equal and their treatment of every tenth man as though he were not" (p. 28). In addition, where Blackness is equated with moral wrongness, they lose, above all else, the right to experience the world free from terror. In educational sites this has meant that students can be verbally assaulted by teachers; Black girls can be thrown, snatched, and pulled; Black students are disproportionately pushed out; Black students are surveilled, expected to justify their standing on campus (Okello, 2022). In this way, to live as Black in an anti-Black world is to bout with the quotidian and mundane acts of terror that, in the current order of ethical regard, efficiently function to infringe on the space, time, energy, and movements of Black (ontology) living in an effort to maintain ordinariness.

4. Expulsion from the capacity to be recognized as fully human—ethical regard—is discerned by ungendering the enslaved subject. As Spillers has noted, the gender calculus that produces and reproduces the idea of the Black as nonhuman and failed human subject circulates on and travels through the Black female.

5. June Jordan, "Poem About My Rights" from *Directed by Desire: The Collected Poems of June Jordan*, Copper Canyon Press, © Christopher D. Meyer, 2007. Reprinted by permission of the Frances Goldin Literary Agency.

Chapter 8

1. Weheliye (2014) made this point when discussing racialization as the process by which Blackness comes into nonbeing. He noted that Blackness exists beyond biological and cultural inscriptions, and more fully, as the amalgamation of "sociopolitical relations that discipline humanity into full humans, not-quite-humans, and non-humans" (p. 6). That is, "Blackness designates a changing system of unequal power structures that apportion and delimit which humans can lay claim to full human status and which humans cannot" (p. 6).

2. Even though Western humanist logics are veiled, they are not impervious to critique. Wynter's (2006) work illuminates the insidious nature of how Western humanism is rendered invisible: "the western Man over-represents[s] a partial

group interest as if it were 'the common interest of all the members of society' and by doing so, to give the ideas that are generated from the perspective of this 'special or partial group interest' the form of universality, representing them 'as the only rational, universally valid ones'" (p. 154).

Chapter 9

1. This is how pessimism is defined in the dictionary.

2. I am also thinking here of Sounds of Blackness—a vocal and instrumental ensemble from Minneapolis/St. Paul, Minnesota who perform music from several genres, including gospel, R&B, soul, and jazz.

3. I am thinking here with what artist Torkwase Dyson calls Black compositional thought, a consideration of "how paths, freeways, waterways, architecture, and geographies are composed by black bodies and how properties of energy, space, and objects interact as networks of liberation" (Long, 2019, para. 13).

References

Abes, E. S., Jones, S. R., & Stewart, D.-L. (2019). *Rethinking college student development theory using critical frameworks.* Stylus.

Ahmed, S., & Ahmed, S. (2004). Affective economies. *Social Text, 22*(2), 117–39.

Alexander, E. (2004). *The Black interior.* Graywolf Press.

Alexander, E. (2020). The Trayvon generation. *New Yorker.* https://www.newyorker.com/magazine/2020/06/22/the-trayvon-generation

Anderson, L. M. (2008). *Black feminism in contemporary drama.* University of Illinois Press.

Anderson, R. E., & Stevenson, H. C. (2019). RECASTing racial stress and trauma: Theorizing the healing potential of racial socialization in African American families. *American Psychologist, 74*(1), 63–75.

Ani, M. (1994). *Yurugu: An African-centered critique of European cultural thought and behavior.* Africa World Press.

Annamma, S. A., Jackson, D. D., & Morrison, D. (2017). Conceptualizing color-evasiveness: Using dis/ability critical race theory to expand a color-blind racial ideology in education and society. *Race, Ethnicity and Education, 20*, 147–62.

Appadurai, A. (1996). *Modernity at large: Cultural dimensions of globalization (Vol. 1).* University of Minnesota Press.

Association of American Colleges and Universities. (2006). Academic freedom and educational responsibility. *Change: The Magazine of Higher Learning, 92*(2), 6–13.

Bacchi, C. L. (1999). *Women, policy, and politics: The construction of policy problems.* Sage. https://doi.org/10.4135/9781446217887

Baldwin, J. (1953). *Go tell it on the mountain.* Alfred A. Knopf.

Baldwin, J. (1955). *Notes of a native son.* Beacon Press.

Baldwin, J. (1962, November 9). Letter from a region in my mind. *New Yorker.* https://www.newyorker.com/magazine/1962/11/17/letter-from-a-region-in-my-mind

Baldwin, J. (1963). *The fire next time.* Dial Press.

Baldwin, J. (1985). *The price of the ticket: Collected nonfiction, 1948–1985*. Macmillan.
Baldwin, J. (2011). *The cross of redemption: Uncollected writings*. Vintage Books.
Baldwin, J., & Clark, K. (1963, May 24). *A conversation with James Baldwin*. https://www.youtube.com/watch?v=zhop-eFB0sI
Banks, J. (2014, August 14). Black kids don't have to be college-bound for their deaths to be tragic. *Kennebec Journal*. https://www.centralmaine.com/2014/08/14/black-kids-dont-have-to-be-college-bound-for-their-deaths-to-be-tragic-2/
Baraka, A. (2000). Black art. In W. J. Harris (Ed.), *The Leroi Jones/Amira Baraka Reader* (pp. 219–20). University of Mississippi Press.
Baszile, D. T. (2015). Rhetorical revolution: Critical race counterstorytelling and the abolition of white democracy. *Qualitative Inquiry, 21*(3), 239–49.
Baszile, D. T. (2019). Rewriting/recurricularizing as a matter of life and death: The coloniality of academic writing and the challenge of black mattering therein. *Curriculum Inquiry, 49*(1), 7–24. https://doi.org/10.1080/03626784.2018.154610
Baxter Magolda, M. B. (1992). *Knowing and reasoning in college: Gender-related patterns in students' intellectual development*. Jossey-Bass.
Baxter Magolda, M. B. (2001). *Making their way: Narratives for transforming higher education to promote self-development*. Stylus Publishing.
Baxter Magolda, M. B. (2008). Three elements of self-authorship. *Journal of College Student Development, 49*(4), 269–84.
Baxter Magolda, M. B. (2009). *Authoring your life: Developing your internal voice to navigate life's challenges*. Stylus.
Baxter Magolda, M., & King, P. M. (2004). *Learning partnerships: Theory and models of practice to educate for self-authorship*. Stylus Publishing.
Baxter Magolda, M. B., & King, P. M. (2007). Interview strategies for assessing self-authorship: Constructing conversations to assess meaning making. *Journal of College Student Development, 48*(5), 491–508.
Beamon, K. K. (2008). "Used Goods": Former African American college student-athletes' perception of exploitation by division I universities. *Journal of Negro Education*, 352–64.
Bell, D. A. (1980). Brown v. Board of Education and the interest-convergence dilemma. *Harvard Law Review, 93*(3), 518–33. https://doi.org/10.2307/1340546
Bell, D. (1995) Who's afraid of critical race theory? *University of Illinois Law Review*, vol. 1995, 893–910.
Benjamin, R. (2016). Racial fictions, biological facts: Expanding the sociological imagination through speculative methods. *Catalyst: Feminism, Theory, Technoscience, 2*(2), 1–28.
Biello, K., Ickovics, J., & Niccolai, L. (2013). Racial differences in age at first sexual intercourse: Residential racial segregation and the Black–White disparity among U.S. adolescents. *Public Health Reports, 128*(1), 23–32.

Biondi, M. (2012). *The Black revolution on campus*. University of California Press.
Bliss, J. (2015). Hope against hope: Queer negativity, black feminist theorizing, and reproduction without futurity. *Mosaic: a journal for the interdisciplinary study of literature*, 83–98.
Boylorn, R. M. (2013). *Sweetwater: Black women and narratives of resilience*. Peter Lang.
Boylorn, R. M., and Orbe, M. P. (2013). *Critical autoethnography: Intersecting cultural identities in everyday life*. Left Coast Press.
Brand, D. (2001). Opening the door: an interview with Dionne Brand by Maya Mavjee. *Read, 2*(1), 28–29.
Burke, T. (2018, November). *MeToo is a movement, not a moment* [Video file]. https://www.ted.com/talks/tarana_burke_me_too_is_a_movement_not_a_moment
Butler, J. (1993). Engendering/endangering: Schematic racism and white paranoia. In R. Gooding-Williams (Ed.), *Reading Rodney King/reading urban uprising* (pp. 15–22). Routledge.
Butler, P. (2018). *Chokehold: Policing Black men*. The New Press.
Callier, D. M., & D. C. Hill. (2019). *Who look at me?!: Shifting the gaze of education through Blackness, Queerness, and the body*. Brill.
Campt, T. M. (2017). *Listening to images*. Duke University Press.
Campt, T. M. (2018, July 18). Refusal. https://www.fotomuseum.ch/en/2018/07/24/refusal/
Campt, T. M. (2019, February). *Black visuality and the practice of refusal*. https://www.womenandperformance.org/amper-sand/29-1/campt
Carr, G. (2020). *Curriculum and instruction*. https://www.drgregcarr.com/curriculum-and-instruction.
Carter, J. K., & Cervenak, S. J. (2016). *The Black outdoors: Humanities futures after property and possession*. Humanities Futures. https://humanitiesfutures.org/contributors/c2-j-kameron-carter-sarah-jane-cervenak/
Castro-Gomez, S. (2002). Social sciences, epistemic violence, and the problem of the invention of the other. *Nepantla: Views from the South, 3*(2), 269–85.
Cavazos-Rehg, P., Krauss, M. J., & Spitznagel, E. L. (2009). Age of sexual debut among U.S. adolescents. *Contraception, 80*(2), 158–62.
Cervenak, S. J., and Carter, J. K. (2017). "Untitled and outdoors: Thinking with Saidiya Hartman. *Women & Performance: A Journal of Feminist Theory, 27*(1), 45–55. doi:10.1080/0740770X.2017.1282116
Chandler, N. D. (2013). *X—The problem of the Negro as a problem for thought*. Fordham University Press.
Childs, D. (2015). *Slaves of the state: Black incarceration from the chain gang to the penitentiary*. U of Minnesota Press.
Clark, V. (1991). Developing diaspora literacy and marasa consciousness. In H. Spillers (Ed.), *Comparative American identities* (pp. 41–61). Routledge.

Clifton, L. (2000). *Blessing the boats: New and selected poems, 1988–2000*. BOA.
Clifton, L. (2012). *The collected poems of Lucille Clifton, 1965–2010*. BOA.
Coates, T., & Hannah-Jones, N. (2020, January 2020). Wise word from Nikole Hannah-Jones. https://www.facebook.com/forharriet/videos/wise-words-from-nikole-hannah-jones/527413141203617/
Cohen, C. (2014). *Male rape is a feminist issue: Feminism, governmentality, and male rape*. Palgrave MacMillan.
Colebrook, C. (2017). What is this thing called education? *Qualitative Inquiry, 23*(9), 649–55.
Coles, J. A. (2023). Storying against non-human/superhuman narratives: Black youth Afro-futurist counterstories in qualitative research. *International Journal of Qualitative Studies in Education, 36*(3), 446–64.
Coles, J. A. (2024). The spiritual aesthetics of Black world creation: A departure from Blackness as the unfree. In r. hampton, S. Habtom, & J. L. Williams (Eds.), *Conceptualizations of Blackness in educational research* (pp. 14–30). Routledge.
Collins, P. H. (2004). *Black sexual politics: African Americans, gender, and the new racism*. Routledge.
Cooper, B. C. (2017). *Beyond respectability: The intellectual thought of race women*. University of Illinois Press.
Corley, C. (2015, August 8). Whether history or hype, 'hands up, Don't shoot' endures. *NPR*. https://www.npr.org/2015/08/08/430411141/whether-history-or-hype-hands-up-dont-shoot-endures
Costa Vargas, J., & James, J. (2012). Refusing blackness-as-victimization: Trayvon Martin and the black cyborgs. *Pursuing Trayvon Martin: Historical contexts and contemporary manifestations of racial dynamics*, 193–204.
Council for the Advancement of Standards. (2006). *CAS professional standards for higher education* (6th ed.).
Cox, A. M. (2015). *Shapeshifters: Black girls and the choreography of citizenship*. Duke University Press.
Cox, J., & Jean-François, I. (2022). Aesthetics of (Black) breathing. *liquid blackness, 6*(1), 98–117.
Crawley, A. T. (2017). *Blackpentecostal breath: The aesthetics of possibility*. Fordham University Press.
Crawley, A. T. (2020). *The lonely letters*. Duke University Press.
Crenshaw, K. (1990). Mapping the margins: Intersectionality, identity politics, and violence against women of color. *Stanford Law Review, 43*, 1241.
Crenshaw, K., Ocen, P., & Nanda, J. (2015). Black girls matter: Pushed out, over-policed, and underprotected. *Center for Intersectionality and Social Policy Studies. Columbia University*.
Cross, W. E., Jr. (1971). Toward a psychology of Black liberation: The Negro-to-Black conversion experience. *Black World, 20*(9), 13–27.

Cross, W. E., Jr. (1991). *Shades of Black: Diversity in African-American identity*. Temple University Press.
Curry, T. J. (2017). *The man-not: Race, class, genre, and the dilemmas of Black manhood*. Temple University Press.
Curry, T. J., & Utley, E. (2018). She touched me: Five snapshots of adult sexual violations of African American boys. *Kennedy Institute of Ethics Journal, 28*(2), 205–41.
Curry, T. J. (2019). Expendables for whom: Terry Crews and the erasure of Black male victims of sexual assault and rape. *Women's Studies in Communication, 42*(3), 287–307.
Dancy, T. E., II, Edwards, K. T., & Earl Davis, J. (2018). Historically White universities and plantation politics: Anti-blackness and higher education in the Black Lives Matter era. *Urban Education, 53*(2), 176–95.
Da Silva, D. F. (2007). *Toward a global idea of race*. University of Minnesota Press.
Da Silva, D. F. (2013). To be announced: Radical praxis or knowing (at) the limits of justice. *Social Text, 31*(1), 43–62.
Da Silva, D. F. (2015). Before man: Sylvia Wynter's rewriting of the modern episteme. In K. McKittrick (Ed.), *Sylvia Wynter: On being human as a praxis* (pp. 90–105). Duke University Press.
Delgado, R., & Stefancic, J. (2012). *Critical race theory: An introduction* (2nd ed). New York University Press.
Dei, G. J. (2017). *Reframing Blackness and Black solidarities through anti-colonial and decolonial prisms*. Springer.
Desai, K., & Sanya, B. N. (2016). Towards decolonial praxis: Reconfiguring the human and the curriculum. *Gender and Education, 28*(6), 1–15. http://dx.doi.org/10.1080/09540253.2016.1221893
Diem, S., Young, M. D., Welton, A. D., Mansfield, K. C., & Lee, P. L. (2014). The intellectual landscape of critical policy analysis. *International Journal of Qualitative Studies in Education, 27*(9), 1068–1090.
Dillard, C. B. (2000). The substance of things hoped for, the evidence of things not seen: Examining an endarkened feminist epistemology in educational research and leadership. *International Journal of Qualitative Studies in Education, 13*(6), 661–81. doi:10.1080/09518390050211565
Dillard, C. B. (2012). *Learning to (re)member the things we've learned to forget: Endarkened feminisms, spirituality, & the sacred nature of research & teaching*. Peter Lang Publishing.
Dixon, J. H. (2019, March 4). The rank-and-file women of the Black Panther Party and their powerful influence. *Smithsonian Magazine*. https://www.smithsonianmag.com/smithsonian-institution/rank-and-file-women-black-panther-party-their-powerful-influence-180971591/
Dotson, K. (2011). Tracking epistemic violence, tracking practices of silencing. *Hypatia, 26*(2), 236–57.

Du Bois, W. E. B. (1899). *The Philadelphia Negro*. In *The Philadelphia Negro*. University of Pennsylvania Press.

Du Bois, W. E. B. (1903). *The souls of Black folk*. A. C. McClurg.

Dumas, M. J. (2014). 'Losing an arm': School as a site of Black suffering. *Race Ethnicity and Education, 17*(1), 1–29.

Dumas, M. J. (2016). Against the dark: Antiblackness in education policy and discourse. *Theory Into Practice, 55*(1), 11–19.

Dumas, M. J., & ross, k. m. (2016). "Be real black for me" imagining BlackCrit in education. *Urban Education, 51*(4), 415–442.

Dumas, M. J. (2018). Beginning and ending with Black suffering: A meditation on and against racial justice in education. In *Toward what justice?* (pp. 29–45). Routledge.

Durham, A. (2014). *Home with hip-hop feminism: Performances in communication and culture*. Peter Lang Publishing.

Editors. (2019, June 10). *Stokely Carmichael. History*. https://www.history.com/topics/black-history/stokely-carmichael

Ellison, R. (1952). *Invisible man*. Random House.

Ellison, R. (1964). *Shadow and act*. Vintage.

Fairclough, N. (2003). *Analyzing discourse: Textual analysis for social research*. Routledge.

Fanon, F. (1952/1967). *Black skin, white masks*. Grove Press.

Fanon, F. (1963). *The wretched of the earth*. Grove Press.

Farmer, A. D. (2017). *Remaking Black power: How Black women transformed an era*. University of North Carolina Press.

Floyd, S. A., Jr. (1996). *The power of black music: Interpreting its history from Africa to the United States*. Oxford University Press.

Fried, J. (2003). Ethical standards and principles. *Student services: A handbook for the profession, 4*, 107–27.

Fried, J. (2010). *Student services: A handbook for the profession*. Jossey Bass.

French, B. H., Tilghman, J., & Malebranche, D. (2015). Sexual coercion context and psychosocial correlates among diverse males. *Psychology of Men and Masculinity, 16*(1), 42–53.

Giddings, P. (2008). *Ida: A sword among lions: Ida B. Wells and the campaign against lynching*. Amistad.

Fleetwood, N. R. (2011). *Troubling vision: Performance, visuality, and Blackness*. University of Chicago Press.

Ferguson, R. (2004). *Aberrations in Black: Toward a queer of color critique*. University of Minnesota Press.

Free Huey rally. (1968). *Six Black women with raised fists*. [Photograph]. https://www.smithsonianmag.com/smithsonian-institution/rank-and-file-women-black-panther-party-their-powerful-influence-180971591/

Gillespie, M. B. (2016). *Film Blackness: American cinema and the idea of Black film*. Duke University Press.

Gildersleeve, R. (2013). Policy, reconfigured: Critical policy studies and the (false) beneficence of subjects. *Journal of critical Thought and Praxis, 2*(1), 1–7.
Glissant, E. *Poetics of Relation*. University of Michigan Press.
Gordon, L. R. (1995). Sartrean bad faith and antiblack racism. In *The prism of the self* (pp. 107–29). Springer, Dordrecht.
Gordon, L. R. (Ed.). (1997). *Existence in Black: An anthology of Black existential philosophy*. Routledge.
Gordon, L. R. (2018). Black aesthetics, Black value. *Public Culture, 30*(1), 19–34.
Gordon, L. R. (2000) *Existentia Africana: Understanding Africana existential thought*. Routledge.
Grand Jury Documents. (2014, November 25). *Documents from the Ferguson grand jury*. CNN. http://www.cnn.com/interactive/2014/11/us/ferguson-grand-jury-docs/
Greig, J. (2020). *40 Black men are accusing a former University of Michigan athletic doctor of sexual assault*.https://blavity.com/40-black-men-are-accusing-a-former-university-of-michigan-athletic-doctor-of-sexual-assault?category1=news
Gumbs, A. P. (2020). *Black feminist lessons from marine mammals*. AK Press.
Hamilton, V. (1985). *The people could fly: American Black folktales*. Alfred A. Knopf.
Harris, C. I. (1993). Whiteness as property. *Harvard Law Review*, 1707–91.
Harris, J. (2017). Centering women of color in the discourse on sexual violence on college campuses. In J. C. Harris & C. Linder (Eds.) *Intersections of identity and sexual violence on campus: Centering minoritized students' experiences* (pp. 42–59). Stylus Publishing.
Harris, J., & Linder, C. (2017). Introduction. In J. C. Harris & C. Linder (Eds.) *Intersections of identity and sexual violence on campus: Centering minoritized students' experiences* (pp. 1–22). Stylus Publishing.
Harney, S., & Moten, F. (2013). *The undercommons: Fugitive planning and black study*. Minor Compositions.
Hartman, S. (1997). *Scenes of subjection: Terror, slavery and self-making in nineteenth-century America*. Oxford University Press.
Hartman, S. (2007). *Lose your mother: A journey along the Atlantic slave route*. Macmillan.
Hartman, S. (2008). Venus in two acts. *Small Axe: A Caribbean Journal of Criticism, 12*(2), 1–14.
Hartman, S. (2019). *Wayward lives, beautiful experiments: Intimate histories of riotous Black girls, troublesome women, and queer radicals*. W. W. Norton.
Hartman, S. & Moten, F. (2016, October 5). The Black outdoors: Humanities futures after property and possession. https://www.youtube.com/watch?v=t_tUZ6dybrc&t=20s
Henson, B. (2021). *Unsettling the coloniality of the researcher: Toward a Black Studies approach to critical humanisms in qualitative inquiry*. Qualitative Inquiry, 27(10), 1200–12.

Hernández, E. (2012). The journey toward developing political consciousness through activism for Mexican American women. *Journal of College Student Development, 53*, 680–702.

Hernández, E. (2016). Utilizing critical race theory to examine race/ethnicity, racism, and power in student development theory and research. *Journal of College Student Development, 57*(2), 168–80.

Hill, D. C. (2016). Blackgirl, one word: Necessary transgressions in the name of imagining Black girlhood. *Cultural Studies ↔ Critical Methodologies, 19*(4), 275–83.

Hill, D. C. (2017). What happened when I invited students to see me? A Black queer professor's reflections on practicing embodied vulnerability in the classroom. *Journal of lesbian studies, 21*(4), 432–42.

Hill, K. K. (2016). *Beyond the Rope: The impact of lynching on Black culture and memory*. Cambridge University Press.

hooks, b. (1989). *Thinking feminist, thinking black*. South End Press.

hooks, b. (1990). *Yearning: Race, gender, and cultural politics*. South End Press.

hooks, b. (1992). *Representing whiteness in the black imagination*. Routledge.

hooks, b. (2004). *We real cool: Black men and masculinity*. Psychology Press.

Hong, L. (2017). *Digging up the roots, rustling the leaves: A critical consideration of the root causes of sexual violence and why higher education needs more courage*. In J. C. Harris & C. Linder (Eds.), *Intersections of identity and sexual violence on campus: Centering minoritized students' experiences* (pp. 23–41). Stylus Publishing.

Howard University orientation. (2014). *Howard University students, hands up, don't shoot*. [Photograph]. https://www.washingtonian.com/2014/08/14/howard-university-students-take-powerful-photo-in-response-to-michael-brown-shooting/

Hurtado, A. (2003). Theory in the flesh: Toward an endarkened epistemology. *International Journal of Qualitative Studies in Education, 16*(2), 215–25.

Jackson, J. L., Jr. (2013). *Thin description: Ethnography and the African Hebrew Israelites of Jerusalem*. Harvard University Press.

Jackson, Z. I. (2013). *Animal: New directions in the theorization of race and posthumanism. Feminist Studies, 39*(3), 669–85.

Jackson, Z.I. (2020). *Becoming human: Matter and meaning in an anti-Black world*. New York University Press.

Jacobs, H. (Linda Brent) (1987). *Incidents in the life of a slave girl*. Harvard University Press.

James, J. (1999). *Shadowboxing: Representations of Black feminist politics*. St. Martin's Press.

James, J. (2013). Afrarealism and the black matrix: maroon philosophy at democracy's border. *The Black Scholar, 43*(4), 124–31.

James, J. (2015). The womb of Western theory: Trauma, time theft, and the captive maternal. *Carceral Notebooks, 12*.

Jenkins, D. A. (2021). Unspoken grammar of place: Anti-Blackness as a spatial imaginary in education. *Journal of School Leadership, 31*(1–2), 107–26.

Jessup-Anger, J. (2018). History of sexual violence in higher education. *New Directions for Student Services, 161*(1), 9–19.

Johnson, E. P. (2003). *Appropriating Blackness: Performance and the politics of authenticity*. Duke University Press.

Johnson, J. W. (1900). *Lift every voice and sing*. https://www.blackpast.org/black-past-features/black-national-anthem/

Johnson, L., & Bryan, N. (2016). Using our voices, losing our bodies: Michael Brown, Trayvon Martin, and the spirit murder of Black male professors in the academy. *Race Ethnicity, and Education, 20*(2), 163–77.

Johnson, L. L., Jackson, J., Stovall, D. O., & Baszile, D. T. (2017). "Loving Blackness to death": (Re) imagining ELA classrooms in a time of racial chaos. *English Journal*, 60–66.

Jones, N. (2010). *Between good and ghetto: African American girls and inner-city violence*. Rutgers University Press.

Jones, S. R. (2019). Waves of change: The evolving history of student development theory. In E. S. Abes, S. R. Jones, & D. L. Stewart (Eds.) *Rethinking college student development theory using critical frameworks* (pp. 7–16). Stylus Publishing.

Jordan, J. (1969). *Who look at me*. Ty Crowell.

Jordan, J. (1980). *Passion: New poems, 1977–1980*. Beacon Press.

Jordan, J. (2003). *Some of us did not die*. Basic Books.

Jordan, J. (2005). *Directed by desire: The collected poems of June Jordan*. Copper Canyon Press.

Kaba, M. (2021). *We do this 'til we free us: Abolitionist organizing and transforming justice*. Haymarket Books.

Kaufman, M. (1998, November 16). Stokely Carmichael, rights leader who coined 'Black power' dies at 57. *New York Times*. https://www.nytimes.com/1998/11/16/us/stokely-carmichael-rights-leader-who-coined-black-power-dies-at-57.html

Kegan, R. K. (1982). *The evolving self: Problem and process in human development*. Harvard University Press.

Kegan, R. (1994). *In over our heads: The mental demands of modern life*. Harvard University Press.

Keeling, R. P. (Ed.). (2004). *Learning reconsidered: A campus-wide focus on the student experience*. Washington, DC: National Association of Student Personnel Administrators & American College Personnel Association.

Kelley, R. D. (2022). *Freedom dreams: The black radical imagination*. Beacon Press.

Kendi, I. (2012). *The Black campus movement: Black students and the racial reconstitution of higher education, 1965–1972*. Palgrave Macmillan.

Kim, D. (2005). *Writing manhood in Black and Yellow: Ralph Ellison, Frank Chin, and the literary politics of identity*. Stanford University Press.

King, J. E. (1992). Diaspora literacy and consciousness in the struggle against miseducation in the Black community. *Journal of Negro Education, 61*(3), 317–40.

King, T. L. (2016). The labor of (re)reading plantation landscapes fungible(ly). *Antipode, 48*(4), 1022–39.

King, T. L. (2019). *The Black shoals: Offshore formations of Black and Native studies*. Duke University Press.

Kitchener, K. S. (1985). Ethical principles and ethical decisions in student affairs. In H. J. Canon, & R. D. Brown (Eds.), *Applied ethics in student services. New directions for student services* (pp. 17–29). Wiley Press.

Kuntz, A. A. (2009). The politics of space in qualitative research. In M. Savin-Baden, & C. H. Major (Eds.), *New approaches to qualitative research: Wisdom and uncertainty*. Routledge.

Ladson-Billings, G. (2004). Landing on the wrong note: The price we paid for Brown. *Educational Researcher, 33*, 3–13.

Lee, J. (2014, August 14). Hands up: Howard U. photo of students in solidarity goes viral. *USA Today*. https://www.usatoday.com/story/news/nation-now/2014/08/14/hands-up-ferguson-michael-brown-howard-brown/14044865/

Linder, C. (2017). Reexamining our roots. In J. C. Harris & C. Linder (Eds.) *Intersections of identity and sexual violence on campus: Centering minoritized students' experiences* (pp. 60–82). Stylus Publishing.

Linder, C., & Harris, J. (2017). Conclusion: History, identity, and power-conscious strategies for addressing sexual violence on college campuses. In J. C. Harris & C. Linder (Eds.). *Intersections of identity and sexual violence on campus: Centering minoritized students' experiences* (pp. 235–50). Stylus Publishing.

Lincoln, Y. S., & Guba, E. G. (2000). Paradigmatic controversies, contradictions, and emerging confluences. In N. K. Denzin & Y.S. Lincoln (Eds.), *Handbook of qualitative research* (2nd ed., pp. 163–88). Sage.

Logan, R. W. (1969). *What the Negro wants*. Notre Dame University.

Long, M. (2019, September 27). Torkwase Dyson tells the history of black liberation through *cartographic art*. https://www.documentjournal.com/2019/09/torkwase-dyson-tells-the-history-of-black-liberation-through-cartographic-art/

Lorde, A. (1982). *Zami: A new spelling of my name*. Crossing Press.

Lorde, A. (1984). *Sister outsider: Essays and speeches*. Crossing Press.

Lorde, A. (1992). *Undersong: Chosen poems, old and new*. W. W. Norton.

Love, B. L. (2019). *We want to do more than survive: Abolitionist teaching and the pursuit of educational freedom*. Beacon Press.

Lugones, M. (2010). Toward a decolonial feminism. *Hypatia, 25*(4), 742–59.

Makalani, M. (2017). Black Lives Matter and the limits of formal Black politics. *South Atlantic Quarterly, 116*(3), 529–52.

Maldonado-Torres, N. (2007). On the coloniality of being: Contributions to the development of a concept. *Cultural studies, 21*(2–3), 240–70.

Marowski, S. (2020, April). Black men were 'particularly vulnerable' to sexual abuse by late University of Michigan doctor, lawyer says. https://www.mlive.com/news/ann-arbor/2020/04/black-men-were-particularly-vulnerable-to-sexual-abuse-by-late-university-of-michigan-doctor-lawyer-says.html

Marriott, D. (2007). *Haunted life: Visual culture and Black modernity*. Rutgers University Press.

Marriott, D. (2011). Inventions of Existence: Sylvia Wynter, Frantz Fanon, Sociogeny, and "the Damned." *CR: New Centennial Review, 11*(3), 45–89.

Maturana, H., & Varela, F. (1972). *Autopoiesis and cognition: The realization of the living*. D. Reidel.

McGuire, D. L. (2010). *At the dark end of the street: Black women, rape, and resistance: A new history of the civil rights movement from Rosa Parks to the rise of Black Power*. Vintage.

McKittrick, K. (2006). *Demonic grounds: Black women and the cartographies of struggle*. University of Minnesota Press.

McKittrick, K. (2011). On plantations, prisons, and a Black sense of place. *Social & Cultural Geography, 12*, 947–63.

McKittrick, K. (2013). Plantation futures. *Small Axe, 17*(3), 1–15.

McKittrick, K. (2014). Mathematics black life. *The Black Scholar, 44*(2), 16–28.

McKittrick, K. (Ed.). (2015). *Sylvia Wynter: On being human as praxis*. Duke University Press.

McKittrick, K. (2015). "Yours in the intellectual struggle: Sylvia Wynter and the realization of the living." In K. McKittrick (Ed.), *Sylvia Wynter: On being human as praxis* (pp. 1–8). Duke University Press.

McKittrick, K. (2016). Rebellion/invention/groove. *Small Axe: A Caribbean Journal of Criticism, 20*(1), 79–91.

McKittrick, K. (2017). Commentary: worn out. *Southeastern Geographer, 57*(1), 96–100.

McKittrick, K. (2021). *Dear science and other stories*. Duke University Press.

McQuirter, M. (2018, December 27). 12 November 1968 & towards a Black university conf @ hu begins tomorrow. https://www.dc1968project.com/blog/2018/12/27/12-november-1968-amp-toward-a-black-university-conf-hu-begins-tomorrow

Menakem, R. (2017). *My grandmother's hands: Racialized trauma and the pathway to mending our hearts and bodies*. Central Recovery Press.

Mignolo, W. (2011). *The darker side of Western modernity: Global futures, decolonial options*. Duke University Press.

Mills, C. W. (1997). *The racial contract*. Cornell University Press.

Milner, H. R., IV (2008). Critical race theory and interest convergence as analytic tools in teacher education policies and practices. *Journal of teacher education, 59*(4), 332–46.

Mirzoeff, N. (2011). The right to look. *Critical Inquiry, 37*(3), 473–96.

Moten, F. (2003). *In the break: The aesthetics of the black radical tradition*. University of Minnesota Press.

Moten, F. (2008). The case of blackness. *Criticism, 50*(2), 177–218.

Moten, F. (2013). *Blackness and nothingness (mysticism in the flesh). South Atlantic Quarterly, 112*(4), 737–80.

Moten, F. (2017). *Black and blur*. Duke University Press.

Moten, F., & Hartman, S. (2014, September 27). Fugitivity and waywardness. https://arika.org.uk/fugitivity-and-waywardness/

Moraga, C., & Anzaldúa, G. (1981). *This bridge called my back: Writings by radical women of color*. Persephone Press.

Morrison, T. (1987). *Beloved*. Plume.

Muncey, T. (2010). *Creating autoethnographies*. Sage.

Murty, K. S., Roebuck, J. B., & McCamey Jr., J. D. (2014). Race and class exploitation: A study of Black male student athletes (BSAs) on white campuses. *Race, Gender & Class*, 156–73.

Mustaffa, J. B. (2017). *Mapping violence, naming life: A history of anti-Black oppression in the higher education system. International Journal of Qualitative Studies in Education, 30*(8), 711–27.

Nash, J. C. (2013). Practicing love: Black feminism, love-politics, and post-intersectionality. *Meridians, 11*(2), 1–24.

Nash, J. C. (2018). *Black feminism reimagined: After intersectionality*. Duke University Press.

Nicholson, G. (2010). *Michigan man*. https://umgoblog.com/end-around/michigan-man/

Nxumalo, F., & ross, k. m. (2019). Envisioning Black space in environmental education for young children. *Race Ethnicity and Education, 22*(4), 502–24.

Ohito, E. O. (2017). Thinking through the flesh: A critical autoethnography of racial body politics in urban teacher education. *Race Ethnicity and Education, 22*(2), 250–68.

Okello, W. K. (2018). *From self-authorship to self-definition: Remapping theoretical assumptions through Black feminism. Journal of College Student Development, 59*(5), 528–44.

Okello, W. K. (2020). "Loving flesh": Self-love, student development theory, and the coloniality of being. *Journal of College Student Development, 61*(6), 717–32.

Okello, W. K. (2022a). "[Existing] while Black": Race, gender, and the surveillance of Blackness. *Educational Studies, 58*(2), 250–66.

Okello, W. K. (2022b). "What are you pretending not to know?": Un/doing internalized carcerality through pedagogies of the flesh. *Curriculum Inquiry.* DOI: 10.1080/03626784.2022.2047579

Okello, W. K. (2024). *Unspeakable joy: On loving Blackness as a practice of Black joy.* Urban Education. https://doi.org/10.1177/00420859241227956

Okello, W. K., & Calhoun, K. (2024) *Affirmations of the flesh*: Explicating the potentialities of self-love beyond the educational context. *Journal of Higher Education.* doi: https://doi.org/10.1080/00221546.2024.2362558

Okello, W. K., & Duran, A. (2021). 'Here and there, then and now': Envisioning a palimpsest methodology International Journal of Qualitative Methods. http://doi:10.1177/16094069211042233

Okello, W. K., Duran, A., & Pierce, E. (2021a). Dreaming from the hold: Suffering, survival, and futurity as contextual knowing. *Journal of Diversity in Higher Education.* Advance online publication. https://doi.org/10.1037/dhe0000321

Okello, W. K., & Stewart, T. J. (2021). Because we know: Toward a pedagogical insistence on Black mattering. *Journal of Effective Teaching in Higher Education, 4*(2), 1–10.

Okello, W. K., Jenkins, D., & Nyachae, T. (forthcoming). (No) humans involved: On the potentialities of Black research approaches in education. *International Journal of Qualitative Methods.*

Okello, W. K., & Turnquest, T. A. (2020). "Standing in the kitchen": Race, gender, history, and the promise of performativity. *International Journal of Qualitative Studies in Education.* https://doi.org/10.1080/09518398.2020.1828653

Okello, W. K., & White, K. (2019). A Black feminist reconstruction of agency. In E. S. Abes, S. R. Jones, D-L. Stewart (Eds.), *Rethinking college student development theory using critical frameworks* (pp. 142–57). Stylus Publishing.

Owunna, M. (2020). *Infinite essence.* https://www.mikaelowunna.com/infinite-essence#1

Parker, C. A. (1977). On modeling reality. *Journal of College Student Personnel, 18,* 419–25.

Patterson, O. (1979). Slavery in human history. *New Left Review, 1*(117), 31–67.

Patterson, O. (1982). *Slavery and social death: A comparative study.* Harvard University Press.

Patton, L. D. (2014). Preserving respectability or blatant disrespect?: A critical discourse analysis of the Morehouse Appropriate Attire Policy and implications for intersectional approaches to examining campus policies. *International Journal of Qualitative Studies in Education, 27*(6), 724–46.

Perez, R. J. (2019). Paradigmatic perspectives and self-authorship: Implications for theory, research, and praxis. *Journal of College Student Development, 60*(1), 70–84.

Perlstein, D. (1990). *Teaching freedom: SNCC and the creation of the Mississippi*

freedom schools. *History of Education Quarterly, 30*(3), 297–324.
Perry, I. (2021). She changed Black literature forever. Then she disappeared. https://www.nytimes.com/2021/09/17/magazine/gayl-jones-novel-palmares.html
Phillip, M. N. (2008). *Zong!* Wesleyan University Press.
Piaget, J. (1950). *The psychology of intelligence* (M. Piercy & D. Berlyne, Trans.). London: Routledge & Kegan Paul.
Pizzolato, J. E. (2003). Developing self-authorship: Exploring the experiences of high-risk college students. *Journal of College Student Development, 44*, 797–812.
Pizzolato, J. E. (2007). Assessing self-authorship. In P. S. Meszaros (Ed.), *Advancing students' intellectual growth through the lens of self-authorship, New Directions for Teaching and Learning* (pp. 31–42). Jossey-Bass.
Pizzolato, J. E., & Olson, A. B. (2016). Exploring the relationship between the three dimensions of self-authorship. *Journal of College Student Development, 57*, 411–27.
Prescod-Weinstein, C. (2021). Public thinker: Katherine McKittrick on Black methodologies and other ways of being.
Quashie, K. (2021). *Black aliveness, or a poetics of being.* Duke University Press.
Rankine, C. (2014). *Citizen: American lyric.* Graywolf Press.
Ransby, B. (2003). *Ella Baker and the Black freedom movement: A radical democratic vision.* University of North Carolina Press.
Reason, R., & Kimball, E. (2012). A new theory-to-practice model for student affairs: Integrating scholarship, context, and reflection. *Journal of Student Affairs Research & Practice, 49*(4), 359–76.
Roberts, N. (2015). *Freedom as marronage.* University of Chicago Press.
Rodgers, R. F., & Widick, C. (1980). Theory to practice: Uniting concepts, logic, and creativity. In F. B. Newton & K. L. Ender (Ed.), *Student development practices: Strategies for making a difference* (pp. 3–25). Springfield, IL: Thomas.
Rodriguez, A., Deane, K. C., & Davis, C. H., III (2022). Towards a framework of racialized policymaking in higher education. In *Higher education: Handbook of theory and research: Volume 37* (pp. 519–99). Springer International Publishing.
Roelefs, M. (2005). Radicalization as an aesthetic production. In G. Yancy (Ed.), *White on white/Black on Black* (pp. 83–124). Rowman & Littlefield.
Rojas, F. (2007). *From Black Power to Black Studies: How a radical social movement became an academic discipline.* Johns Hopkins University Press.
Rose, E. (2019). Neocolonial mind snatching: Sylvia Wynter and the curriculum of man. *Curriculum Inquiry, 49*(1), 25–43.
Saldana, J. (2009). *The coding manual for qualitative researchers.* Sage.
Samatar, S. (2015). Against a normative world. https://thenewinquiry.com/against-the-normative-world/
Schwandt, T. A. (2007). *The SAGE dictionary of qualitative inquiry* (3rd ed.). Sage.

Scott, D. (2002). The sovereignty of the imagination: An interview with George Lamming. *Small Axe, 6*(2), 72–200.

Scott, D. (2010). *Extravagant abjection: Blackness, power, and sexuality in the African American literary imagination*. New York University Press.

Scott, J. C. (1990). *Domination and the arts of resistance: Hidden transcripts*. Yale University Press.

Shange, S. (2019). Black girl ordinary: Flesh, carcerality, and the refusal of ethnography. *Transforming Anthropology, 27*(1), 3–21. https://doi.org/10.1111/traa.12143

Sharpe, C. (2016). *In the wake: On Blackness and being*. Duke University Press.

Siddle-Walker, V. (2013). Ninth annual Brown lecture in education research: Black educators as educational advocates in the decades before Brown v. Board of Education. *Educational Researcher, 42*, 207–22.

Sexton, J. (2008). *Amalgamation schemes: Antiblackness and the critique of multiracialism*. University of Minnesota Press.

Sexton, J. (2011). The social life of social death: On Afro-pessimism and Black optimism. https://doi.org/10.25071/1913-5874/37359

Sexton, J. (2018). *Black men, Black feminism: Lucifer's nocturne*. Springer.

Shahid, K. T. (2018). *Anti-Black racism and epistemic violence*. Sentia Publishing.

Sharpe, C. (2016). *In the wake: On Blackness and being*. Duke University Press.

Sharpe, C. (2023). *Ordinary notes*. Farrar, Straus and Giroux.

Skrivan, L. (2014). *Hands up, don't shoot* [Photograph]. https://mizzoumag.missouri.edu/2014/11/protest/index.html

Smith, A. (2005). *Conquest: Sexual violence and American Indian genocide*. South End Press.

Smith, B. (1979). Toward a Black feminist criticism. *Women's Studies International Quarterly, 2*(2), 183–94.

Spillers, H. (1987). Mama's baby, papa's maybe: An American grammar book. *Diacritics, 17*(2), 65–81.

Spillers, H. J. (1996). "All the things you could be by now if Sigmund Freud's wife was your mother": Psychoanalysis and race. *Critical Inquiry, 22*(4), 710–34.

Spillers, H. J. (2003). The crisis of the Negro intellectual: A postdate. In *Black, white, and in color: Essays on American literature and culture* (pp. 428–70). University of Chicago Press.

Spillers, H., Hartman, S., Griffin, F. J., Eversley, S., & Morgan, J. L. (2007). "Whatcha gonna do?": Revisiting "Mama's baby, papa's maybe": An American grammar book: A conversation with Hortense Spillers, Saidiya Hartman, Farah Jasmine Griffin, Shelly Eversley, & Jennifer L. Morgan. *Women's Studies Quarterly, 35*(2), 299–309.

Standley, F. L., & Pratt, L. H. (1989). *Conversations with James Baldwin*. University Press of Mississippi.

Stevenson, H. C. (2014). *Promoting racial literacy in schools: Differences that make a difference.* Teachers College Press.

Stewart, D. L. (2019). Ideologies of absence: Anti-Blackness and inclusion rhetoric in student affairs practice. *Journal of Student Affairs, 28,* 15–30.

Stewart, D. L. (2022). Performing goodness in qualitative research methods. *International Journal of Qualitative Studies in Education, 35*(1), 58–70.

The Lyrics (n.d.). Star Spangled Banner. https://amhistory.si.edu/starspangledbanner/the-lyrics.aspx

Thelin, J. R. (2004). *A history of American higher education.* Johns Hopkins University Press.

Thomas, G. (2006). Proud flesh inter/views: Sylvia Wynter. *Proud Flesh: New Afrikan Journal of Culture, Politics and Consciousness, 4.*

Tichavakunda, A. A. (2021). *Black campus life: The worlds Black students make at historically white institutions.* State University of New York Press.

Tinsley, J. (2020, July). Jon Vaughn and the cost of being a Michigan man. https://theundefeated.com/features/jon-vaughn-and-the-cost-of-being-a-michigan-man/

Torres, V. (2009). The developmental dimensions of recognizing racist thoughts. *Journal of College Student Development, 50,* 504–20.

Torres, V., & Hernández, E. (2007). The influence of ethnic identity on self-authorship: A longitudinal study of Latino/a college students. *Journal of College Student Development, 48,* 558–73.

Trouillot, M. R. (1995). *Silencing the past: Power and the production of history.* Beacon Press.

Ture, K., & Hamilton, C. V. (1967). *Black power: The politics of liberation in America.* Vintage.

Van Dijk, T. A. (1993). Principles of critical discourse analysis. *Discourse & Society, 4*(2), 249–83.

Van Dijk, T. A. (2003). Critical discourse analysis. In D. Schiffrin, D. Tannen, & H. E. Hamilton (Eds.), *The handbook of discourse analysis* (pp. 352–71). Blackwell.

Vargas, J. C., & James, J. A. (2013). Refusing blackness-as-victimization: Trayvon Martin and the Black cyborgs. In G. Yancy & J. Jones (Eds.), *Pursuing Trayvon Martin: Historical contexts and contemporary manifestations of racial dynamics* (pp. 193–204). Lanham, MD: Lexington Books.

Walcott, R. (2009). *Black like who? Writing Black Canada.* Insomniac Press.

Wa Thiong'o, N. (1986). *Decolonizing the mind: The politics of language in African literature.* London: James Currey.

Wa Thiong'o, N. (1986). *Something torn and new: An African renaissance.* Basic Civitas Books.

Wall, C. (1989) (Ed.). *Changing our own words: Essays on criticism, theory, and writings by Black women.* Rutgers University Press.

Wall, C. A. (2018). *On freedom and the will to adorn: The art of the African American essay.* University of North Carolina Press Books.

Wallace, D. S. (2018, April 30). Fred Moten's radical critique of the present. https://www.newyorker.com/culture/persons-of-interest/fred-motens-radical-critique-of-the-present

Warren, C. (2016). Black interiority, freedom, and the impossibility of living. *Nineteenth Century Contexts, 38*(2), 107–21.

Warren, C. L. (2017). Black mysticism: Fred Moten's phenomenology of (black) spirit. *Zeitschrift für Anglistik und Amerikanistik, 65*(2), 219–29.

Warren, C. A. (2021). From morning to mourning: A meditation on possibility in Black education. *Equity & Excellence in Education, 54*(1), 92–102.

Watkins, W. H. (2001). *The white architects of Black education: Ideology and power in America, 1865–1954*. Teachers College Press.

Weheliye, A. (2014a). Introduction: Black studies and Black life. *Black Scholar, 44*(2), 5–10. https://doi.org/10.1080/00064246.2014.11413682

Weheliye, A.G. (2014b). *Habeas viscus: Racializing assemblages, biopolitics, and Black feminist theories of the human*. Duke University Press.

West, C. (2000). *Race matters*. Beacon Press.

Wheatle, K. I., & Commodore, F. (2019). Reaching back to move forward: The historic and contemporary role of student activism in the development and implementation of higher education policy. *Review of Higher Education, 42*(5), 5–35.

Wilder, C. S. (2013). *Ebony & ivy: Race, slavery, and the troubled history of America's Universities*. Bloomsbury Press.

Wilderson, F. B., III (2003). The prison slave as hegemony's (silent) scandal. *Social Justice, 30*(2), 18–27.

Wilderson, F. B., III (2010). *Red, white & Black: Cinema and the structure of US antagonisms*. Duke University Press.

Williams, P. J. (1992). *The alchemy of race and rights*. Harvard University Press.

Williams, B. C., Squire, D. D., Tuitt, F. A. (2021). *Plantation politics and campus rebellions: Power, diversity, and the emancipatory struggle in higher education*. State University of New York Press.

Williamson, T. L. (2016). *Scandalize my name*. Fordham University Press.

Wilmer Hale (2021, May). Report of independent investigation: Allegations of sexual misconduct against Robert E. Anderson. https://regents.umich.edu/files/meetings/01-01/WH_Anderson_Report.pdf

Womack, A. (2021). *The matter of Black living: The aesthetic experiment of racial data, 1880–1930*. University of Chicago Press.

Woodson, C. G. (1933). *The miseducation of the Negro*. Associated Publishers.

Wynter, S. (1970.) "Jonkonnu in Jamaica: Towards the interpretation of folk dance as a cultural process. *Jamaica Journal, 4*(2), 34–48.

Wynter, S. (1971). Novel and history, plot and plantation. *Savacou, 5*(1), 95–102.

Wynter, S. (1984). The ceremony must be found: After humanism. *Boundary 2, 12/13*(3), 19–70.

Wynter, S. (1989). Beyond the word of man: Glissant and the new discourse of the Antilles. *World Literature Today, 63*(4), 637–48.

Wynter, S. (1990). Afterword: Beyond Miranda's meanings: Un/silencing the 'demonic ground of Caliban's 'woman.' In C. B. Davies & E. S. Fido (Eds.), *Out of the Kumbla: Caribbean women and literature* (pp. 355-72). Trenton: Africa World Press.

Wynter, S. (1992a). 'Do not call us negros': How multicultural textbooks perpetuate racism. Aspire Books.

Wynter, S. (1992b). Rethinking "aesthetics": Notes towards a deciphering practice. *Exiles: Essays on Caribbean cinema*, 245.

Wynter, S. (1994). No humans involved: An open letter to my colleagues. *Forum N.H.I. Knowledge for the 21st Century*, 1(1), 42-73.

Wynter, S. (1995a). 1492: A new world view. In V. L. Hyatt & R. M. Nettleford (Eds.), *Race, discourse, and the origin of the Americas: A new world view* (pp. 5-57). Smithsonian Institution Press. doi:10.1086/ahr/102.3.875

Wynter, S. (1995b). The Pope must have been drunk, the king of Castile a madman: Culture as actuality, and the Caribbean rethinking modernity. In *The reordering of culture: Latin America, the Caribbean and Canada in the hood*, 17-41.

Wynter, S. (2003). 'Unsettling the coloniality of being/power/truth/freedom: Towards the human, after man, its overrepresentation—An argument. *New Centennial Review*, 3(3), 257-337.

Wynter, S. (2006). On how we mistook the map for the territory, and re-imprisoned ourselves in our unbearable wrongness of being, of *desetre*: Black studies toward the human project. In L. R. Gordon & J. A. Gordon (Eds.), *Not only the master's tools: African-American studies in theory and practice* (pp. 107-69). Paradigm.

Wynter, S., & Scott, D. (2000). The re-enchantment of humanism: An interview with Sylvia Wynter. *Small Axe*, 8(1), 119-207.

Wynter, S. (2015). The ceremony found: Towards the autopoetic turn/overturn, its autonomy of human agency and extraterritoriality of (self-)cognition. In *Black knowledges/black struggles: Essays in critical epistemology*, 184-252.

Wynter, S., & McKittrick, K. (2015). Unparalleled catastrophe for our species? Or, to give humanness a different future: Conversations. In *Sylvia Wynter* (pp. 9-89). Duke University Press.

Wynter, S. (n.d.). Black metamorphosis. Unpublished manuscript.

Yale University. (1968). Yale cheerleaders raise Black power fist. [Photograph]. https://www.gazettenet.com/-The-Game--Football-as-a-microcosm-of-the-dramatic-1960s-20622688

Young, M. D., Diem, S. (2018). Doing critical policy analysis in education research: An emerging paradigm. In C. Lochmiller (Eds.), *Complementary research methods for educational leadership and policy studies* (pp. 79-98). Palgrave Macmillan.

Zuberi, T., & Bonilla-Silva, E. (Eds.). (2008). *White logic, white methods: Racism and methodology*. Rowman & Littlefield.

Index

Bold page numbers refer to figures

abjection, 31, 33, 42, 149, 157
abolitionism, 2, 203, 217, 236
academic writing, 4, 175
accessibility, 47, 83, 220–24, 235
accommodation, 48, 203
aesthetic errantry, 5
aesthetics, 2, 6, 76–77, 136, 151, 165–66, 239, 245, 253; Black aesthetics, 77, 86, 96, 143, 164, 208–10, 215–16, 222–23, 248–49; and Black Study, 7; and conquistador humanism, 211; as life-making, 18–20; and presence, 148; refusing anti-Blackness, 4–5. *See also* Black Aesthetics Movement
affect, 19, 75, 82, 84–85, 94, 138, 163, 242–43, 248, 253; affective enclosure, 54; and the Black essay, 141; and Black liveliness and living, 41; and Black shoals/Black outdoors, 179–80; and embodiment, 80; politics of, 38; and presence, 147, 152, 165; and sexual violence, 104, 118. *See also* love
Afro-pessimism, 35, 37, 58; and anti-Blackness, 75, 251–52. *See also* pessimism

afterlife of slavery, 17, 19–20, 29–30, 33–35, 57, 106, 126, 129–30, 137, 140, 153, 175–77, 182, 239, 262n2. *See also* the wake
Alawuala, **45–46**
Alexander, Elizabeth, 150, 166
alienation, 57, 107, 135, 260n4
American grammar, 55, 146, 185, 261n1, 262n1
Amma, **15, 169, 199**–200
Anderson, Robert: sexual assault by, 104, 114–16, 121
annotations, 6, 62, 137, 139–40, 151, 164, 238–39, 251, 253; and anti-Blackness, 102, 111; and the Black intimate, 10; as Black reading practice, 41–42; and self-definition, 95–96
anti-Blackness, 4, 42, 54–55, 59, 86, 89, 97, 138, 139, 142, 146–47, 165, 170–78, 184–85, 221, 224, 232, 241; and aesthetics, 4–5; and Afro-pessimism, 75, 251–52; and American grammar, 262n1; and annotations, 95, 102, 111; anti-Black enclosures, 36, 148; and Audre Lorde, 77–78, 84–85, 88, 90,

anti-Blackness *(continued)*
92; and biocentrism, 25; and the Black essay, 135–36, 141; and the Black intimate, 126, 133–34; and Black liveliness and living, 20, 246; and Black Study, 68; and breathing, 64; and countergravity, 261n1; and critical race theory, 52; definition, 6, 29; and education, 61–62, 70–71, 96, 192, 200–218, 251, 262n2; and fear, 43; and humanism, 263n4; and internal voice, 81–82; and James Baldwin, 77–78, 84–85, 137, 141, 244; and June Jordan, 189, 191, 194; and limbos, 83; and love, 38, 231; and the nation-state, 236; and police, 111; resisting, 4–5, 18, 32–35, 157, 163, 166, 249–50; and self-authorship, 78–80, 120; and sexual violence, 112; and social death, 22; and student development theory, 9–10; and theorizing from the hold, 76; as the weather, 30–31, 74. *See also* racism; white supremacy

Appadurai, Arjun, 217
Armstrong, Samuel, 204
Aristotelian thinking, 106–7, 171
Asé, 43, 98, 253–54
August, 6; and breathing, 72; and desire, 195; and intimacy, 142–43; and naming, 97–98; and parenting, 43; and presence, 167; and schooling, 225–27; and the shoreline, 122; and the telescope, 254
autonomy, 29, 36, 53, 55, 131, 137, 140, 176–77, 181–82, 190, 212
autopoiesis, 23–26, 76, 210–11

Baker, Ella, 217

Baldwin, James, 32, 86–93, 97, 133, 138; and anti-Blackness, 77–78, 85; *The Fire Next Time*, 84; *Go Tell It on the Mountain*, 84; interview with Kenneth Clark, 232, 234–36, 239–40, 242–44; letter to his nephew, 126, 136–37, 140–41; and methodology of book, 83–84; *Notes of a Native Sun*, 84; on pessimism, 230–31, 234–36, 240
Bambara, Toni Cade, 1, 3–4, 195
Banks, Jasmine, 162
Baraka, Amiri, 32
Baszile, Denise Taliaferro, 175, 205
Baxter Magolda, Marcia, 78, 81–82, 95
Be Chukwu, **101**–102
Becton, Dejerra, 137
being human, 7, 11, 24, 76, 93, 96, 106, 223; as praxis, 4, 77, 218, 225, 242
beneficence, 181, 183
Benjamin, Ruha, 253
biocentricity, 23–26, 59, 76, 112, 118, 148, 246
Black aesthetics, 77, 86, 96, 143, 164, 208–10, 215–16, 222–23, 248–49
Black Aesthetics Movement, 4–5, 10, 32, 60, 70, 83, 201, 205, 218
Black aliveness, 61–62, 125, 135–36, 140, 218, 241
Black Arts Movement, 4, 10, 32, 60, 83, 201, 205, 218, 238
Black Atlantic, 2
Black being, 32, 60, 79, 102, 137, 146, 150, 152, 178, 186, 201, 231, 250; and anti-Blackness, 52, 55, 82, 163; and Black males, 103; and Black Power salute, 157; and Black Study, 238–39; and breathing, 64, 69; and childhood, 226; and education, 58,

61, 165, 213; and ethics, 185; and intimating, 138; and inventiveness, 10; as knowledge-producing site, 148; and limbos, 83; and liveliness, 3–5, 19, 151, 164, 237; and love, 39; and methodology of book, 40; and optimism, 236; otherwise possibilities of, 25; and pessimism, 234; and policy making, 221; and self-definition, 204; and student/early-adult development theory, 35; in the wake, 29; and the weather, 134

Black capaciousness, 2, 6, 11, 35, 141, 241, 249, 253
Black cyborg, 138
Black dispositional ethics, 185–86, 192–95
blackened knowledge, 30–31
Black essay, 126, 135–36, 140–41
Black feminism, 1, 22, 38–39, 66, 84, 103, 259n1
Black futures, 11, 149, 159–63, 216, 230–32, 238, 242–45, 253
Black intimate, 123–43; definition, 10
Black liberation, 68, 148, 159, 163, 166, 177, 208, 265n3
Black Lives Matter, 28
Black males, 103–21
Black matter/mattering, 89, 155, 248–49
Black methodology, 21, 60, 61–64
Blackness, definition, 6
Black outdoors, 178–80
Black Panther Party, 158
Black people, definition, 7
Black policy praxis (BPP), 11, 208–20
Black possibility, 3, 16, 33, 79, 149, 206, 235, 260n5
Black Power fist/salute, 148, 153, 155–60, 164, 166–67

Black Power Movement, 10, 32, 111, 154–60, 166–67, 205
Black shoals, 178–80
black specificity, definition, 2
Black Studies, 22, 26, 32, 40, 42, 48, 60, 69–70, 83, 111, 209–10; conceptual categories in, 62–63
Black Studies Movement, 10, 32, 201, 205
Black Study, 59–60, 65, 67–71, 208, 232, 238–39, 242–50, 253, 256; definition, 7; and Freedom Schools, 62; and otherwise possibility, 46–47; and territory, 58
Bliss, James, 55, 107
Bonilla-Silva, Eduardo, 209
Brand, Dionne, 16–17, 19, 31
breathing, 16, 19, 43, 76, 85, 97, 103, 111, 116, 121–22, 143, 147, 166, 184, 226, 230, 235, 243–46, 249–53, 256, 261n2; and Black liveliness and living, 41; and Black specificity, 2; and human development, 45–72
Brit (student), 64, 66–69
Brown, Bill, 156–57, 159
Brown, Michael, 29, 86, 105, 155, 161–62
Brown v. Board of Education, 204, 233
Burke, Tarana, 119
Butler, Judith, 165
Butler, Octavia, 261n2
Butler, Paul, 110

Callier, Durell, 238
Campt, Tina, 9, 148–49, 152, 155, 157–58, 160, 251
Capitol insurrection (2021), 29
carceral imagination, 209, 216, 237–38
carcerality, 54, 236; carceral imagination, 11, 209, 216–17, 231, 237–48; and education, 129, 231,

carcerality *(continued)*
  239, 244; internalized, 133; and policy making, 209
care ethics, 5
Carlos, John, 155
Carlton, Mary Ann, **158**
Carmichael, Stokely. *See* Ture, Kwame (formerly Stokely Carmichael)
Carr, Greg, 236
Cartesian dualism, 54–55, 148. *See also* subject-object relationship
Castro-Gomez, Santiago, 263n2
ceremony, 4, 218
Césaire, Aimé, 216, 231
Chi, **101**
Childs, Dennis, 261n2
chokehold, 42, 105, 110–17, 120–21
Christianity, 8, 173, 181, 204
Chukwu, **73**, **145**–46
cisgender men, 59, 75, 78
citizenship, 28, 46, 57, 86, 130–31, 147, 174, 178, 208, 216, 232, 245; conditional, 210; denial of, 21, 24, 30–34, 52, 233–39, 261n2
civil rights movement, 136, 147, 154
Civil War (US), 203
Clark, Kenneth, 230–36, 242–43
Clifton, Lucille, 35
Coates, Ta-Nehisi, 170
Cobb, Charlie, 205
Cohen, Claire, 110
Collins, Patricia Hill, 37–38
colonialism/imperialism, 18, 35, 62, 75, 87, 132, 150, 210, 213, 232, 245, 260n5; and anti-Blackness, 25, 28–29, 36, 54, 139, 200, 215, 224; and Blackness, 21–22, 27–29, 55, 173–75, 183, 190, 192, 232; and Christianity, 181; and flesh, 7, 25; gendered, 105, 116; and humanism, 8, 34, 211, 212; and social science, 3

color-evasive ideology, 79, 109
Congress of Racial Equality, 204
conquistador humanism, 211
constructivism, 9, 40, 48–57, 79, 81, 95
content studies, 70
Costa Vargas, João, 138–39
Council for the Advancement of Standards in Higher Education (CAS), 171–72, 181–85
countergravity, 74, 261n1
Cox, Aimee Meredith, 90
Crawley, Ashon, 46, 151, 244, 252
critical autoethnography, 77
critical discourse analysis, 105, 112–13
critical fabulation, 1
critical policy studies, 209, 213–15, 219
critical race feminism, 109
critical race theory (CRT), 50–51, 109, 163, 184, 215
Curry, Tommy J., 108, 110

damnation (Fanon), 212
Dartmouth College, 156
da Silva, Denise Ferreira, 46, 259n1
DEEP Breathing Practices, 64–71
Dei, George J. Sefa, 38
Delgado, Richard, 118
Deluca, Tad, 114
demonic ground, 37, 41, 148, 194
diaspora, 2, 16, 136, 161, 190, 201
Diem, Sarah, 219
dignity, 64–65, 69, 71, 98, 154, 157, 183, 221, 260n4
Dillard, C. D., 63, 66, 89
Dillard, Cynthia D., 131
Dionne (student), 62, 65–69
dissonance, 48–49, 59, 80, 104, 249
diversity, 183, 207, 214, 222, 253
Dixon, Janelle Harris, 158

Dogon people, **15, 169,** 199
doll test, 233
door of no return, 31
the door of no return (Brand), 16–17, 19
Dream Defenders, 217
Du Bois, W. E. B., 46–47, 52, 70, 209, 259n4, 263n3
Dumas, Michael, 24
Dunham, Katherine, 1
Dyson, Torkwase, 265n3

Eke-Nnechukwu, **45, 73,** 145
Eke-Nwe-Ohia, **45**
Ellison, Ralph, 118, 146–47
emancipation, 29, 33–34, 40, 59, 89, 107, 130, 132, 136, 142, 203, 223, 233, 253
enclosure, 17, 35–36, 54, 57, 61, 70, 88, 96, 106, 111, 148, 167, 178–80, 232, 236, 243, 247, 249, 261n1
endarkenment, 64–67, 71, 133, 175
ethics, 5, 31–32, 41, 61–64, 80, 84, 116, 121–22, 139, 146–47, 209, 211, 225, 234, 245, 264n4; abolitionist, 217, 236; and anti-Blackness, 135, 138, 141, 252; Black dispositional ethics, 185–86, 192–95; and Black Study, 70, 78, 244; of care, 40, 67, 180; definition, 7; and education, 10–11, 169–95, 239; and humanism, 263n3; and love, 40, 42; maroon ethic, 179; normative, 57; of poesis, 253
Eurocentrism, 36, 59, 92, 128, 174, 181, 231
Executive Order 1395042, 175–76

Fanon, Frantz, 25, 27, 38, 70, 74–76, 79, 86, 96, 102, 153, 212, 218, 263n3
Farmer, Ashley D., 158

feminism, 27, 58; Black, 1, 22, 38–39, 66, 84, 103, 259n1; critical race, 109
Ferguson, MO, 161–63
Ferguson, Roderick, 146
FESTAC 77, 1
Fleetwood, Nicole, 165
flesh (Spillers), 11, 25, 33, 35–37, 56, 59, 117, 126, 157, 160, 163–65, 182, 241–43, 246; and American grammar, 261n1; and articulation, 194; and Black specificity, 253; definition, 7; hieroglyphics of the flesh, 34, 138, 152; loving Black flesh, 15–43, 133, 136–37, 195, 208, 231, 262n2; and presence, 147–51; and vitality, 249–50
Floyd, George, 103
Fourteenth Amendment, 182
Freedmen's Bureau, 202–4, 222, 233
freedom dreaming, 2, 165, 201
Freedom Schools, 62, 202, 204–8, 216
Free Huey Newton Rally (1968), **158**–160
French colonialism, 17
fugitivity, 3, 17, 39, 151, 244, 248
fungibility, 58, 107, 126, 128, 148–49, 166, 176

gender *vs.* sex, 103
genocide, 1, 62, 211
genre, 4, 59; definition, 7; genres of the human, 7–8, 26, 34, 76–77, 106, 150, 175, 207, 245; otherwise genres of being, 11, 60, 150, 207, 215
Georgia, **229**
Gilroy, Paul, 111
Glissant, Édouard, 236
Gordon, Lewis R., 25, 263n3
governance, 62–63, 202, 215, 232, 236–42, 246–47, 250
grammar, 2, 5, 33, 155, 157, 175, 185, 250, 261n1, 263n2; of Black

grammar *(continued)*
  futurity, 159; and Blackness, 55, 102, 146, 246, 262n1; definition, 4; and ethics, 173; of the outside, 178–81; of possibility, 35
Gumbs, Alexis, 72

Haiti, 17, 125, 139
Haitian Revolution, 17
Hamilton, Virginia, 154
Hampton Institute, 204
hands up, don't shoot, 148, 153, 155, 160–64, 167
Hannah-Jones, Nikole, 170, 172, 179, 195
Harris, Jessica C., 109, 121
Hartman, Saidiya, 1, 29, 31, 46, 90, 102, 130–31, 148–49, 182, 187
Henderson, Delores, **158**
Herero Genocide, 1
Hernández, Ebelia, 50, 80
hieroglyphics of the flesh, 34, 138, 152, 153
Hill, Dominique C., 238
Hill, Paula, **158**
the hold, 17, 76, 95, 111, 127–42, 239, 252, 261
hooks, bell, 8, 210
Howard University, 161–62
the human, definition, 8
human development theory, 6, 23, 42, 78, 244, 260n5; and breathing, 45–72. *See also* student/early-adult development theory
humanism, 40–42, 106, 118, 133, 157, 166, 174, 217–18, 224–25, 230–39, 242–44, 259n2, 264n2; and academic publishing, 175; and Blackness, 20, 27–28, 65, 102, 107, 111, 137, 155, 181–85, 192, 201–12, 249, 251–52, 263n3; and colonialism/imperialism, 8, 34, 211, 212; conquistador, 211; and education, 170; and embodiment, 26; and freedom, 32; and genre, 8; liberal, 27–28, 32, 34, 58–59, 178, 184; and sexual violence, 119–20; and student/early-adult development theory, 10, 34–35
humanities, 6–7, 79, 146
human/not-quite/nonhuman, 28–29, 33, 103, 132, 175–76
human sciences, 26. *See also* social science
hypersexualization, 108, 110, 115

Igbo Landing, **229**
Igbo people, **45**, **73**, **123**, **145**, **229**, Igbo people101
imagining otherwise, 53, 151, 157, 166, 208, 244, 260n5. *See also* otherwise
inclination, 11, 140, 146, 192–93, 195, 240, 263
Indigenous Peoples, 151, 173, 211, 215
individualism, 36
interdependence, 49, 56–57
interdisciplinarity, 3, 5, 40–41, 61, 63, 209, 222–23
interiority, 3, 28, 135, 240, 250; and annotation, 10; erasure of, 117–19; and photography, 20; as resisting anti-Blackness, 84, 90, 95, 126, 133, 164
internalization, 54, 80, 84, 118, 131, 133
internal voice, 81–82
the interpersonal, 47
intersectionality, 38, 40, 59, 109, 121, 177
intimacy. *See* Black intimate
intimating, 88–91, 134–40, 180, 247–48, 250; as praxis, 78, 85–86, 97, 135, 138, 140–42, 245

invention/inventiveness, 2, 10, 49, 92–93, 150–51, 182, 191, 212, 218, 233–34, 240, 245–47, 260n7; and Black ontology, 101–22; and the human, 26, 32; as praxis, 78, 85–88, 97, 112, 120–21

Jackson, Zakiyyah Iman, 231
Jacobs, Harriet, 239
James, Joy, 83, 104–5, 138–39, 163
Jessup-Anger, Jody E., 109
Jim Crow, 125, 140
Johnson, James Weldon, 156
Jones, Nikki, 90
Jordan, June, 37, 39, 186–95, 238–39
justice, 30, 52, 153, 181, 183–84, 204, 222

Kantian reason, 54, 56
Kegan, Robert, 48–50, 78
Kelley, Robin D. G., 208
Key, Francis Scott, 156
Kimball, Ezekiel W., 220
King, Rodney, 28, 60, 105
King, Tiffany Lethabo, 149, 166, 179, 211
Kinshasha, DRC, 1
Kitchener, Karen Strohm, 171–72, 185
Komosu, **73–74**

Lee, Joyce, **158**
Leigh, Simone, 1, 3
liberalism, 18, 40, 83, 126, 129, 130–34, 177, 180; liberal humanism, 27–28, 32, 34, 58–59, 178, 184; liberal progressivism, 31, 139, 214, 222, 233; liberal redactions, 138–42
"Lift Every Voice and Sing," 156
limbos, 77, 83–85, 163
listening to images, 42, 148, 152–54, 156, 164

literary criticism, 42, 77, 82–86
liveliness and living, 11, 20, 77, 94, 97, 102, 121, 132, 146, 193, 201, 231, 237–41, 245; and Black specificity, 2; and the chokehold, 110; and education, 64, 69–71, 75, 125, 206; and ethics, 171, 179; and interdisciplinarity, 3, 223; and otherwise genres of the human, 150–52; and policy making, 209, 212; as praxis, 41–42, 195, 218
Lorde, Audre, 27, 32, 56, 77–78, 83–94, 97
Los Angeles Police Department: "no humans involved" (NHI) designation, 28, 53, 60
love, 9, 22, 37–40, 72, 98, 124, 127, 137, 152, 167, 188, 193, 195, 225, 227, 230, 238, 251, 253; Blackness as source of, 46; definition, 8; and education, 96; and freedom, 166; loving Black flesh, 133, 136–38, 208; loving Blackness, 37–40, 43, 217, 234–35; self-, 262n2
Lugones, María, 105
Lumumba, Patrice, 187
Lumumba, Pauline, 1
lynching, 105, 108

Makalani, Minkah, 212
Maldonado-Torres, Nelson, 175
Man-as-human, 9, 34, 46, 48, 146, 222, 245, 259n2; and anti-Blackness, 52, 252; and Blackness, 58–59, 132, 136, 174, 177, 212, 253; critique of, 9, 22, 121, 150; definition, 8; and education, 32, 133, 244; Eurocentric, 92, 181; and optimism, 236; racialized, 22, 28; and territory, 38, 41. *See also* humanism; Western Man
Manuel, Warde, 114

map/mapping, 71, 104, 116, 148, 159, 165, 171, 178, 184, 202, 210–13, 246; definition, 8; *versus* territory, 27, 38, 40–42, 58–60, 224
marronage, 2, 32, 151–52, 160–62, 164, 223, 239, 253; maroon ethics, 178–79
Martin, Trayvon, 29, 105, 125, 137, 140
masculinity, 10, 104, 108, 116–19, **145,** 158–59
master's tools, 27
Maturana, Humberto, 24
McKittrick, Katherine, 17, 36, 46, 108, 149–50, 206, 260n7
Means, Joyce, **158**
Meredith, James, 154
methodology of book, 4, 40–42, 82–86, 95–96, 112, 148. *See also* critical autoethnography; storytelling
#MeToo, 119. *See also* sexual violence
Michigan Man, 113, 116–17, 121
Michigan State University, 114, 116
Mills, Charles W., 209
Milner, H. Richard, 214
misogynoir, 158, 189
Mkpuke, **73**
Morrison, Toni, 39
Moses, Bob, 205
Moten, Fred, 33–34, 36–38, 111, 150, 185, 224
multiculturalism, 183–84
Mustaffa, Jalil Bishop, 206
Myers, Josh, 259n4

Nash, Jennifer C., 38–39
Nassar, Larry, 114, 116
Negritude, 1, 18
Negro Question, 202, 233
neoliberalism, 70, 126, 131, 184, 213, 225, 239

Nigerian-Swedish Americans, 20
noise, 236–38
Nommo, **15, 169**
nonbeing, 25, 27, 29, 58, 103, 194, 205, 264n1
nonhuman/not-quite-human, 103, 105, 115, 132, 149, 151, 262n1; as anti-Blackness, 29; and Blackness, 8, 22–23, 25, 28, 33, 53, 56, 173–77, 189, 191, 200, 203, 211–12, 261n2

objectivity, 27, 47, 56, 58, 64, 67, 70, 95, 140, 153, 177, 180, 208, 210, 216, 238
Odachi Nne Ebere, **73**
Ogo, **15**
Oku na Mmiri, **123**–124
Olson, Avery B., 81
Olympics (Mexico City, 1968), 155–56
onto-epistemologies, 17, 21, 25, 61, 77, 82, 84, 96, 148, 151, 174–77, 183, 185, 201, 213, 224, 236, 245, 252–53
ontology, 38, 55, 66, 182, 189, 222, 232, 245, 263n3; and anti-Blackness, 85–88; and Blackness, 5, 22, 24, 55–56, 173–78; Black ontological possibility, 11, 31, 35, 37, 40–42, 106, 121, 146, 148, 170, 186, 201, 252–53; and Black Studies, 26; and flesh, 34, 37; and intimacy, 123–43; narrating, 101–22; and presence, 145–67, 250
optimism, 35, 38, 230, 234–36, 240, 242–43, 253
Orlando (student), 65, 68
otherwise, 6, 40, 42, 58, 67, 71, 133, 165, 178, 216–17, 232, 236, 238–39, 243, 253; and aesthetics, 16, 19–21; and the Black intimate, 135, 137, 141; and the Black shoals, 179–80; definition, 8; imagining

otherwise, 53, 151, 157, 166, 208, 244, 260n5; and inventiveness, 10; otherwise genres of the human, 11, 60, 76, 150, 206–7, 215; otherwise knowing and being, 96–97, 102, 112, 149, 164, 208, 218, 248; otherwise narrations, 93; otherwise possibilities, 5, 9, 25, 32, 46–47, 92, 94, 141, 151–53, 180, 244, 250; and praxis, 3, 119, 200, 209; and refusal, 9; and revision, 170, 250
Owunna, Mikael, 42, 253; *The Flying African,* **229**–230, 245–52; *Infinite Essence,* 5–6, **15, 20**–21, 35, **45, 73, 101, 123, 145**, 169, 199, 229

Palestine, 2
Parker, Clyde A., 220
Parker, Greg, 156–57, 159
patriarchy, 18, 108–10, 116–17, 119–21, 177; hetero-, 146, 166
Patterson, Orlando, 31, 57, 259n3, 260n4
Perez, Rosemary J., 79–80
Perry, Imani, 21, 97
pessimism, 58, 240, 265n1; James Baldwin on, 230, 234–36, 240. *See also* Afro-pessimism
Philadelphia, PA, 47, 52, 62
Philadelphia Freedom Schools, 62
Philip, M. NourbeSe, 111–12
Piaget, Jean, 49
Pizzolato, Jane, 81–82
plantation, 42, 152, 204, 252; logic of, 17; plantation futures, 201, 206; politics of, 104, 200–201
poesis, 223, 236, 238–39, 242, 244, 253
police violence, 29, 103, 155, 160; "no humans involved" (NHI) designation, 28, 53, 60. *See also* chokehold; white supremacy

positivism, 18, 26, 40, 52, 177–78, 209
praxis, 2, 21, 32, 35, 126, 151, 180, 233, 235; being human as, 4, 77, 218, 225, 242; Black specificity as, 3; Black Study as, 46, 62, 67, 70; DEEP breathing as, 71; definition, 3, 9; education as, 204–6; of ethics, 11; and flesh, 31, 160; intimating as, 78, 85–86, 97, 135, 138, 140–42, 245; invention as, 78, 85–88, 97, 112, 120–21; liveliness and living as, 41, 195; and otherwise, 3, 119, 200, 209; policy praxis, 11, 200, 202, 208–20, 222; presence as, 78, 85–86, 91, 97, 147, 167, 245; revision as, 11, 78, 85–86, 97, 185–95, 245, 251; self-defining, 77–78, 93, 95–97, 223, 231–32, 244–45, 252–53
presence/presencing, 10, 18, 57–58, 90, 92–94, 124, 179–80, 193, 195, 236, 239, 241, 248–50, 262n2; and Black ontology, 145–67; and intimacy, 142–43; as praxis, 78, 85–86, 91, 97, 147, 167, 245
progressivism, 30, 83, 132–34, 137–38, 140–42, 157, 177, 214; liberal, 31, 139, 214, 222, 233

queerness, 20, 58–59, 84, 177

racelessness, 55, 79
racial socialization, 134
racism, 11, 51, 80, 130, 134, 138, 154, 173, 233; *vs.* Blackness approach, 69, 70, 76, 79, 132, 212–15; and Black specificity, 52; and education, 75; and epistemology, 54–55; and gender violence, 116, 120; internalized, 84; and self-authorship, 51. *See also* anti-Blackness; white supremacy

Rankine, Claudia, 30
rape crisis centers, 109
Reason, Robert D., 220
Reconstruction, 130, 202, 207
redaction, 41–42, 125, 138–42, 238–41
revision, 35, 92–94, 194, 249; and critical race theory, 51–52; and otherwise, 170, 250; as praxis, 11, 78, 85–86, 97, 185–95, 245, 251
Rice, Tamir, 137
Rittenhouse, Kyle, 29
Rodgers, Robert, 220
rooted errantry, 236

Sanchez, Sonia, 230
schooling, 85, 88, 200–208, 262n2; definition, 77
scopic regimes, 10
Scott, David, 106, 153
Scott, Dred and Harriet, 30
self-authorship, 9–10, 22–23, 47–51, 54–57, 78–81, 94, 97
self-defining praxis, 32, 77–78, 86–97, 223, 231–32, 244–45, 252–53
self-definition, 36, 42, 73–77, 117, 133, 171, 193, 202, 204, 215; and literary criticism, 82–86; and self-authorship, 78–82, 94–97. See also self-defining praxis
Sexton, Jared, 35, 107
sexual violence, 10, 56, 104–21, 176–77, 187–90. See also #MeToo; patriarchy
Sharpe, Christina, 29–30, 238, 262
Sims, Megan, 161
sitting with history, 17, 19, 31
slavery, 16, 18, 22, 62, 125, 132, 151, 166, 185, 192, 206, 215, 261nn1–2; afterlife of, 17, 19–20, 29–30, 33–35, 57, 106, 126, 129–30, 137, 140, 153, 175–77, 182, 239, 262n2; and American grammar, 262n1; and the Black essay, 136; and carcerality, 133, 239; and education, 157, 200–203, 262n2; and flesh, 37, 137; and gender/sexual violence, 106–10, 115; and the human, 25, 28–30, 55, 58, 86, 103, 211, 264n4; and presence, 148–49; slave rebellions, **229**; and social death, 23–24, 260nn4–5. See also plantation; the wake
slave ships, 112, 127–28, 261nn1–2. See also the hold
Smith, Tommie, 155–57
Social Darwinism, 53
social death, 23–24, 35, 52, 57, 79, 112, 130, 149, 159, 260nn4–5
social science, 2–3, 52, 62, 79, 95, 127–31, 146, 204, 209; anti-Blackness in, 10; Blackness in, 54, 60, 65–66, 248–49; versus Black Study, 47. See also human sciences
sociogeny, 76, 106
Sounds of Blackness, 265n2
South Carolina, **229**
Southern Christian Leadership Conference, 204
sovereignty, 18–19, 32, 126, 130, 132, 178–79, 181, 244
speculation, 19, 21, 71, 215–17, 250, 253
Spillers, Hortense, 1, 25–26, 29, 31, 33–34, 37, 107–8, 147, 149, 152, 191, 224, 260n6, 261n1, 262n1, 264n4
stasis, 152–56, 160, 163
Stefancic, Jean, 118
storytelling, 4, 76, 87
student/early-adult development theory, 30, 76–77, 117, 220–21, 232, 244; anti-Blackness in, 9–10; Blackness in, 5–6, 22–23, 35, 58–61, 69; and Black specificity, 32, 64;

and Black Studies, 40, 58, 70–71; and flesh, 34, 39; second wave, 48, 58–59; self-authorship in, 9, 22–23, 47–52, 78–80, 94–95; third-wave, 10, 40, 54, 58–59; wave framework, 48. *See also* human development theory
Student Nonviolent Coordinating Committee (SNCC), 154
subjection, 34, 89, 132–33, 246, 250
subject-object relationship, 48, 50, 54–55, 175. *See also* Cartesian dualism
Suggs, Baby, 37, 39

Take Back the Night, 109
the talk, 10, 126, 134–35
Taylor, Breonna, 29
territory, 27, 38, 40–42, 58–60, 107, 176, 202, 213, 224, 247; definition, 9
theoretical practice, 40, 220, 223–24
theory in the flesh, 95–96, 221
Torres, Vasti, 80
Toward a Black University conference, 213–14
Trayvon Generation, 166
Ture, Kwame (formerly Stokely Carmichael), 154

University of California, Berkeley, 154
University of Michigan, 104–5, 112, 114–20
Utley, Ebony A., 110

van Dijk, Teun, 113
Varela, Francisco J., 24
vitality, 3, 21, 34–35, 103, 125, 152, 249, 260n6

the wake, 1, 17, 19, 34, 93, 126, 194, 221, 241, 262n2; anti-Blackness as, 43, 61–62, 78, 81–85, 88–92, 95, 178, 185, 192; and Black being, 29; definition, 30–31, 262n2; and the human, 33; and pedagogy, 96. *See also* afterlife of slavery
Wall, Cheryl A., 136
Warren, Calvin, 55, 107
Watkins, William H., 203
the weather, 29, 31, 74, 134
Weheliye, Alexander G., 26, 148, 264n1
West, Cornell, 200
Western Enlightenment, 8, 56–57, 61, 65–66, 132, 174, 181, 185, 203, 232, 262n2
Western humanism. *See* humanism
Western Man, 32, 41, 59, 65, 75, 87, 93–94, 141, 152, 154, 174, 176, 184, 233–37, 243, 245, 248, 264n2; and Blackness, 10, 22, 26, 33, 35, 103, 107, 111, 118–20, 126, 131, 194, 210–16, 263n3; and education, 126, 146–47, 244, 252–53, 262n2; and social death, 24; terminology of, 259n2. *See also* humanism; Man-as-human
White, Jamie, 114–15
White, Mya, 161
white masculinity, 108
white supremacy, 38, 104–5, 109, 112, 115–17, 120, 204, 210. *See also* police violence; racism
Widdick, Carole, 220
Wilderson, Frank, 31, 124, 172
Williams, Patricia J., 140
Williamson, Terrion L., 34
Wilson, Darren, 86, 155
Winston (student), 2–3, 6, 124–25, 137–40, 142
Woodson, Carter Godwin, 165
Wynter, Sylvia, 25, 33, 38, 53, 57, 70, 76, 87, 132, 147, 151, 205, 206, 211–12, 221, 223, 233, 242, 245,

Wynter, Sylvia *(continued)*
259n2, 260n7; on being human, 4, 218; on Black Aesthetics/Black Arts, 10, 32, 60, 83, 201; on Black Studies, 26; critique of Man-as-human, 9, 22, 26–28, 41, 150, 173–74, 244, 264n2; on demonic ground, 37, 41; on genres of the human, 8, 26, 106; on the map and territory, 40, 58–60, 202

Yale University, 156–57, 159
Ya Sa Dyongou, **169**–170
Youngstown City Schools, 127

Zuberi, Tukufu, 209